Called to Be Saints

An Anthology on Holiness

Called to Be Saints

An Anthology on Holiness

Ralph I. Tilley, Editor

LITS Books
PO Box 405
Sellersburg, Indiana 47172

ISBN: 10: 0990395014
ISBN: 13: 978-0-9903950-1-0

LITS Books
PO Box 405
Sellersburg, Indiana 47172

Ralph I. Tilley is the executive director of Life in the Spirit Ministries and online
editor of *Life in the Spirit Journal*. For further information, contact
Ralph I. Tilley, editor@litsjournal.org.

Books available at Amazon.com; for discounts, contact
Ralph I. Tilley, editor@litsjournal.org.

For all available books, go to litsjournal.org.

*This volume is affectionately and gratefully dedicated
to each of those writers—whose names are without number—
who, though unknown to them, have been immeasurably
used by God, since my conversion, to shape my mind
and warm my heart in the pursuit of holiness.*

Contents

Acknowledgements

Grateful acknowledgement is made to the following publishers/authors for permission to quote from copyrighted material.

Baker Publishing Group. "How to Be a Living Sacrifice" is taken from *Mind Renewal in a Mindless Age* by James Montgomery Boice. Copyright © 1993 by James Montgomery Boice. Used by permission of Baker Books, a division of Baker Publishing Group, Grand Rapids, MI.

"The Ongoing Warfare—the Spirit Against the Flesh" is taken from *Paul, the Spirit, and the People of God* by Gordon D. Fee. Copyright © 1996 by Gordon D. Fee. Used by permission of Baker Academic, a division of Baker Publishing Group, Grand Rapids, MI.

"What Holiness is and Why it Matters" is taken from *Rediscovering Holiness* by J. I. Packer. Copyright © 1992 by J. I. Packer. Used by permission of Baker Books, a division of Baker Publishing Group, Grand Rapids, MI.

Beacon Hill Press. "Toward Christian Maturity" is taken from *God, Man, and Salvation* by W. T. Purkiser, Richard S. Taylor, Willard H. Taylor. Copyright © 1977 by Beacon Hill Press of Kansas City, MO. Used by permission of Beacon Hill Press. All rights reserved.

Brown, Allan. "Holiness and the Spirit-filled Life." Copyright © 2014 by Allan Brown. Used by permission

Christian Focus Publications. "Service" is taken from *Living Holiness* by Helen Roseveare. Copyright © 1986 by Helen Roseveare. Used by permission of Christian Focus Publications, Ross-shire, Scotland, UK. The chapter from which this is taken was originally titled "Service."

Wm. B. Eerdmans Publishing Co. "The Letter and the Spirit" is taken from *Studies in the Sermon on the Mount,* Vol. One, by D. Martyn Lloyd-Jones. Copyrighted © 1959 Wm. B. Eerdmans Publishing Co. Used by permission of Wm. B. Eerdmans Publishing Co., Grand Rapids, MI.

Francis Asbury Society. "Look Not to Your Own Interests" is taken from *The Mind of Christ* by Dennis F. Kinlaw. Copyright © 1998 The Francis Asbury Society. Used by permission of The Francis Asbury Society, Wilmore, KY.

Kregel Publications. "Transfiguration of Character" is taken from *A New Call to Holiness* by J. Sidlow Baxter, pp. 161-172. Copyright © 1973 J. Sidlow Baxter. Used by permission of Kregel Publications, Grand Rapids, MI.

Moody Publishers. "Christ's Ideal of Character" is taken from *Spiritual Maturity* by J. Oswald Sanders. Copyright © 1962 Moody Publishers. Used by permission of Moody Publishers, Chicago, IL, www.moodypublishers.com.

Grateful acknowledgement is made to the memory of those authors whose quoted material is now in the public domain (according to the editor's knowledge).

Johann Arndt. "Some Rules for Living the Holy Life" is taken from http://www.gutenberg.org/files/34736/34736-h/34736-h.html.

Horatius Bonar. "Counsels and Warnings" is taken from http://grace-ebooks.com/library/Horatius%20Bonar/HB_Gods%20Way%20of%20Holiness.pdf, by Horatius Bonar.

Samuel L. Brengle. "Francis of Assisi: Re-formed by Love" is taken from *The Guest of the Soul* by Samuel L. Brengle. Noblesville, IN: Newby Book Room, 1971 edition; originally published 1934. The chapter from which this is taken was originally titled "A Thirteenth-Century Salvationist."

Thomas Brooks. "Hungering for Holiness" is taken from http://www.ccel.org/ccel/ryle/holiness.iii.xx.html?highlight=complain#highlight. From Brooks' *Crown and Glory of Christianity; or, Holiness the only way to*

Happiness—Brooks' Works, vol. 4. Grosart's edition. 1866.

Thomas Cook. "Arbiter of the Heart" is taken from *New Testament Holiness* by Thomas Cook. London: The Epworth Press, 1958; originally published 1902.

J. Gregory Mantle. "The Indwelling Christ" is taken from *The Way of the Cross* by J. Gregory Mantle. Revised edn., New York: George H. Doran Co., 1922.

Andrew Murray. "The Rest" is taken from *The Holiest of All* by Andrew Murray. Grand Rapids: Baker Books, 1993; originally published 1894.

J. C. Ryle. "Holiness" is taken from *A Call to Holiness* by J. C. Ryle. Grand Rapids: Baker Books, 1976, an excerpt from Ryle's original work titled *Holiness*.

W. E. Sangster. "Attention and Obedience" is taken from *The Pure in Heart* by W. E. Sangster. London: The Epworth Press, 1954. The chapter from which this is taken was originally titled "The Way is Worship."

Erich Sauer. "Pressing On to the Mark!" is taken from *In the Arena of Faith* by W. E. Sangster. Grand Rapids: Wm. B. Eerdmans Publishing Co., 1956.

A. W. Tozer. "The Holiness of God" is taken from *The Knowledge of the Holy*. New York: Harper & Brothers, 1961.

Introduction

Ralph I. Tilley

God is holy—in his total personhood, and in all his ways and works. In using a metaphor for God's holiness, the beloved apostle wrote, "God is light and in him is no darkness at all" (1 John 1:5).[1] God is absolutely and perfectly holy: "in him is no darkness at all."

Because God is who he is—a holy God—he calls his people in every age to a holy life. The Holy Spirit, through the Apostle Peter, delivered this call to the first-century believers, citing God's call to Israel centuries before (1 Peter 1:15-16): "As obedient children, do not be conformed to the passions of your former ignorance, but as he who called you is holy, you also be holy in all your conduct, since it is written, 'You shall be holy, for I am holy.'"

This book is about holiness. I realize the topic is offensive to many professing Christians in the contemporary church—as has always been the case in every generation. Just the same, while the subject has been fraught with many controversies, theories, and caricatures of its reality, the call remains—God's call for every disciple of the Lord Jesus Christ is to live a life unlike the common sinner. God calls Christians to live-up to their name.

God has raised up men and women in every generation of the church to herald his call to holiness. One of those voices was heard in the eighteenth-century and still reverberates today, the voice of J. C. Ryle (1816-1900), an Anglican Church minister. Distressed over the observable lack of Christlikeness among believers of his own day, Ryle took up his pen and wrote extensively on this subject, which in time became a classic. In the heart of his volume, this concerned pastor and church leader wrote:

I have no desire to make an idol of holiness. I do not wish to dethrone Christ, and put holiness in His place. But I must candidly say, I wish sanctification was more thought of in this day than it seems to be, and I therefore take occasion to press the subject on all believers into whose hands these pages may fall. I fear it is sometimes forgotten that God has married together justification and sanctification. They are distinct and different things, beyond question, but one is never found without the other. All justified people are sanctified, and all sanctified are justified. What God has joined together let no man dare to put asunder. Tell me not of your justification, unless you have also some marks of sanctification. Boast not of Christ's work *for you*, unless you can show us the Spirit's work *in you*. Think not that Christ and the Spirit can ever be divided. I doubt not that many believers know these things, but I think it good for us to be put in remembrance of them. Let us prove that we know them by our lives. Let us try to keep in view this text more continually: "Follow holiness, without which no man shall see the Lord."

I must frankly say I wish there was not such an excessive *sensitiveness* on the subject of holiness as I sometimes perceive in the minds of believers. A man might really think it was a dangerous subject to handle, so cautiously is it touched! Yet surely when we have exalted Christ as "the way, the truth, and the life," we cannot err in speaking strongly about what should be the character of His people. Well says Rutherford, "The way that crieth down duties and sanctification, is not the way of grace. Believing and doing are blood-friends."

I would say it with all reverence, but say it I must—I sometimes fear if Christ were on earth now, there are not a few who would think His preaching *legal*; and if Paul were writing his Epistles, there are those who would think he had better not write the latter part of most of them as he did. But let us remember that the Lord Jesus *did* speak the Sermon on the Mount, and that the Epistle to the Ephesians contains six chapters and not four. I grieve to feel obliged to speak in this way, but I am sure there is a cause.[2]

Yes, "there is a cause," as there has always been, but so much more in our day. One need not list a litany of concerns presently afflicting the church in arguing for the need of this message. The concerns are many; the needs are great. The question is: Will we listen to the Spirit as he speaks?

Will we heed the voice of Jesus to love him, to follow him, to obey him?

God is calling each of us to be a wholehearted, totally devoted disciple of the Lord Jesus Christ—from the inside out. Atonement has been made by the once-for-all sacrificial death of Christ on the cross; our Lord has risen from the dead and is presently interceding for us as our great High Priest; and the Holy Spirit has been given to indwell all born-from-above believers. If this is so—and it is, according to God's holy Word—what is keeping us from living better lives—imperfect, to be sure, but day-by-day lives that are being transformed more and more into the image of the Lord Jesus (see 2 Cor. 3:18)?

Sin is the only barrier to this call to holiness being realized in our heart and conduct. If we are in earnest about being a follower of the Lord Jesus, we must be willing to confront and put away everything that impedes our walk with God: "let us also lay aside every encumbrance and the sin which so easily entangles us . . ." (Heb. 12:1 NASB). And we must actively and daily pursue God's call: "walk by the Spirit, and you will not gratify the desires of the flesh" (Gal. 5:16).

While the call to holiness may be tainted by many who have translated this call into self-righteous attitudes and behavior, the high calling still stands. One must not be deterred from heeding the call just because there are those who have descended into a lesser way, a bypath. The Word and the Spirit will lead all who are willing to listen.

A word about the title of this volume—Called to Be Saints. In the words of Timothy George, dean of Beeson Divinity School, the word "saints" "recognizes that all followers of Jesus are saints in the New Testament sense of the word. We have been set apart and called to live a life of holiness and devotion to Christ. . . . We are called to live lives that reflect the character of Christ in a world that knows too little of God's love and grace."[3]

This is what this book is about; we are merely reiterating this biblical call—calling Christ's followers to follow him and pursue this call, first voiced by the prophets, then iterated and delineated by his holy apostles, and later affirmed by a host of saints in life and word throughout the ages.

Concerning the contents of the book. One of my objectives in compiling this anthology was to avoid a narrow, sectarian view on the subject. I realize this will not please some, maybe not many. However, it must be said that God's call to holiness is a call to the whole Church, not just one segment. While I am personally convinced that some branches of Christ's Church have a better apprehension as to what constitutes God's call to holiness than others, that doesn't presume there are not true followers of Christ in all branches of his church and who take the call to holy living seriously. Therefore, while I cannot subscribe to particular points of doctrine that some of the authors in this volume hold, I wholeheartedly subscribe to their *heart* for God, their *love* for his Word, and their *earnestness* in the pursuit of a holy life.

A variety of denominations are represented among these writers: Anglican, Lutheran, Baptist, Salvation Army, Church of the Nazarene, Assemblies of God, Presbyterian, Methodist, Christian & Missionary Alliance, and Nondenominational. Also, various theological persuasions are represented among the writers: Calvinist, Arminian, Wesleyan, Pentecostal, Lutheran, and Keswickian. Personally, I have drawn deeply from their respective *wells* through the years with great profit.

Furthermore, while this book is not exhaustive in its exploration of the subject of holiness, nonetheless I have included a wide range of headings—including both doctrinal and practical. God's call to holiness is a call to be *informed* by the Word, as well as a call to be *transformed* by the Spirit.

A few remarks about the older writings. I have slightly modernized the language in some of the material—to make it more readable to the modern ear. Also, a few chapter titles have been altered, which I have noted in the Acknowledgements.

Now, dear reader, I invite you to listen to two words of the Lord Jesus as you read this volume: "Blessed are those who hunger and thirst for righteousness, for they shall be satisfied" (Matt. 5:6), and "Whoever follows me will not walk in darkness, but will have the light of life" (John 8:12).

If our Lord is pleased to use any, or all, of these writings in your walk with him, to him alone belongs the glory.

Ralph I. Tilley, Editor
Soli Deo Gloria

Holy, Holy, Holy

Holy, holy, holy! Lord God Almighty!
Early in the morning our song shall rise to Thee;
Holy, holy, holy, merciful and mighty!
God in three Persons, blessèd Trinity!

Holy, holy, holy! All the saints adore Thee,
Casting down their golden crowns around the glassy sea;
Cherubim and seraphim falling down before Thee,
Who was, and art, and evermore shall be.

Holy, holy, holy! though the darkness hide Thee,
Though the eye of sinful man Thy glory may not see;
Only Thou art holy; there is none beside Thee,
Perfect in power, in love, and purity.

Holy, holy, holy! Lord God Almighty!
All Thy works shall praise Thy Name, in earth, and sky, and sea;
Holy, holy, holy; merciful and mighty!
God in three Persons, blessèd Trinity!

(Reginald Heber, 1783-1826)

1

Called to Be Saints

Ralph I. Tilley

Ralph I. Tilley (b. 1944) was converted to the Lord Jesus Christ at the age of 16. He is a graduate of God's Bible School & College (Th.B.; Bible, theology, New Testament Greek); Andrews University (M.A.; New Testament Studies); and Trinity Theological Seminary (D.R.S.; Religious Studies).

Ralph pastored for 38 years and has taught at the Bible college, university and seminary levels. He was the editor and publisher *Life in the Spirit Journal* for 20 years, and presently serves as the journal's online editor. He has served as the executive director of Life in the Spirit Ministries since 1993. *Called to Be Saints* is the eleventh book he has either authored or edited. He and his wife Emily reside in Sellersburg, Indiana; they have two married daughters and three grandchildren.

The call of the Holy Spirit to follow the Lord Jesus Christ is a call to *holiness*. It is a call to *leave*; it is a call to *cleave*—to leave our sins, and to cleave to God's Son, the Lord Jesus Christ.

After God made woman from the first man, Adam joyfully exclaimed,

"This at last is bone of my bones
   and flesh of my flesh;
she shall be called Woman,
   because she was taken out of Man."[1]

Following this human union of our original parents, God announced,

1

"Therefore a man shall leave his father and his mother and hold fast [cleave] to his wife, and they shall become one flesh" (Gen. 2:24). Just as there is a leaving and a cleaving in marriage between a man and a woman, so there is a leaving and a cleaving on the part of the repentant, believing disciple of the Lord Jesus Christ. In marriage, the leaving and the cleaving precedes as well as follows the union of a man and woman in covenant relationship. It is no different in our union with Christ, for in authentic Christian discipleship the leaving and the cleaving precedes as well as follows one's mystical union with the heavenly Bridegroom.

The Challenge Every Seeker Faces

The challenge every seeker faces in contemplating the call of Christ is the cost: "What will it cost me?" The convicting Holy Spirit brings each sinner, sooner or later, to face this question. The initiated know the answer: "Everything!"

The call of Christ is a call to *self*-denial—rejecting one's right to rule his life; *death*—death to one's self-centered ego; *obedience*—following the Lord Jesus in total and joyful submission: "If anyone would come after me, let him deny himself and take up his cross and follow me. For whoever would save his life will lose it, but whoever loses his life for my sake will find it" (Matt. 16:24-25).

When it comes to fundamental issues of the heart one faces when contemplating the call of Christ, I know of no better word picture drawn by a person (outside the sacred Scripture) than John Bunyan (1628-1688) drew, when he portrayed a man—under deep, Spirit-induced conviction— weighing his impoverished spiritual condition. In Bunyan's allegory—*The Pilgrim's Progress*—we first meet an unconverted man living in the "City of Destruction" with his family, holding "a Book in his hand with a great Burden on his back." When he began to read the Book "he wept and trembled." Not knowing what to do, he goes home—heavily agitated in spirit. Upon entering his house, he gathers his wife and children about him, pouring out his soul.

> "O, my dear wife, . . . and you the children of my bowels, I, your dear friend, am in myself undone by reason of a burden that lieth hard upon me; moreover, I am certainly informed that this our city

will be burnt with fire from heaven; in which fearful overthrow, both myself, with thee my wife, and you my sweet babes, shall miserably come to ruin, except (the which yet I see not) some way of escape can be found whereby we may be delivered."

Believing her husband and the father of her children had become delusional, his wife quickly put him to bed. But that night and following days did not alter the man's internal trauma. However, in the kind providence of God, he finally meets an evangelist of the gospel one day, and inquires as to what he should do. Whereupon the evangelist gave the seeker a "Parchment Roll, and there was written within, 'Fly from the wrath to come.'" Wishing to know where he should flee to,

Evangelist, (pointing with his finger over a very wide field,) "Do you see yonder wicket-gate?" The man said, "No." Then said the other, "Do you see yonder shining light?" He said, "I think I do." Then said Evangelist, "Keep that light in your eye, and go up directly thereto, so shalt thou see the gate; at which, when thou knockest, it shall be told thee what thou shalt do."

Immediately the man, though carrying a heavy load upon his back, "began to run." But he had no sooner left his house when "his Wife and Children perceiving it, began to cry after him to return; but the Man put his fingers to his ears, and ran on crying, 'Life! Life! Eternal Life!'" Then Bunyan writes: "So he looked not behind him, but fled towards the middle of the plain"—eventually being directed to the "wicket-gate" (the cross of Christ), where he loses his burden—his burden of sin.[2]

City of Destruction

Spiritually dead. Every sinner, whether he realizes it or not, dwells in the "City of Destruction." Every Christian formerly lived in the same *City*. The Scriptures are replete with texts underscoring this fact. Here is one example. Writing to the converted Ephesian Christians (2:1-3), the apostle wrote:

And you were dead in the trespasses and sins in which you once walked, following the course of this world, following the prince of the power of the air, the spirit that is now at work in the sons of disobedience—among whom we all once lived in the passions of our flesh, carrying out the desires of the body and the mind, and were by nature children of wrath, like the rest of mankind.

Prior to God's gracious justifying, regenerating work for us and in us, each one of us was spiritually dead; living in one way or another like every other sinner; unwittingly being led by Satan and his minions; disobedient to God and his righteous and holy laws. We were controlled by our depraved passions, just doing what came naturally—sinning against God. We were not children of God; we were "children of wrath"—living under the righteous judgment of God. We were living like everyone else around us. True, because of the culture in which we were raised, we may have been considered a *respectable* person in society; the education we received may have been from the best schools; our standard of living might have been comparable to the middle or upper classes. Regardless, "All we like sheep have gone astray; we have turned every one to his own way" (Isa. 53:6). The apostle underscores this truth in Romans 3:10-18. Quoting a variety of OT passages, he writes:

> "None is righteous, no, not one; [11]no one understands; no one seeks for God. [12]All have turned aside; together they have become worthless; no one does good, not even one."[13]"Their throat is an open grave; they use their tongues to deceive." "The venom of asps is under their lips." [14]"Their mouth is full of curses and bitterness."[15]"Their feet are swift to shed blood; [16]in their paths are ruin and misery, [17]and the way of peace they have not known." [18]"There is no fear of God before their eyes."

Now, that was our state, our condition before coming to Christ. Every sinner can find himself somewhere in the above texts (and many more); we were all there. We have all sinned—regardless of our respective stations in life.

When God's persistent grace overcame Blaise Pascal (1623-1662), he was an inventor, philosopher, mathematician, and physicist—but a sinner. When God's forgiving grace invaded the life of John Newton (1725-1807), he was a slave-trader and womanizer—a sinner. And when John Wesley

(1703-1791), an ordained Anglican minister, was listening to Martin's Luther's Preface to the Letter of Romans being read one evening in 1738, he was a sinner when his heart was "strangely warmed" by God's regenerating grace. It makes no difference to God what our appearances and standing before others were when his mercy and grace found us. Whether we were like the self-righteous Pharisee in Jesus' parable (Luke 18:9-14), or like the licentious Samaritan woman in John 4, we all stood condemned before a holy God; we were all deserving (and are still deserving) of eternal death and hell. God in Christ calls each sinner to flee the City—the "City of Destruction." But be warned: We can't leave the City by our own human effort!

The Good News

The good news is, "But God, being rich in mercy, because of the great love with which he loved us, [5]even when we were dead in our trespasses, made us alive together with Christ—by grace you have been saved—" (Eph. 2:4-5).

The cross of Christ is God's magnificent demonstration of mercy. The death of Christ occurred *for* us when we were yet spiritually dead in our sins. We who are saved were resurrected—made alive "with Christ"—when he arose from the grave. And what Christ did *for* us on the cross and the empty tomb became an experiential reality *in* us when we repented of our sins, placed our faith in God's gift of salvation, the Lord Jesus Christ, receiving the mercy of God. All of this is of grace—God's grace *for* us, God's grace *in* us. All of this is of mercy—God's mercy *for* us, God's mercy *in* us.

> *Oh, the love that drew salvation's plan!*
> *Oh, the grace that brought it down to man!*
> *Oh, the mighty gulf that God did span at Calvary!*
> *Mercy there was great, and grace was free;*
> *Pardon there was multiplied to me;*
> *There my burdened soul found liberty at Calvary.*[3]

> *'Tis mercy all, immense and free,*
> *For O my God, it found out me!*[4]

5

The Before and After

Returning to the Ephesian Letter, we discover a *before* and *after* in our relationship with God and the Lord Jesus Christ. The apostle reminds these converts to Christ that prior to their conversion they were "separated from Christ, alienated from the commonwealth of Israel and strangers to the covenants of promise, having no hope and without God in the world" (Eph. 2:12). Separated! Alienated! Strangers! No hope! Without God! Paul says, that's what you Ephesian disciples of Christ "were"! And that is precisely what all of us who are now in Christ once "were." The apostle wants these believers to remember that; and we need to remember that as well. No matter how far back it was when we first trusted in Christ, we never want to forget that we were once separated, alienated, strangers, without hope, and without God. That's what we *were*.

But something fundamentally altered our "were" in the atoning death and resurrection of Jesus Christ. Paul says, "But now in Christ Jesus . . ." (Eph. 2:13f). That's the answer to the "were"! That is God's answer to our sins and sinfulness! God in Christ made the difference—essentially and fundamentally altering a believing sinner's relationship with God and their future in God's plan. "In Christ," Paul writes, "you who once were far off have been brought near" How? "By the blood of Christ"! By God's atoning Substitute for sinners! By Christ's very own blood! Peter emphasizes the identical truth when writing to the first-century Diaspora (1 Pet. 1:18-19, emphasis added):

> . . . you were ransomed from the futile ways inherited from your forefathers, not with perishable things such as silver or gold, [19]but *with the precious blood of Christ*, like that of a lamb without blemish or spot.

We were ransomed "with the precious blood of Christ"! We were "brought near by the blood of Christ"! God is saying to us through Peter that we need to remember that! God is saying to us through Paul that we need to remember that! Have we forgotten? Have we forgotten the incredible and unfathomable price paid for our salvation? Do we feel it? Does it still *move* us? Are we still awed by Christ's shedding of his very own blood for our deliverance from eternal death and hell?

My mind is drawn to the great evangelical text in Isaiah 53. I often meditate on this passage on the Sundays when the wine and bread are being distributed in our church pews—to reinforce my memory, lest I forget. And I must say, I wonder that I am not moved more by this truth whenever I read and reflect about the promised Suffering Servant. Is my heart cold? Have I grown accustomed in reading about it? Why doesn't this text affect me more? My tears are too few.

I think of a story once shared by the late Scottish preacher Sidlow Baxter (1903-1999). I quote it in full because of the impact it had on me more than thirty years ago—and it still affects me whenever I reread it, as I just now did.

Most of us, in these days of rush and speed, spend far too little time in rapt contemplation of that Cross. We are needing to relearn the need and enrichment of lingering there. We preachers need to spend hours of aloneness before that Cross, with our Bible open at Isaiah 53, slowly going over it, line by line. If we are really to preach the Cross of Christ with compelling influence, we need inwardly to see it, as Isaiah did, with a vividness which breaks and melts and disturbs and inspires us. Every sermon on the Cross should come to our hearers wet with the preacher's tears.

Years ago I knew a fine Christian man in Canada. He was born and bred among the poor. At an early age he had to leave school and go to work. While still young he came to know the Lord Jesus as his Savior. He started a small business, and covenanted to give one-tenth of all his earnings to God. His business grew and grew until it was one of the largest of its kind in Canada. Faithfully he gave his tithe to the Lord. Then he made it a fifth, then a quarter, then a half, then three-quarters, then nine-tenths, until eventually he was running the whole business practically to make money for supporting the Lord's work in various ways. Thousands received financial help from him without ever knowing where it came from.

One day I asked him what brought about his conversion to Christ. He replied, "It was the example of my godly father." Then he told me he was one of four boys who grew up in the little old home. From their youngest days their father used to gather them round his knee, while he read to them from the Bible and then prayed with them. On Sunday evenings he always read Isaiah 53.

With a glow on his face he would start to read it. Then, on reaching verse 4, "Surely he hath borne our griefs," or verse 5, "He was wounded for our transgressions; he was bruised for our iniquities," his voice would falter, his throat would become husky, the tears would begin to drip down his cheeks, and he would have to say in broken syllables, "I'm sorry, boys, I canna' go on; it's too up-settin'—that such a dear, divine Savior should suffer for us sinners . . . like *that!*"

My friend added, "Sometimes my dad would struggle on a bit, but I never once knew him to get right through Isaiah 53. Even if he managed to get beyond verses 5 and 6, he never got beyond verse 7—'He is led as a lamb to the slaughter.' It broke him down to think that the Son of God should suffer for us 'like that.'"[5]

Yes, dear reader, this was both the Father's and the Son's price for our undeserving salvation. It *cost* the Father to send his Son into the world, and to look upon his Only Begotten One's death; it *cost* the Son his very own life, his very blood! And it will *cost* us!

O love divine, what hast thou done!
The incarnate God hath died for me!
The Father's coeternal Son
Bore all my sins upon the tree!
The Son of God for me hath died:
My Lord, my Love is crucified.

***

Then let us sit beneath his cross,
And gladly catch the healing stream;
All things for him account but loss,
And give up all our hearts to him;
Of nothing think or speak beside:
My Lord, my Love is crucified.[6]

Called to Be Saints

Back to the first two sentences of this chapter: "The call of the Holy Spirit to follow the Lord Jesus Christ is a call to *holiness*. It is a call to *leave*; it is a call to *cleave*—to leave our sins and to cleave to God's Son." This is a forgotten truth in today's church: God's call to holiness, God's call to holy living, God's call to Christlikeness.

Christians in every age have had to grapple with the ethical implications of being a follower of the Lord Jesus Christ. Authentic disciples of Christ are taught both by Word and Spirit, that there is an ongoing price to be paid to walk in fellowship and obedience to the Lord Jesus: the "gate is narrow" (Matt. 7:13). But again and again typical church-goers are told in effect by the pulpit, "Dear friends, our loving and merciful Father in heaven doesn't expect you to be holy, to live holy. Be careful that you don't take your Christianity too seriously. After all, there was only one Person who ever walked this earth who was perfect, and that wasn't *you*. You're not perfect—just forgiven!" Having heard this repeatedly from a shepherd of the sheep week after week, the average believer understandably leaves the church affirmed in his and her *sinning*.

In commenting on the folk theology slogan that "Christian's aren't perfect—just forgiven," the late Southern Baptist philosopher and writer, Dallas Willard (1935-2013), wrote,

> Well, it certainly needs to be said that Christians are forgiven. And it needs to be said that forgiveness does not depend on being perfect. But is that really what the slogan communicates? Unfortunately, it is not. What the slogan really conveys is that forgiveness alone is what Christianity is all about, what is genuinely essential to it.
>
> It says that you can have a faith in Christ that brings forgiveness, while in every other respect your life is no different from that of others who have no faith in Christ at all. This view so pleasingly presented on bumpers and trinkets has deep historical roots. It is by now worked out in many sober tomes of theology, lived out by multitudes of those who sincerely self-identify as Christians.[7]

Our Adversary has insidiously and pervasively deluded many of our pulpits and pews into believing that the *only* difference between Christians and non-Christians is that they have been forgiven. "Don't trouble yourselves about a so-called biblical call to holiness. Who do you think you are—a *saint*?!"

The Word of God answers, "Yes, that's precisely what God calls each person who is in Christ Jesus—a *saint*!" Sixty-one times the New Testament writers refer to true believers as "saints" (ESV).[8] The first occurrence is found in Matthew's Gospel (27:51-53, emphasis added), where the writer recounts remarkable miracles at the moment of Christ's death:

> And behold, the curtain of the temple was torn in two, from top to bottom. And the earth shook, and the rocks were split. [52]The tombs also were opened. And many bodies of the *saints* who had fallen asleep were raised, [53]and coming out of the tombs after his resurrection they went into the holy city and appeared to many.

The final occurrence of the word is located in Revelation 3:3 (emphasis added), when the Lamb opens the seventh seal.

> And another angel came and stood at the altar with a golden censer, and he was given much incense to offer with the prayers of all the *saints* on the golden altar before the throne, . . .

Of the sixty-one occurrences of the word saint, or its plural in the New Testament, fifty-five are employed by the Apostle Paul (fifty-seven if he is the writer of Hebrews). Luke, the historian, uses the term four times in the book of Acts, which are illuminatingly beautiful descriptions of the first-century believers (emphases added).

> Acts 9:13: (Ananias speaking of the recently converted Saul of Tarsus): "Lord, I have heard from many about this man, how much evil he has done to your *saints* at Jerusalem."

> Acts 9:32: Now as Peter went here and there among them all, he came down also to the *saints* who lived at Lydda.

> Acts 9:41 (Peter's ministry to Dorcas): And he gave her his hand and raised her up. Then calling the *saints* and widows, he presented her alive.

> Acts 26:10 (Paul testifying before Agrippa): "I not only locked up many of the *saints* in prison after receiving authority from the chief priests, but when they were put to death I cast my vote against them."

Who is a Saint?

Who is a "saint"? Understandably we have a problem in wrapping our brains around the word "saint," because we are mostly uninformed as to its biblical meaning and usage. If we were to ask a variety of Christians, "Who do you think is a saint?" The answers probably would range between "Someone who has been canonized by the church," to "A monk who gives himself to the vocation of prayer," or to "A very godly person."

The New Testament writers employ a variety of terms when referring to followers of the Lord Jesus Christ. For example, they are called "Christians," "disciples" (primarily in the Gospel and Acts), people belonging to "the Way," "believers," "brothers," "witnesses," "righteous," "servants of God" and "servants of Christ," "children of God" and "sons of God" (and other designations as well). But since in this book and chapter we are addressing the specific subject of holiness, the word Paul uses in reference to Christians, more than any other, is the term we are interested in here: the word "saint."

The English word for "saint" is derived from the Latin word *sanctus* (meaning sacred), eventually evolving into the French word *seint*, or *saint*. The Greek word (the original language of the New Testament) rendered as "saint(s)" in most English translations of the Bible is the word *agios*. The word literally means "holy." When it is used in the nominative case, most translators of the Bible have rendered the word as *saint(s)*. However, the translators of the *New Living Translation* of the Bible have chosen to adhere to its literal meaning: "holy." For example, the NLT's rendering of Romans 1: 1:7 is: "I am writing to all of you in Rome who are loved by God and are called to be his own holy people."

Whether the word is translated "saint" or "holy," it has reference to a people who have been both set apart to God, and who the Holy Spirit is conforming to the likeness of Jesus Christ. For example, in greeting the Corinthian believers in his first letter, the Apostle Paul has both ideas in mind: "To the church of God which is at Corinth, to those who have been *sanctified* in Christ Jesus, *saints* by calling . . ." (1 Cor. 1:2 NASB, emphasis added). We understand from this text that those who comprise the true church have been both "sanctified in Christ Jesus" and are "saints by calling," or "called to be saints" (as some other versions render this phrase, such as the ESV). The Greek root word *agios* (holy) is used in both "sanctified" and "saints" in

11

this text. So a "saint" is a person who is *in Christ*, and a person who is called to a *holy life*, an uncommon life, a life fundamentally unlike the non-Christian, the unsaved, the sinner. In the words of H. C. G. Moule (1841-1920),

> Its usage gives us the thought of dedication to God, connection with Him, separation to His service, His will. The saints are those who belong to Him, His personal property, for His ends. It is used generally in the Scriptures for all Christians, supposed to be true to their name. All, not just an inner circle, bear the title. It is not only a glorified aristocracy but the ordinary believers; not the stars of the eternal sky but the flowers sown by the Lord in the common field — even in such a tract of that field as "Caesar's household" was (Phil. 4:22).[9]

What is meant by the term "saint"? All true Christians are "saints" in the sense that all Christians are "in Christ Jesus." All true Christians are "saints" in the sense that all Christians are called to a holy life. This dual truth is at the core of the entire New Testament scriptures, and could be summed up in these words: "But God's firm foundation stands, bearing this seal: 'The Lord knows those who are his,' and, 'Let everyone who names the name of the Lord depart from iniquity'" (2 Tim. 2:19).

Of course, this call to holiness is not dependent on merely *one word* used by the Holy Spirit in inspiring the writers of the Old and New Testament documents. The entirety of God's written revelation (The Word of God) informs us as to what God is like, what God has done and will do, and what God has called his people to be. The call for believers to live a holy life originated in the heart of a holy God, who revealed himself on earth most perfectly in the person of his holy Son, and who through the Cross and Resurrection of Christ and the indwelling of the promised Paraclete, enables Christ's unworthy and unprofitable servants to *approximate* his Son's own likeness in this present world.

While it can be said that none of God's servants through the ages have experienced *perfect* conformity to the Lord Jesus in this world, the thirsty-hearted follower of Jesus takes this call to holiness seriously. He will not allow his *imperfections* as an excuse for explicit *obedience*:

As obedient children, do not be conformed to the passions of your former ignorance, [15]but as he who called you is holy, you also be holy in all your conduct, [16]since it is written, "You shall be holy, for I am holy."[10]

God calls believers in both Testaments to a separated, devout, holy life, fully trusting in Yahweh and the Lord Jesus Christ. Whether it was Able, who offered a more perfect sacrifice than his brother Cain; or Joseph, who fled the sexual solicitations of his master's wife; or Moses, who ascended the holy mount to receive the holy commandments; or Isaiah, who saw the holy God high and lifted up; or the apostles, who followed the holy Lord Jesus; or the 120, who were filled with the Holy Spirit—every dispensation of believers from the beginning of time through the end of time—were, are, and will be called to live a life wholly unto the Lord.

Conclusion

I conclude this chapter with two words on God's call to holiness: the first from of one of God's faithful servants, who was a Scottish Baptist and Holiness Movement evangelist and teacher, Oswald Chambers (1874-1917). The second quote is from the inspired pen of the Apostle Paul, writing to first-century believers, who were greatly in need of a reminder of God's high calling in Christ Jesus our Lord.

Oswald Chambers:

Do I believe I need to be holy? Do I believe that God can come into me and make me holy? If through your preaching you convince me that I am unholy, I then resent your preaching. The preaching of the gospel awakens an intense resentment because it is designed to reveal my unholiness, but it also awakens an intense yearning and desire within me. God has only one intended destiny for mankind—holiness. His only goal is to produce saints. God is not some eternal blessing-machine for people to use, and He did not come to save us out of pity—He came to save us because He created us to be holy. Atonement through the Cross of Christ means that God can put me back into perfect oneness with Himself through the death of Jesus Christ, without a trace of anything coming between us any longer.

Never tolerate, because of sympathy for yourself or for others, any practice that is not in keeping with a holy God. Holiness means absolute purity of your walk before God, the words coming from your mouth, and every thought in your mind—placing every detail of your life under the scrutiny of God Himself. Holiness is not simply what God gives me, but what God has given me that is being exhibited in my life.[11]

Apostle Paul:

Therefore, having these promises, beloved, let us cleanse ourselves from all defilement of flesh and spirit, perfecting holiness in the fear of God.[12]

Yes, dear reader, this is God's call. Will we listen? Will we follow? Or will we choose a lesser path?

2

The Holiness of God

A. W. Tozer

In 1919, five years after his conversion to Christ and without formal theological training, A. W. Tozer (1897-1963) accepted an offer to pastor his first
church in Nutter Fort, West Virginia. This began forty-four fruitful years of
ministry with The Christian & Missionary Alliance Church, thirty of which
he served as pastor of the Southside Alliance Church in Chicago (1928-
1959). His final years were spent pastoring the Avenue Road Alliance
Church in Toronto, Canada.

Considered by many to be a modern-day prophet, Tozer felt that the
church was on a dangerous course toward compromising with worldly
concerns. In 1950 he was appointed editor of the Alliance Week-
ly magazine (now *Alliance Life*), the official publication of the C&MA. In
his first editorial, dated June 3, 1950, he wrote, "It will cost something to
walk slow in the parade of the ages, while excited men of time rush about
confusing motion with progress. But it will pay in the long run, and the
true Christian is not much interested in anything short of that."

⚬⤙⤘⚬

*Glory be to God on high. We praise Thee, we bless Thee, we worship Thee, for Thy
great glory. Lord, I uttered that I understood not; things too wonderful for me
which I knew not. I heard of Thee by the hearing of the ear, but now mine eye seeth
Thee and I abhor myself in dust and ashes. O Lord, I will lay my hand upon my
mouth. Once have I spoken, yea, twice, but I will proceed no further.*

*But while I was musing the fire burned. Lord, I must speak of Thee, lest by my
silence I offend against the generation of Thy children. Behold, Thou has chosen the*

foolish things of the world to confound the wise, and the weak things of the world to confound the mighty. O Lord, forsake me not. Let me show forth Thy strength unto this generation and Thy power to everyone that is to come. Raise up prophets and seers in Thy Church who shall magnify Thy glory and through Thine almighty Spirit restore to Thy people the knowledge of the holy. Amen.

The moral shock suffered by us through our mighty break with the high will of heaven has left us all with a permanent trauma affecting every part of our nature. There is disease both in ourselves and in our environment.

The sudden realization of his personal depravity came like a stroke from heaven upon the trembling heart of Isaiah at the moment when he had his revolutionary vision of the holiness of God. His pain-filled cry, "Woe is me! for I am undone; because I am a man of unclean lips, and I dwell in the midst of a people of unclean lips: for mine eyes have seen the King, the Lord of hosts," expresses the feeling of every man who has discovered himself under his disguises and has been confronted with an inward sight of the holy whiteness that is God. Such an experience cannot but be emotionally violent.

Until we have seen ourselves as God sees us, we are not likely to be much disturbed over conditions around us as long as they do not get so far out of hand as to threaten our comfortable way of life. We have learned to live with unholiness and have come to look upon it as the natural and expected thing. We are not disappointed that we do not find all truth in our teachers of faith, fullness in our politicians or complete honesty in our merchants or full trustworthiness in our friends That we may continue to exist we make such laws as are necessary to protect us from our fellow men and let it go at that.

Neither the writer nor the reader of these words is qualified to appreciate the holiness of God. Quite literally a new channel must be cut through the desert of our minds to allow the sweet waters of truth that will heal our great sickness to flow in. We cannot grasp the true meaning of the divine holiness by thinking of someone or something very pure and then raising the concept to the highest degree we are capable of. God's holiness is not simply the best we know infinitely bettered. We know nothing like the divine holiness. It stands apart, unique, unapproachable, incomprehensible and unattainable. The natural man is blind to it. He may fear God's power and admire His wisdom, but His holiness he cannot even imagine.

Only the Spirit of the Holy One can impart to the human spirit the knowledge of the holy. Yet as electric power flows only through a conductor, so the Spirit flows through truth and must find some measure of truth in the mind before He can illuminate the heart. Faith wakes at the voice of truth but responds to no other sound. "Faith cometh by hearing, and hearing by the word of God." Theological knowledge is the medium through which the Spirit flows into the human heart, yet there must be humble penitence in the heart before truth can produce faith. The Spirit of God is the Spirit of truth. It is possible to have some truth in the mind without having the Spirit in the heart, but it is never possible to have the Spirit apart from truth.

In his penetrating study of the holy, Rudolf Otto makes a strong case for the presence in the human mind of something he names the "numinous," by which, apparently, he means a sense that there is in the world a vague, incomprehensible Something, the *Mysterium Tremendum*, the awesome Mystery, surrounding and enfolding the universe. This is an It, an awful Thing, and can never be intellectually conceived, only sensed and felt in the depths of the human spirit. It remains as a permanent religious instinct, a feeling for that unnamed, undiscoverable Presence that "runs quick-silver-like through creation's veins" and sometimes stuns the mind by confronting it with a supernatural, suprarational manifestation of itself. The man thus confronted is brought down and overwhelmed and can only tremble and be silent.

This nonrational dread, this feeling for the uncreated Mystery in the world, is back of all religion. The pure religion of the Bible, no less than the basest animism of the naked tribesman, exists only because this basic instinct is present in human nature. Of course, the difference between the religion of an Isaiah or a Paul and that of the animist is that one has truth and the other has not; he has only the "numinous" instinct. He feels after an unknown God, but an Isaiah and a Paul have found the true God through His own self- disclosure in the inspired Scriptures.

The feeling for mystery, even for the Great Mystery, is basic in human nature and indispensable to religious faith, but it is not enough. Because of it men may whisper, "That awful Thing," but they do not cry, "Mine Holy One!" In the Hebrew and Christian Scriptures God carries forward His self-revelation and gives it personality and moral content. This awful Presence is shown to be not a Thing but a moral Being with all the warm qualities of genuine personality. More than this, He is the absolute quintessence of moral excellence, infinitely perfect in righteousness, purity, rectitude, and incomprehensible holiness. And in all this He is uncreated, self-sufficient and beyond the power of human thought to conceive or human speech to utter.

Through the self-revelation of God in the Scriptures and the illumination of the Holy Spirit the Christian gains everything and loses nothing. To his idea of God there are added the twin concepts of personality and moral character, but there remains the original sense of wonder and fear in the presence of the world-filling Mystery. Today his heart may leap up with the happy cry, "Abba Father, my Lord and my God!" Tomorrow he may kneel with the delighted trembling to admire and adore the High and Lofty One that inhabiteth eternity.

Holy is the way God is. To be holy He does not conform to a standard. He is that standard. He is absolutely holy with an infinite, incomprehensible fullness of purity that is incapable of being other than it is. Because He is holy, His attributes are holy; that is, whatever we think of as belonging to God must be thought of as holy.

God is holy and He has made holiness the moral condition necessary to the health of His universe. Sin's temporary presence in the world only accents this. Whatever is holy is healthy; evil is a moral sickness that must end ultimately in death. The formation of the language itself suggests this, the English word holy deriving from the Anglo-Saxon *halig, hal,* meaning, "well, whole."

Since God's first concern for His universe is its moral health, that is, its holiness, whatever is contrary to this is necessarily under His eternal displeasure. To preserve His creation God must destroy whatever would destroy it. When He arises to put down iniquity and save the world from irreparable moral collapse, He is said to be angry. Every wrathful judgment in the history of the world has been a holy act of preservation. The holiness of God, the wrath of God, and the health of the creation are inseparably united. God's wrath is His utter intolerance of whatever degrades and destroys. He hates iniquity as a mother hates the polio that take the life of her child.

God is holy with an absolute holiness that knows no degrees, and this

He cannot impart to His creatures. But there is a relative and contingent holiness which He shares with angels and seraphim in heaven and with redeemed men on earth as their preparation for heaven. This holiness God can and does impart to His children. He shares it with them by imputation and by impartation, and because He has made it available to them through the blood of the Lamb, He requires it of them. To Israel first and later to His Church God spoke, saying, "Be ye holy; for I am holy." He did not say "Be ye as holy as I am holy," for that would be to demand of us absolute holiness, something that belongs to God alone.

Before the uncreated fire of God's holiness angels veil their faces. Yea, the heavens are not clean, and the stars are not pure in His sight. No honest man can say "I am holy," but neither is any honest man willing to ignore the solemn words of the inspired writer, "Follow peace with all men, and holiness, without which no man shall see the Lord."

Caught in this dilemma, what are we Christians to do? We must like Moses cover ourselves with faith and humility while we steal a quick look at the God whom no man can see and live. The broken and the contrite heart He will not despise. We must hide our unholiness in the wounds of Christ as Moses hid himself in the cleft of the rock while the glory of God passed by. We must take refuge from God in God. Above all we must believe that God sees us perfect in His Son while He disciplines and chastens and purges us that we may be partakers of His holiness.

By faith and obedience, by constant meditation on the holiness of God, by loving righteousness and hating iniquity, by growing acquaintance with the Spirit of holiness, we can acclimate ourselves to the fellowship of the saints on earth and prepare ourselves for the eternal companionship of God and the saints above. Thus, as they say when humble believers meet, we will have a heaven to go to heaven in.

How dread are Thine eternal years,
  O everlasting Lord!
By prostrate spirits day and night
  Incessantly adored!

How beautiful, how beautiful
  The sight of Thee must be,

Thine endless wisdom, boundless power,
  And awful purity!

Oh how I fear Thee, living God!
  With deepest, tenderest fears,
And worship Thee with trembling hope,
  And penitential tears.
(Frederick W. Faber)

3

Holiness

J. C. Ryle

J. C. Ryle (1816-1900) was educated at Eton and Christ Church, Oxford. He was ordained as an Anglican minister in 1842, and eventually consecrated a bishop in 1880, which office he held until shortly before his death.

Ryle was thoroughly evangelical in his doctrine and uncompromising in his principles; he was a prolific writer, and a passionate preacher and faithful pastor. Ryle's classic work *Holiness* (written from a Reformed perspective) deserves a supreme place among the great works on this subject.

J. I. Packer says of Ryle, "As a pastor he taught Christian conduct, devotion, and character transformed by the Holy Spirit in a way that the great seventeenth-century Puritans had done before him. . . . He was a big man both physically and spiritually, and his brains, energy, vision, drive, independence, clear head, kind heart, . . . good sense, impatience with stupidity, firmness of principle, and freedom from inhibitions would have made him a leader in any field." Thankfully for the Church, God called and gifted him, using him to bless his people. And God continues to use him through his writings.

Let me try to show what true practical holiness is—what sort of persons are those whom God calls holy.

A man may go to great lengths, and yet never reach true holiness. It is not knowledge—Balaam had that; nor great profession—Judas Iscariot had that; nor doing many things—Herod had that; nor zeal for certain matters in religion—Jehu had that; nor morality and outward respectability of conduct—the young ruler had that; nor taking pleasure in hearing preachers—the Jews in Ezekiel's time had that; nor keeping company with godly people—Joab and Gehazi and Demas had that. Yet none of these was holy! These things alone are not holiness. A man may have any one of them, and yet never see the Lord.

What then is true practical holiness? It is a hard question to answer. I do not mean that there is any lack of scriptural matter on the subject. But I fear lest I should give a defective view of holiness, and not say all that ought to be said; or lest I should say things about it that ought not to be said, and so do harm. Let me, however, try to draw a picture of holiness, that we may see it clearly before the eyes of our minds. Only let it never be forgotten, when I have said all, that my account is but a poor imperfect outline at the best.

What Sort of Persons are Those Whom God Calls Holy?

1. *Holiness is the habit of being of one mind with God, according as we find His mind described in Scripture.* It is the habit of agreeing in God's judgment, hating what He hates, loving what He loves, and measuring everything in this world by the standard of His Word. He who most entirely agrees with God, he is the most holy man.

2. *A holy man will endeavor to shun every known sin, and to keep every known commandment.* He will have a decided bent of mind toward God, a hearty desire to do His will, a greater fear of displeasing Him than of displeasing the world, and a love to all His ways. He will feel what Paul felt when he said, "I delight in the law of God after the inward man" (Rom. 7:22), and what David felt when he said, "I esteem *all* Thy precepts concerning all things to be right, and I hate *every* false way" (Ps. 119:128).

3. *A holy man will strive to be like our Lord Jesus Christ.* He will not only live the life of faith in Him, and draw from Him all his daily peace and strength, but he will also labor to have the mind that was in Him, and to be "conformed to His image" (Rom. 8:29). It will be his aim to bear with and forgive others, even as Christ forgave us, to be unselfish—even as Christ pleased not Himself—to walk in love, even as Christ loved us, to be lowly-minded and humble, even as Christ made Himself of no reputation and

humbled Himself. He will remember that Christ was a faithful witness for the truth; that He came not to do His own will; that it was His meat and drink to do His Father's will; that He would continually deny Himself in order to minister to others; that He was meek and patient under undeserved insults; that He thought more of godly poor men than of kings; that He was full of love and compassion to sinners; that He was bold and uncompromising in denouncing sin; that He sought not the praise of men, when He might have had it; that He went about doing good; that He was separate from worldly people; that He continued instant in prayer; that He would not let even His nearest relations stand in His way when God's work was to be done. These things a holy man will try to remember. By them he will endeavor to shape his course in life. He will lay to heart the saying of John, "He that saith he abideth in Christ ought himself also so to walk, even as He walked" (1 John 2:6); and the saying of Peter, that "Christ suffered for us, leaving us an example that ye should follow His steps" (1 Peter 2:21). Happy is he who has learned to make Christ his "all," both for salvation and example! Much time would be saved, and much sin prevented, if men would oftener ask themselves the question, "What would Christ have said and done, if He were in my place?"

4. *A holy man will follow after meekness, longsuffering, gentleness, patience, kind tempers, government of his tongue.* He will bear much, forbear much, overlook much, and be slow to talk of standing on his rights. We see a bright example of this in the behaviour of David when Shimei cursed him, and of Moses when Aaron and Miriam spoke against him. (2 Sam. 16:10; Num. 12:3).

5. *A holy man will follow after temperance and self-denial. He will labor to mortify the desires of his body; to crucify his flesh with his affections and lusts; to curb his passions; to restrain his carnal inclinations, lest at any time they break loose.* Oh, what a word is that of the Lord Jesus to the Apostles, "Take heed to yourselves, lest at any time your hearts be overcharged with surfeiting and drunkenness, and cares of this life" (Luke 21:34); and that of the Apostle Paul, "I keep under my body, and bring it into subjection, lest that by any means when I have preached to others, I myself should be a castaway" (1 Cor. 9:27).

6. *A holy man will follow after charity and brotherly kindness. He will endeav-or to observe the golden rule of doing as he would have men do to him, and speaking as he would have men speak to him.* He will be full of affection towards his brethren—towards their bodies, their property, their characters, their feelings, their souls. "He that loveth another," says Paul, "hath fulfilled the law." (Rom. 8:8). He will abhor all lying, slandering, backbiting, cheating, dishonesty, and unfair dealing, even in the least things. The shekel and cubit of the sanctuary were larger than those in common use. He will strive to adorn his religion by all his outward demeanor, and to make it lovely and beautiful in the eyes of all around him. Alas, what condemning words are the 13th chapter of 1 Corinthians, and the Sermon on the Mount, when laid alongside the conduct of many professing Christians!

7. *A holy man will follow after a spirit of mercy and benevolence towards others.* He will not stand all the day idle. He will not be content with doing no harm; he will try to do good. He will strive to be useful in his day and generation, and to lessen the spiritual needs and misery around him, as far as he can. Such was Dorcas, "full of good works and alms deeds, which she did"—not merely purposed and talked about, *but did.* Such an one was Paul: "I will very gladly spend and be spent for you," he says, "though the more abundantly I love you the less I be loved" (Acts 9:36; 2 Cor. 12:15).

8. *A holy man will follow after purity of heart.* He will dread all filthiness and uncleanness of spirit, and seek to avoid all things that might draw him into it. He knows his own heart is like tinder, and will diligently keep clear of the sparks of temptation. Who shall dare to talk of strength when David can fall? There is many a hint to be gleaned from the ceremonial law. Under it the man who only *touched* a bone, or a dead body, or a grave, or a diseased person, became at once unclean in the sight of God. And these things were emblems and figures. Few Christians are ever too watchful and too particular about this point.

9. *A holy man will follow after the fear of God.* I do not mean the fear of a slave, who only works because he is afraid of punishment, and would be idle if he did not dread discovery. I mean rather the fear of a child, who wishes to live and move as if he was always before his father's face, because

he loves him. What a noble example Nehemiah gives us of this! When he became governor at Jerusalem he might have been chargeable to the Jews and required of them money for his support. The former Governors had done so. There was none to blame him if he did. But he says, "So did not I, because of the fear of God" (Neh. 5:15).

10. *A holy man will follow after humility.* He will desire, in lowliness of mind, to esteem all others better than himself. He will see more evil in his own heart than in any other in the world. He will understand something of Abraham's feeling, when he says, "I am dust and ashes"; and Jacob's, when he says, "I am less than the least of all Thy mercies"; and Job's, when he says, "I am vile"; and Paul's, when he says, "I am chief of sinners." Holy Bradford, that faithful martyr of Christ, would sometimes finish his letters with these words, "A most miserable sinner, John Bradford." Good old Mr. Grimshaw's last words, when he lay on his death-bed, were these, "Here goes an unprofitable servant."

11. *A holy man will follow after faithfulness in all the duties and relations in life.* He will try, not merely to fill his place as well as others who take no thought for their souls, but even better, because he has higher motives, and more help than they. Those words of Paul should never be forgotten, "Whatever ye do, do it heartily, as unto the Lord"; "Not slothful in business, fervent in spirit, serving the Lord." (Col. 3:23; Rom. 12:11). Holy persons should aim at doing everything well, and should be ashamed of allowing themselves to do anything ill if they can help it. Like Daniel, they should seek to give no "occasion" against themselves, except "concerning the law of their God" (Dan. 6:5). They should strive to be good husbands and good wives, good parents and good children, good masters and good servants, good neighbors, good friends, good subjects, good in private and good in public, good in the place of business and good by their firesides. Holiness is worth little indeed, if it does not bear this kind of fruit. The Lord Jesus puts a searching question to His people, when He says, "What do ye more than others?" (Matt. 5:47).

12. *Last, but not least, a holy man will follow after spiritual-mindedness.* He will endeavor to set his affections entirely on things above, and to hold

things on earth with a very loose hand. He will not neglect the business of the life that now is; but the first place in his mind and thoughts will be given to the life to come. He will aim to live like one whose treasure is in heaven, and to pass through this world like a stranger and pilgrim traveling to his home. To commune with God in prayer, in the Bible, and in the assembly of His people—these things will be the holy man's chiefest enjoyments. He will value everything and place and company, just in proportion as it draws him nearer to God. He will enter into something of David's feeling, when he says, "My soul followeth hard after Thee." "Thou art my portion" (Ps. 62:8; 99:57).

Some Reasons Why Practical Holiness is So Important

Can holiness save us? Can holiness put away sin, cover iniquities, make satisfaction for transgressions, pay our debt to God? No, not a whit. God forbid that I should ever say so. Holiness can do none of these things. The brightest saints are all "unprofitable servants." Our purest works are no better than filthy rags, when tried by the light of God's holy law. The white robe which Jesus offers, and faith puts on, must be our only righteousness, the name of Christ our only confidence, the Lamb's book of life our only title to heaven. With all our holiness we are no better than sinners. Our best things are stained and tainted with imperfection. They are all more or less incomplete, wrong in the motive or defective in the performance. By the deeds of the law shall no child of Adam ever be justified. "By grace are ye saved through faith, and that not of yourselves, it is the gift of God: not of works, lest any man should boast" (Eph. 2:8-9).

Why then is holiness so important? Why does the apostle say, "Without it no man shall see the Lord"? (Heb. 12:14). Let me set out in order a few reasons.

1. *For one thing, we must be holy, because the voice of God in Scripture plainly commands it.* The Lord Jesus says to His people, "Except your righteousness shall exceed the righteousness of the scribes and Pharisees, ye shall in no case enter into the kingdom of heaven" (Matt. 5:20). "Be ye perfect, even as your Father which is in heaven is perfect" (Matt. 5:48). Paul tells the Thessalonians, "This is the will of God, even your sanctification" (1 Thess. 4:3). And Peter says, "As He which hath called you is holy, so be ye holy in all

manner of conversation; because it is written, 'Be ye holy, for I am holy.'" (1 Peter 1:15-16.) "In this," says Leighton, "law and Gospel agree."

2. *We must be holy, because this is one grand end and purpose for which Christ came into the world.* Paul writes to the Corinthians, "He died for all, that they which live should not henceforth live unto themselves, but unto Him which died for them and rose again" (2 Cor. 5:15). And to the Ephesians, "Christ loved the Church, and gave Himself for it, that He might sanctify and cleanse it" (Eph. 5:25-26). And to Titus, "He gave Himself for us, that He might redeem us from all iniquity, and purify unto Himself a peculiar people, zealous of good works" (Titus 2:14). In short, to talk of men being saved from the guilt of sin, without being at the same time saved from its dominion in their hearts, is to contradict the witness of all Scripture. Are believers said to be elect?—it is "through sanctification of the Spirit." Are they predestinated?—it is "to be conformed to the image of God's Son." Are they chosen?—it is "that they may be holy." Are they called?—it is "with a holy calling." Are they afflicted?—it is that they may be "partakers of holiness." Jesus is a complete Savior. He does not merely take away the guilt of a believer's sin, He does more—He breaks its power (1 Peter 1:2; Rom. 8:29; Eph. 1:4; Heb. 12:10).

3. *We must be holy, because this is the only sound evidence that we have a saving faith in our Lord Jesus Christ.* The Twelfth Article of our Church [Church of England] says truly, that "Although good works cannot put away our sins, and endure the severity of God's judgment, yet are they pleasing and acceptable to God in Christ, and do spring out necessarily of a true and lively faith; insomuch that by them a lively faith may be as evidently known as a tree discerned by its fruits." James warns us there is such a thing as a dead faith—a faith which goes no further than the profession of the lips, and has no influence on a man's character (James 2:17).

True saving faith is a very different kind of thing. True faith will always show itself by its fruits—it will sanctify, it will work by love, it will overcome the world, it will purify the heart. I know that people are fond of talking about death-bed evidences. They will rest on words spoken in the hours of fear, and pain, and weakness, as if they might take comfort in them about the friends they lose. But I am afraid in ninety-nine cases out of a hundred such evidences are not to be depended on. I suspect that, with rare exceptions, men die just as they have lived. The only safe evidence that we are one with Christ, and Christ in us, is a holy life. They that live unto the Lord are generally the only people who die in the Lord. If we would die the death of the righteous, let us not rest in slothful desires only; let us seek to live His life. It is a true saying of Traill's, "That man's state is naught, and his faith unsound, that finds not his hopes of glory purifying to his heart and life."

4. *We must be holy, because this is the only proof that we love the Lord Jesus Christ in sincerity.* This is a point on which He has spoken most plainly, in the fourteenth and fifteenth chapters of John. "If ye love Me, keep my commandments"; "He that hath my commandments and keepeth them, he it is that loveth Me"; "If a man love Me he will keep my words"; "Ye are my friends if ye do whatsoever I command you" (John 14:15, 21, 23; 15:14). Plainer words than these it would be difficult to find, and woe to those who neglect them! Surely that man must be in an unhealthy state of soul who can think of all that Jesus suffered, and yet cling to those sins for which that suffering was undergone. It was sin that wove the crown of thorns; it was sin that pierced our Lord's hands, and feet, and side; it was sin that brought Him to Gethsemane and Calvary, to the cross and to the grave. Cold must our hearts be if we do not hate sin and labor to get rid of it, though we may have to cut off the right hand and pluck out the right eye in doing it.

5. *We must be holy, because this is the only sound evidence that we are true children of God.* Children in this world are generally like their parents. Some, doubtless, are more so, and some less, but it is seldom indeed that you cannot trace a kind of family likeness. And it is much the same with the children of God. The Lord Jesus says, "If ye were Abraham's children ye would do the works of Abraham"; "If God were your Father ye would love Me" (John 8:39, 42). If men have no likeness to the Father in heaven, it is vain to talk of their being His "sons." If we know nothing of holiness we may flatter ourselves as we please, but we have not got the Holy Spirit dwelling in us: we are dead, and must be brought to life again; we are lost and must be found. "As many as are led by the Spirit of God, they," and they only, "are the sons of God" (Rom. 8:14). We must show by our lives

the family we belong to. We must let men see by our good behaviour that we are indeed the children of the Holy One, or our sonship is but an empty name. "Say not," says Gurnall, "that thou hast royal blood in thy veins, and art born of God, except thou canst prove thy pedigree by daring to be holy."

6. *We must be holy, because this is the most likely way to do good to others.* We cannot live to ourselves only in this world. Our lives will always be doing either good or harm to those who see them. They are a silent sermon which all can read. It is sad indeed when they are a sermon for the devil's cause, and not for God's. I believe that far more is done for Christ's kingdom by the holy living of believers than we are at all aware of. There is a reality about such living which makes men feel, and obliges them to think. It carries a weight and influence with it which nothing else can give. It makes religion beautiful, and draws men to consider it, like a lighthouse seen afar off. The day of judgment will prove that many besides husbands have been won "without the word" by a holy life, (1 Peter 3:1.)

You may talk to persons about the doctrines of the Gospels, and few will listen, and still fewer understand. But your life is an argument that none can escape. There is a meaning about holiness which not even the most unlearned can help taking in. They may not understand justification, but they can understand love. I believe there is far more harm done by unholy and inconsistent Christians than we are aware of. Such men are among Satan's best allies. They pull down by their lives what ministers build with their lips. They cause the chariot wheels of the Gospel to drive heavily. They supply the children of this world with a never-ending excuse for remaining as they are. "I cannot see the use of so much religion," said an irreligious tradesman not long ago; "I observe that some of my customers are always talking about the Gospel, and faith, and election, and the blessed promises, and so forth; and yet these very people think nothing of cheating me of pence and half-pence, when they have an opportunity. Now, if religious persons can do such things, I do not see what good there is in religion." I grieve to be obliged to write such things, but I fear that Christ's name is too often blasphemed because of the lives of Christians. Let us take heed lest the blood of souls should be required at our hands. From murder of souls by inconsistency and loose walking, good Lord, deliver us! Oh, for the sake of others, if for no other reason, let us strive to be holy!

7. *We must be holy, because our present comfort depends much upon it.* We cannot be too often reminded of this. We are sadly apt to forget that there is a close connection between sin and sorrow, holiness and happiness, sanctification and consolation. God has so wisely ordered it, that our well-being and our well-doing are linked together. He has mercifully provided that even in this world it shall be man's interest to be holy. Our justification is not by works—our calling and election are not according to our works—but it is vain for anyone to suppose that he will have a lively sense of his justification, or an assurance of his calling, so long as he neglects good works, or does not strive to live a holy life. "Hereby we do know that we know Him, if we keep His commandments"; "Hereby we know that we are of the truth, and shall assure our hearts." (1 John 2:3; 3:19.)

A believer may as soon expect to feel the sun's rays upon a dark and cloudy day, as to feel strong consolation in Christ while he does not follow Him fully. When the disciples forsook the Lord and fled, they escaped danger, but they were miserable and sad. When, shortly after, they confessed Him boldly before men, they were cast into prison and beaten; but we are told "they rejoiced that they were counted worthy to suffer shame for His name." (Acts 5:41.) Oh, for our own sakes, if there were no other reason, let us strive to be holy! He that follows Jesus most fully will always follow Him most encouragingly.

8. *Lastly, we must be holy, because without holiness on earth we shall never be prepared to enjoy heaven.* Heaven is a holy place. The Lord of heaven is a holy Being. The angels are holy creatures. Holiness is written on everything in heaven. The book of Revelation says expressly, "There shall in no wise enter into it anything that defileth, neither whatsoever worketh abomination, or maketh a lie" (Rev. 21:27).

4

Hungering for Holiness

Thomas Brooks

Thomas Brooks (1608-1680) entered Emmanuel College, Cambridge, in 1625, where such New England Puritans as Thomas Hooker, John Cotton, and Thomas Shepard were also educated, but he appears to have left before graduating. Brooks was ordained as a preacher of the gospel in 1640 and became a chaplain to the parliamentary fleet, serving for some years at sea. That ministry is mentioned in some of his "sea-devotions" as well as his statement: "I have been some years at sea and through grace I can say that I would not exchange my sea experiences for England's riches."

After the Civil War, Brooks became minister at the church of St. Thomas the Apostle, Queen Street, London (1648-1651). He was often called to preach before Parliament. In 1652, he became rector of St. Margaret's, New Fish Street Hill. Later he became minister of a congregation at Moorfields, near St. Margaret's. Unlike many ministers, he stayed in London during the Great Plague of 1665, faithfully tending his flock. John Reeve, who preached his funeral, said Brooks had "a sweet nature, great gravity, large charity, wonderful patience, and strong faith."

Consider the necessity of holiness. It is impossible that ever you should be happy, except you are holy. No holiness here, no happiness hereafter. The Scripture speaks of three bodily inhabitants of heaven—Enoch, before the law; Elijah, under the law; and Jesus Christ, under the Gospel: all three eminent in holiness, to teach us, that even in an ordinary course there is no going to heaven without holiness. There are many thousand thousands now in heaven, but not one unholy one among them all; there is not one sinner among all those saints; not one goat among all those sheep; not one weed among all those flowers; not one thorn or prickle among all those roses; not one pebble among all those glistering diamonds. There is not one Cain among all those Abels; nor one Ishmael among all those Isaacs; nor one Esau among all those Jacobs in heaven. There is not one Ham among all the patriarchs; not one Saul among all the prophets; nor one Judas among all the apostles; nor one Demas among all the preachers; nor one Simon Magus among all the professors.

Heaven is only for the holy man, and the holy man is only for heaven; heaven is a garment of glory, that is only suited to him that is holy. God, who is truth itself, and cannot lie, hath said it, that "without holiness no man shall see the Lord" (Heb. 12:14). Mark that word, "no man." Without holiness the rich man shall not see the Lord; without holiness the poor man shall not see the Lord; without holiness the nobleman shall not see the Lord; without holiness the mean man shall not see the Lord; without holiness the prince shall not see the Lord; without holiness the peasant shall not see the Lord; without holiness the ruler shall not see the Lord; without holiness the ruled shall not see the Lord; without holiness the learned man shall not see the Lord; without holiness the ignorant man shall not see the Lord; without holiness the husband shall not see the Lord; without holiness the wife shall not see the Lord; without holiness the father shall not see the Lord; without holiness the child shall not see the Lord; without holiness the master shall not see the Lord; without holiness the servant shall not see the Lord. "For faithful and strong is the Lord of hosts that hath spoken it" (Josh. 23:14).

In this day some cry up one form, some another; some cry up one Church state, some another; some cry up one way, some another; but certainly the way of holiness is the good old way (Jer. 6:16); it is the King of kings' highway to heaven and happiness: "And a highway shall be there, and a way, and it shall be called the way of holiness; the unclean shall not pass over it; but it shall be for those: the wayfaring men, though fools, shall not err therein" (Isa. 35:8). Some men say, "Lo, here is the way"; other men say, "Lo, there is the way"; but certainly the way of holiness is the surest, the safest, the easiest, the noblest, and the shortest way to happiness.

Among the heathen, no man could enter into the temple of honour, but must first enter the temple of virtue. There is no entering the temple of happiness, except you enter into the temple of holiness. Holiness must first enter into you, before you can enter into God's holy hill. As Rachel cried out, "Give me children, or I die"; so all unsanctified souls may well cry out, "Lord, give me holiness, or I die: give me holiness or I eternally die." If the angels, those princes of glory, fall once from their holiness, they shall be forever excluded from everlasting happiness and blessedness. If Adam in paradise falls from his purity, he shall quickly be driven out from the presence of divine glory. Augustine would not be a wicked man, an unholy man, one hour for all the world, because he did not know but that he might die that hour; and should he die in an unholy estate, he knew he should be forever separated from the presence of the Lord and the glory of His power.

O, sirs, do not deceive your own souls; holiness is of absolute necessity; without it you shall never see the Lord (2 Thess. 1:8-10). It is not absolutely necessary that you should be great or rich in the world; but it is absolutely necessary that you should be holy; it is not absolutely necessary that you should enjoy health, strength, friends, liberty, life; but it is absolutely necessary that you should be holy. A man may see the Lord without worldly prosperity, but he can never see the Lord except he be holy.

Ah, sirs, holiness is a flower that grows not in nature's garden. Men are not born with holiness in their hearts, as they are born with tongues in their mouths; holiness is of a divine offspring; it is a pearl of price, that is to be found in no nature but a renewed nature, in no bosom but a sanctified bosom. There is not the least beam or spark of holiness in any natural man in the world. "Every imagination of the thoughts of man's heart is only evil continually" (Gen. 6:5). "How can man be clean that is born of a woman?" (Job 25:4). The interrogation carries in it a strong negation, "How can man be clean?" That is, man cannot be clean that is born of a woman; a man that is born of a woman is born in sin, and born both under wrath and under the curse. "And who can bring a clean thing out of an unclean?" "But we are all as an unclean thing, and all our righteousnesses are as filthy rags" (Job 14:4; Isa. 64:6). "There is none righteous, no not one; there is none that understandeth, there is none that seeketh after God." (Rom. 3:10-11.) Every man by nature is a stranger, yea, an enemy to holiness. (Rom. 8:7). Every man that comes into this world comes with his face towards sin and hell, and with his back upon God and holiness.

Such is the corruption of our nature, that, propound any divine good to it, it is entertained as fire by water, or wet wood, with hissing. Propound any evil, then it is like fire to straw; it is like the foolish satyr that made haste to kiss the fire; it is like that unctuous matter which, the naturalists say, sucks and snatches the fire to it, with which it is consumed. All men are born sinners, and there is nothing but an infinite power that can make them saints. All men would be happy, and yet they naturally loathe to be holy. By all which you may clearly see that food is not more necessary for the preservation of natural life, than holiness is necessary for the preservation and salvation of the soul. If a man had the wisdom of Solomon, the strength of Samson, the courage of Joshua, the policy of Ahithophel, the dignities of Haman, the power of Ahasuerus, and the eloquence of Apollos, yet all those without holiness would never save him.

The days and times wherein we live call aloud for holiness. If you look upon them as days and times of grace, what greater and higher engagements to holiness were ever put upon a people, than those that God hath put upon us, who enjoy so many ways, means, and helps to make us holy? Oh, the pains, the care, the cost, the charge, that God hath been at, and that God is daily at, to make us holy! Hath He not sent, and doth He not still send His messengers, rising up early, and going to bed late, and all to provoke you to be holy? Have not many of them spent their time, and spent their strength, and spent their spirits, and spent their lives to make you holy? O, sirs, what do holy ordinances call for, but holy hearts and holy lives? What do days of light call for, but walking in the light, and casting off the deeds of darkness? What is the voice of all the means of grace, but this: Oh, labour to be gracious? And what is the voice of the Holy Spirit, but this: Oh, labour to be holy? And what is the voice of all the miracles of mercy that God hath wrought in the midst of you, but this: "Be ye holy, be ye holy"?

O, sirs, what could the Lord have done that He hath not done to make you holy? Hath He not lifted you up to heaven in respect of holy helps? Hath He not to this very day followed you close with holy offers, and holy entreaties, and holy counsels, and holy encouragements, and all to make you holy? And will you be loose still, and proud still, and worldly still, and malicious still, and envious still, and contentious still, and unholy still? Oh, what is this, but to provoke the Lord to put out all the lights of heaven, to drive your teachers into corners, to remove your candlesticks, and to send His everlasting Gospel, that hath stood long a tip-toe, among a people that may more highly prize it, and dearly love it, and stoutly defend it, and conscientiously practice it, than you have done to this very day? (Rev. 2:4-5; Isa. 42:25).

I suppose there is nothing more evident than that the times and seasons wherein we live call aloud upon everyone to look after holiness, and to labour for holiness. Never complain of the times, but cease to do evil, and labour to do well, and all will be well; get but better hearts and better lives, and you will quickly see better times (see Isa. 1:16-19).

5

What Holiness is, and Why it Matters

J. I. Packer

James I. Packer (b. 1926) is a conservative evangelical Anglican, author, and theologian. He currently serves as the Board of Governors' Professor of Theology at Regent College in Vancouver, British Columbia. He is considered to be one of the most important evangelical theologians of the late twentieth and early twenty-first centuries. Born in England, the son of a clerk for the Great Western Railway, Packer won a scholarship to Oxford University. It was as a student at Oxford where he first met C. S. Lewis, whose teachings would become a major influence in his life.

Packer became recognized as a leader in the Evangelical movement in the Church of England. In 1978, he signed the Chicago Statement on Biblical Inerrancy, which affirmed the conservative position on inerrancy. In 1979, Packer moved to Vancouver to take up a position with Regent College. He is a frequent contributor to and an executive editor of *Christianity Today*. Packer served as general editor for the *English Standard Version of the Bible*. The author of many works, one of Packer's most popular books is *Knowing God*.

⟨⟨⟨⟩⟩⟩

"Just as he who called you is holy, so be holy in all you do; for it is written: 'Be holy, because I am holy'" (1 Peter 1:15-16).

"Make every effort . . . to be holy; without holiness no one will see the Lord" (Heb. 12:14).

Loss of the Precious Past

Our grandfather clock, which tells us not only the hours, minutes, and seconds, but also the days of the week, the months of the year, and the phases of the moon, is something of a veteran. Scratched on one of its lead weights is the date 1789—the year of the French Revolution and George Washington's first term as president. I am writing these words in 1991, the 200th anniversary of John Wesley's death: our clock was going before he stopped going, if I may put it so. It is a musical clock, too, of a rather unusual sort Not only does it strike the hour, but it also has a built-in carillon (knobs on a brass cylinder tripping hammers that hit bells which play a tune for three minutes every three hours). Two of its four tunes we recognize, for we hear them still today. However, the other two, which sound like country dances, are unknown—not just to us but to everyone who has heard them played.

Over the years they were forgotten, which was a pity, for they are good tunes; and we would like to know something about them.

In the same way, the historic Christian teaching on holiness has been largely forgotten, and that also is a pity, for it is central to the glory of God and the good of souls.

It is nearly sixty years since I learned at school the opening verse of a poem by Rudyard Kipling, titled "The Way through the Woods." It goes like this:

> *They shut the road through the woods*
> *Seventy years ago.*
> *Weather and rain have undone it again*
> *And now you would never know*
> *There was once a road through the woods.*

I suppose it is because I love walking through woods that these lines move me so deeply. Again and again, when I find myself mourning the loss of a good thing that has perished through stupidity, carelessness, or neglect (and I confess that, both as a conservationist and a Christian, I have that experience often), Kipling's verse jumps into my mind. It haunts me now, as I contemplate the church's current loss of biblical truth about holiness.

Our Christian Heritage of Holiness. There was a time when all Christians laid great emphasis on the reality of God's call to holiness and spoke with deep insight about his enabling of us for it. Evangelical Protestants, in particular, offered endless variations on the themes of what God's holiness requires of us, what our holiness involves for us, by what means and through what disciplines the Holy Spirit sanctifies us, and the ways in which holiness increases our assurance and joy and usefulness to God.

The Puritans insisted that all life and relationships must become "holiness to the Lord." John Wesley told the world that God had raised up Methodism "to spread scriptural holiness throughout the land." Phoebe Palmer, Handley Moule, Andrew Murray, Jessie Penn-Lewis, F. B. Meyer, Oswald Chambers, Horatius Bonar, Amy Carmichael, and L. B. Maxwell are only a few of the leading figures in the "holiness revival" that touched all evangelical Christendom between the mid-nineteenth and mid-twentieth centuries.

On the other side of the Reformation divide, Seraphim of Sarov (Russian Orthodox) and Teresa of Avila, Ignatius Loyola, Madame Guyon, and Père Grou (all Roman Catholics) ministered as apostles of holiness in a similar way. We must realize that, as John Wesley, for one, clearly saw, the Reformation cleavage was much less deep on sanctification and the Spirit than it was on justification and the Mass.

Formerly, then, holiness was highlighted throughout the Christian church. But how different it is today! To listen to our sermons and to read the books we write for each other, and then to watch the zany, worldly, quarrelsome way we behave as Christian people, you would never imagine that once the highway of holiness was clearly marked out for Bible-believers, so that ministers and people knew what it was and could speak of it with authority and confidence. "Weather and rain have undone it again." Now we have to rebuild and reopen the road, starting really from scratch.

In the Old Testament we read how Isaac, forced to relocate his large household, "reopened the wells that had been dug in the time of his father Abraham, which the Philistines had stopped up after Abraham died" (Gen. 26:18). Isaac thus secured the water supply without which neither his family, nor his servants, nor his cattle, nor he himself, could have survived. He did not prospect for new wells in a water-divining quest that might or might not have succeeded, but he went straight to the old wells. He knew he would find water in them, once he had cleared them of the earth and debris that malevolent Philistines had piled on top of them. Isaac's action reflects two simple spiritual principles that apply here in a very direct way:

1. The recovering of old truth, truth which has been a means of blessing in the past, can under God become the means of blessing again in the present, while the quest for newer alternatives may well prove barren;

2. No one should be daunted from attempting such recovery by any prejudice, ill will, or unsympathetic attitudes that may have built up against the old truth during the time of its eclipse.

These are the principles whose guidance I follow in this [chapter]. No novelties will be found here. I shall draw, gratefully, from an older Christian wisdom.

The Lost World. Sir Arthur Conan Doyle, the creator of Sherlock Holmes, also wrote an adventure story called *The Lost World.* In it Professor Challenger and his friends climb to a supposedly inaccessible plateau in South America and find there both dinosaurs and a previously unknown pattern of human life. The story was clearly meant for boys from nine to ninety, and I vividly recall being thrilled by it, I think at the age of ten, when I heard it serialized on British radio's Children's Hour. It ends with Challenger battling frozen disbelief among his scientific peers as he tells them what he had found.

In this [chapter] I try to testify to the reality of the lost world of authentic Christian holiness. Will what I say about the supernaturalizing of our disordered lives be believed, I wonder? Will my account of what will appear to many as an unknown pattern of human life have any credibility at all? And what sort of spiritual dinosaur shall I be seen as for producing such ancient ideas? Never mind. In the memorable words of Cary Grant, "A man's got to do what a man's got to do." For me that means moving without fuss into my expository task, whether or not I am going to be taken seriously. To this task I now turn.

School of Holiness, School of Prayer

One of the tides I proposed for this book was *With Christ in the School of*

Holiness. That was a deliberate echo, almost a steal, of *With Christ in the School of Prayer* by Andrew Murray, a much appreciated South African devotional author of two generations ago. I adapted Murray's title in this manner in order to highlight three truths that to me seem basic to all I propose to say. (Murray would—indeed, did—chilly agree with all three, as his own many books make plain.)

First Truth. Holiness, like prayer (which is indeed part of it), is something which, though Christians have an instinct for it through their new birth, as we shall see, they have to learn in and through experience. As Jesus "learned obedience from what he suffered" (Heb. 5:8)—learned what obedience requires, costs, and involves through the experience of actually doing his Father's will up to and in his passion—so Christians must, and do, learn prayer from their struggles to pray, and holiness from their battles for purity of heart and righteousness of life.

Talented youngsters who go to tennis school in order to learn the game soon discover that the heart of the process is not talking about tactics but actually practicing serves and strokes, thus forming new habits and reflexes, so as to iron out weaknesses of style. The routine, which is grueling, is one of doing prescribed things over and over again on the court, against a real opponent, in order to get them really right

Prayer and holiness are learned in a similar way as commitments are made, habits are formed, and battles are fought against a real opponent (Satan, in this case), who with great cunning plays constantly on our weak spots. (That these are often what the world sees as our strong points is an index of Satan's resourcefulness: presumptuous self-reliance and proud overreaching on our part serve his turn just as well as do paralyzing timidity, habits of harshness and anger, lack of discipline, whether inward or outward, evasion of responsibility, lack of reverence for God, and willful indulgence in what one knows to be wrong.) Satan is as good at judo throws as he is at frontal assaults, and we have to be on guard against him all the time.

Second Truth. The process of learning to be holy, like the process of learning to pray, may properly be thought of as a school—God's own school, in which the curriculum, the teaching staff, the rules, the discipline, the occasional prizes, and the fellow pupils with whom one studies, plays, debates, and fraternizes, are all there under God's sovereign providence.

As pushing ahead on the path of prayer and holiness is a prime form of spiritual warfare against sin and Satan, so it is an educational process that God has planned and programmed in order to refine, purge, enlarge, animate, toughen, and mature us. By means of it he brings us progressively into the moral and spiritual shape in which he wants to see us.

Physical education in grade school and adult workouts in fitness centers offer perhaps the closest parallels to what is going on here. They, too, require us to endure things we find it hard to enjoy. As a schoolboy I was gangling and clumsy. I loathed "P. T." (physical training, as it was called in those days). I was in fact very bad at it, but I do not doubt that it was very good for me. Having to heave and bump my dogged way over a period of years through physical jerks that others found easy (and treated as fun and did much better than I could) may well have helped me grasp the virtue of keeping on keeping on in other disciplines that are not immediately gratifying; and God's program of holiness training always includes quite a number of these.

We must be clear in our minds that whatever further reasons there may be why God exposes us to the joys and sorrows, fulfillments and frustrations, delights and disappointment, happinesses and hurts, that make up the emotional reality of our lives, all these experiences are part of his curriculum for us in the school of holiness, which is his spiritual gymnasium for our reshaping and rebuilding in the moral likeness of Jesus Christ

It is reported that on one occasion when Teresa of Avila was traveling, her conveyance dumped her in the mud. The spunky saint's first words as she struggled to her feet were: "Lord, if this is how you treat your friends, it is no wonder that you have so few!" One of the most attractive things about Teresa is that she could be playful like this with her God. But none knew better than she that the ups and downs of her life were divinely planned in order to mold her character, enlarge her heart, and deepen her devotion. And what was true for her is true for us all.

Third Truth. In God's school of holiness our Lord Jesus Christ (the Father's Son and the Christian's Savior) is with us, and we with him, in a controlling relationship of master and servant, leader and follower, teacher and student. It is crucially important to appreciate this. Why is it that in the school of holiness, as in the schools to which we send our own children, some move ahead faster than others? How are the different rates of progress to be explained? Fundamentally, the factor that makes the difference is neither one's intelligence quotient, nor the number of books one has read nor the conferences, camps, and seminars one has attended, but the quality of the fellowship with Christ that one maintains through life's vicissitudes.

Jesus is risen. He is alive and well. Through his Word and Spirit he calls us to himself today, to receive him as our Savior and Lord and become his disciples and followers. Speaking objectively—with reference to how things really are, as distinct from how they might feel at any particular moment—the "there-ness" of Jesus, and the personal nature of his relationship with us as his disciples, are as truly matters of fact as were his bodily presence and his words of comfort and command when he walked this earth long ago. Some, however, do not reckon with this fact as robustly and practically as others do. That is what makes the difference.

I mean this. Some who trust Jesus as their Savior have formed the habit of going to him about everything that comes up, in order to become clear on how they should react to it as his disciples. ("Going to him" is an umbrella phrase that covers three things: praying; meditating, which includes thinking, reflecting, drawing conclusions from Scripture, and applying them directly to oneself in Jesus' presence; and holding oneself open throughout the process to specific illumination from the Holy Spirit) These Christians come to see how events are requiring them to:

- consecrate themselves totally to the Father, as Jesus did;
- say and do only what pleases the Father, as Jesus did;
- accept pain, grief, disloyalty, and betrayal, as Jesus did;
- care for people and serve their needs without either compromise of principle or ulterior motives in practice, as Jesus did;
- accept opposition and isolation, hoping patiently for better things and meantime staying steady under pressure, as Jesus did;
- rejoice in the specifics of the Father's ways and thank him for his wisdom and goodness, as Jesus did;

and so on.

Kept by this means from bitterness and self-pity, these Christians cope with events in a spirit of peace, joy, and eagerness to see what God will do next. Others, however, who are no less committed to Jesus as their Savior, never master this art of habitually going to him about life's challenges. Too often they start by assuming that their life as children of God will be a bed of roses all the way. Then when the storms come, the best they can do is stagger through in a spirit of real if unacknowledged disappointment with God, feeling all the time that he has let them down. It is easy to understand why those in the first category advance farther and faster in the love, humility, and hope that form the essence of Christ-like holiness than those in the second category.

Defining Holiness

But what exactly is holiness? We need a full-scale definition, and my next task is to attempt one.[1]

Consider first the word itself. *Holiness* is a noun that belongs with the adjective *holy* and the verb *sanctify*, which means to make holy. (It is a pity in one way that we have to draw on two word-groups in English to cover what is a single word-group in both Hebrew and Greek, but the verb *holify* would be so ugly that maybe we should be glad it does not exist) *Holy* in both biblical languages means separated and set apart for God, consecrated and made over to him. In its application to people, God's "holy ones" or "saints," the word implies both devotion and assimilation: devotion, in the sense of living a life of service to God; assimilation, in the sense of imitating, conforming to. and becoming like the God one serves. For Christians, this means taking God's moral law as our rule and God's incarnate Son as our model; this is where our analysis of holiness must start . . .[2]

Aspects of Holiness

Holiness Has to Do with My Heart. I speak of the heart here in the biblical sense, according to which it means, not the body's blood pump, but the center and focus of one's inner personal life; the source of motivation, the seat of passion, the spring of all thought processes and particularly of conscience. The assertion that I make, and must myself face, is that holiness begins with the heart. Holiness starts inside a person, with a right purpose that seeks to express itself in a right performance. It is a matter, not just of the motions that I go through, but of the motives that prompt me to go through them.

A holy person's motivating aim, passion, desire, longing. aspiration, goal, and drive is to please God, both by what one does and by what one avoids doing. In other words, one practices good works and cuts out evil ones. Good works begin with praise, worship, and honoring and exalting of God as the temper of one's whole waking life. Evil works start with neglect of these things, and coolness with regard to them. So I must labor to keep my heart actively responsive to God.

Of George Herbert, his favorite poet, the Puritan Richard Baxter said: "*heart-work* and *heaven-work* make up his books."[3] By "heart-work" Baxter meant cultivating the spirit of grateful, humble, adoring love to one's divine Lover and Savior, as Herbert does in this poem (nowadays a familiar hymn):

> *King of glory, King of peace,*
> *I will love thee;*
> *And that love may never cease*
> *I will move [ask] thee.*
> *Thou hast granted my request*
> *Thou hast heard me;*
> *Thou didst note my working breast*
> *Thou hast spared me.*
> *Wherefore with my utmost art*
> *I will sing thee.*
> *And the cream of all my heart*
> *I will bring thee . . .*

This kind of heart-love to God is the taproot of all true holiness. So asceticism, as such—voluntary abstinences, routines of self-deprivation and grueling austerity—is not the same thing as holiness, though some forms of asceticism may well find a place in a holy person's life. Nor is formalism, in the sense of outward conformity in word and deed to the standards God has set anything like holiness, though assuredly there is no holiness without such conformity. Nor is legalism, in the sense of doing things to earn God's favor or to earn more of it than one has already, to be regarded as holiness. Holiness is always the saved sinner's response of gratitude for grace received.

The Pharisees of Jesus' day made all three mistakes, yet were thought to be very holy people until Jesus told them the truth about themselves and the inadequacies of their supposed piety. After that, however, we dare not forget that holiness begins in the heart. Who wants to line up with those Pharisees?

Charles Wesley wrote:

O for a heart to praise my God,
  A heart from sin set free;
A heart that always feels thy blood
  So freely shed for me;
A heart resigned, submissive, meek,
  My great redeemer's throne,
Where only Christ is heard to speak.
  Where Jesus reigns alone;
A heart in every thought renewed
  And full of love divine,
Perfect and right and pure and good:
  A copy, Lord, of thine.

It is with this focus, and this prayer, that real holiness begins.

Holiness Has to Do with My Temperament. By temperament I mean the factors that make specific ways of reacting and behaving natural to me. To use psychologists' jargon, it is my temperament that inclines me to *transact* with my environment (situations, things, and people) in the way I usually do.

Drawing on the full resources of this jargon, psychologist Gordon Allport defines temperament as "the characteristic phenomena of an individual's nature, including his susceptibility to emotional stimulation, his customary strength and speed of response, the quality of his prevailing mood, and all the peculiarities of fluctuation and intensity of mood, these being regarded as dependent on constitutional make-up, and therefore largely hereditary in origin."[4] Allport's statement is cumbersome but clear. Temperament, we might say, is the raw material out of which character is formed. Character is what we do with our temperament. Personality is the final product, the distinct individuality that results.

Temperaments are classified in various ways: positive and negative, easy and difficult, introverted and extroverted, outgoing and withdrawn, active and passive, giving and taking, sociable and forthcoming as distinct from manipulative and self-absorbed, shy and uninhibited, quick and slow to warm up, stiffly defiant as contrasted with flexibly acquiescent, and so on.

While these classifications are useful in their place, perhaps the most useful of all, certainly to the pastoral leader, is the oldest one which Greek physicians had already worked out before the time of Christ. It distinguishes four basic human temperaments:

- the sanguine (warm, jolly, outgoing, relaxed, optimistic);
- the phlegmatic (cool, low-key, detached, unemotional, apathetic);
- the choleric (quick, active, bustling, impatient, with a relatively short fuse); and
- the melancholic (somber, pessimistic, inward-looking, inclined to cynicism and depression).

It then acknowledges the reality of mixed types, such as the phlegmatic-melancholic and the sanguine-choleric, when features of two of the temperaments are found in the same person. In this way it covers everybody. The ancient beliefs about body fluids that supported this classification are nowadays dispelled, but the classification itself remains pastorally helpful. People do observably fall into these categories and recognizing them helps one to understand the temper and reactions of the person with whom one is dealing.

The assertion that I now make, and must myself face, is that I am not to become (or remain) a victim of my temperament. Each temperament has its own strengths and also its weaknesses. Sanguine people tend to live thoughtlessly and at random. Phlegmatic people tend to be remote and unfeeling, sluggish and unsympathetic. Choleric people tend to be quarrelsome, bad-tempered, and poor team players. Melancholic people tend to see everything as bad and wrong and to deny that anything is ever really good and right. Yielding to my temperamental weaknesses is, of course, the most natural thing for me to do, and is therefore the hardest sort of sin for me to deal with and detect. But holy humanity, as I see it in Jesus Christ, combines in itself the strengths of all four temperaments without any of the weaknesses. Therefore, I must try to be like him in this, and not indulge the particular behavioral flaws to which my temperament tempts me.

Holiness for a person of sanguine temperament, then, will involve learning to look before one leaps, to think things through responsibly, and to speak wisely rather than wildly. (These were among the lessons Peter learned with the Spirit's help after Pentecost.) Holiness for a person of phlegmatic temperament will involve a willingness to be open with people, to feel with them and for them, to be forthcoming in relationships, and to become vulnerable, in the sense of risking being hurt. Holiness for a choleric person will involve practicing patience and self-control. It will mean redirecting one's anger and hostility toward Satan and sin, rather than toward fellow human beings who are obstructing what one regards as the way forward. (These were among the lessons Paul learned from the Lord after his conversion.) Finally, holiness for a melancholic person will involve learning to rejoice in God, to give up self-pity and proud pessimism, and to believe, with the medieval mystic Julian of Norwich, that through sovereign divine grace, "All shall be well, and all manner of things shall be well." What are my temperamental weaknesses? If I am to be holy, as I am called to be, I must identify them (that is the hard part) and ask my Lord to enable me to form habits of rising above them.

Holiness Has to Do with My Humanness. Our Lord Jesus Christ is both God for man and man for God; he is God's incarnate Son, fully divine and fully human. We know him as both the mediator of divine grace and the model of human godliness. And what is human godliness, the godliness that is true holiness, as seen in Jesus? It is simply human life lived as the Creator intended—in other words, it is perfect and ideal humanness, an existence in which the elements of the human person are completely united in a totally God-honoring and nature-fulfilling way. (Since God made humanity for himself, godliness naturally fulfills human nature at the deepest level. As experience proves, no contentment can match the contentment of obeying God, however costly this may prove.)

Human lives that are lived differently from this, however, though human in a biological and functional sense, are less than fully human in terms of their quality. Holiness and humanness are correlative terms and mutual implicates (as the logicians would put it). To the extent that I fall short of the first, I fall short of the second as well.

All members of our fallen race who, because they do not know Jesus Christ, still live under the power of that self-deifying, anti-God syndrome in our spiritual system which the Bible calls sin, are living lives that are quali-tatively subhuman. Sin in our minds says otherwise, but in this, as always, sin is lying.

The twentieth century will doubtless go down in history as the century of secular humanism. It began with the euphoric, sin-spawned confidence that human endeavor in science, education, the harnessing of nature, and the increase of wealth would generate human happiness to the point of achieving something like heaven on earth. It ends, however, with none of these hopes realized, but with sickening memories of many great evils com-mitted, and with hearts everywhere full of restless and gloomy unease re-garding humanity's future prospects and life's present worth.

Our proud humanism, so-called, has made the world more like hell than heaven. "What the world hungers for today," say British writers Brain and Warren, rightly, is:

> the discovery of what it means to be truly human. The world sees the destructive effect of devotion to the pursuit of money, sex and power in the lives of many of its heroes. What people long for is a way of integrating the various parts of themselves, and the insights of modem psychology and sociology, in a way that leads to whole-ness. Humanism cannot provide the answer. It is through the per-son of Jesus Christ alone that true humanity can be found. . . . Holi-ness is not primarily about submission to authoritarian rules or narrow or conformist notions of acceptable behavior. It is about the celebration of our humanity.

To hammer this home, they subjoin a telling quotation from the Scottish preacher James Philip:

> Above all the life of the early church was characterized—and sure-ly this is a paramount need in evangelical life today—by humanity. The deepest word that can be spoken about sanctification is that it is a progress towards true humanity. Salvation is, essentially con-sidered, the restoration of humanity to men. This is why the slight-ly inhuman, not to say unnatural, streak in some forms and expres-sions of sanctification is so far removed from the true work of grace in the soul. The greatest saints of God have been characterized, not by haloes and an atmosphere of distant unapproachability, but by their humanity. They have been intensely human and lovable peo-

ple with a twinkle in their eyes.[5]

The assertion I make, and must now myself face, is that Brain, Warren, and Philip are right. Genuine holiness is genuine Christ-likeness, and genuine Christ-likeness is genuine humanness—the only genuine humanness there is. Love in the service of God and others, humility and meekness under the divine hand, integrity of behavior expressing integration of character, wisdom with faithfulness, boldness with prayerfulness, sorrow at people's sins, joy at the Father's goodness, and single-mindedness in seeking to please the Father morning, noon, and night, were all qualities seen in Christ, the perfect man.

Christians are meant to become human as Jesus was human. We are called to imitate these character qualities, with the help of the Holy Spirit, so that the childish instability, inconsiderate self-seeking, pious play acting, and undiscerning pigheadedness that so frequently mar our professedly Christian lives are left behind. "Holiness, rightly understood, is a beautiful thing, and its beauty is the beauty and tenderness of divine love"[6]—which is precisely the beauty of truly mature humanity. I need to remember all this, and take it to heart, and set my sights accordingly.

Holiness Has to Do with My Relationships. Sometimes it has been thought that a state of isolation and solitude, permanently detached from ordinary human involvements, is a help, or perhaps even a necessity, for the practice of holiness. It is true that holy living calls for regular times of aloneness with God. But the notion here is that one gains freedom to move ahead with God by cutting oneself off from the communal life of family and church and society, and that does not seem to be true at all. This idea, it seems, broke surface in the fourth century when pioneer Christian monks habitually went off on their own to practice the bodily austerities and spiritual athletics by which holiness was defined at that time. Thus, Antony withdrew into the Egyptian desert for twenty years. Simeon Stylites mounted his pillar and lived on top of it for thirty years. There was much of this kind of thing.

In turn, people in the Middle Ages cherished the thought of holiness as an optional "higher life" of prayerful austerity for the super-serious. They took for granted the propriety of seeking the detachment that was supposedly necessary for such a life by renouncing marriage and wealth and becoming a monk, a nun, or a hermit. It was thus revolutionary for social life and thought when the Reformers reconceived holiness as the fulfilling of one's relationships, the stewarding of one's talents and time, and the maintaining of love, humility, purity, and zeal for God in one's heart. The ideal of isolationism was then jettisoned completely and replaced by an insistence that holiness—viewed now as the consecrated life of the grateful, forgiven sinner—must be worked out in the way in which, as worshiper, worker, and witness, one relates to one's family, church, and wider community. It is not open to dispute, however, that the Reformers had the Bible on their side.

No doubt the Reformers went too far when, in the heat of their reaction against the prevailing pattern, they sought to close all monasteries and denied there ever was such a thing as a call to serve God in the solitude of withdrawal from the world's affairs. But they were certainly right to negate the idea that such withdrawal is a necessary condition of thoroughgoing holiness, and that involvement in the world rules out all possibility of a full-scale holy life. Biblical holiness is in this sense an unambiguously worldly holiness. Without conforming to the world by becoming materialistic, extravagant, or a grabber and empire-builder of any kind, the Christian must operate as a servant of God in the world, serving others for the Lord's sake. So the assertion I make, and must now myself face, is that the way I relate to others is the essence of my holiness in the sight of God, just as it is one index of it in the sight of men and women.

Here I recall something I once read about a lady who was a popular speaker on holiness platforms and a fluent writer on holiness themes over a hundred years ago. (To avoid scandal, I will not give her name, or reference the quotation that follows.) Her son-in-law wrote that many thought her "a sage and a saint," but he himself "came gradually to think of her as one of the wickedest people I had ever known." Why? His list of reasons began thus: "Her treatment of her husband, whom she despised, was humiliating to the highest degree. She never spoke to him or of him except in a tone that made her contempt obvious. It cannot be denied that he was a silly old man, but he did not deserve what she gave him, and no one capable of mercy could have given it."

The son-in-law was not a Christian, but there is nothing unchristian about this bit of reasoning. For love to be replaced by resentful contempt between husband and wife, or for that matter between parent and child, or colleague and colleague, is a negation of holiness, whatever stuff one may display in books or relay from pulpits and platforms. I need to remember that, and I do not think I am the only one.

In the book that Brain and Warren cited, James Philip points to the way in which some Christians are unwilling to show any kind of empathetic feelings (the macho-syndrome of those who fancy themselves as God's tough guys), and to give up their love of the limelight and the desire to control others (the Diotrephes disease of 3 John 9); all these things, he tells us, induce a hardness of heart that from God's standpoint ruins their relationships.

> There are many Christians who have never learned to say "Thank you" graciously, and who cause their best friends much distress by their apparent thoughtlessness and lack of gratitude, when they take so much costly love and friendship . . . for granted. . . . There is nothing so calculated to cause trouble . . . as persisting in holding unrealistic estimates of oneself. . . . Very often, of course, it is the relentless drive of an inferiority complex that expresses itself in high and exalted ideas of one's own importance, out of all proportion to reality. The problem of inferiority complex is more closely allied to self-centeredness than most of us would like to believe. . . . We must recognize the root of the problem for what it is. This is why, ultimately, the gospel is the only true psychology, for no less a power can break the tyranny of self in the human heart.

The essential problem is "a self that has not learned to die." But "a true surrender to Christ shrinks our inflated ego to its proper size in relation to him and our fellows, and imparts reality to our lives."[7] Wise words! Let none suppose that they advance in holiness while such lapses in Christian relationships still mark their path.

To summarize, then, it appears that Christian holiness is a number of things together. It has both outward and inward aspects. Holiness is a matter of both action and motivation, conduct and character, divine grace and human effort, obedience and creativity, submission and initiative, consecration to God and commitment to people, self-discipline and self-giving, righteousness and love. It is a matter of Spirit-led law-keeping, a walk, or course of life, in the Spirit that displays the fruit of the Spirit (Christ-likeness of attitude and disposition). It is a matter of seeking to imitate Jesus' way of behaving, through depending on Jesus for deliverance from carnal self-absorption and for discernment of spiritual needs and possibilities.

It is a matter of patient, persistent uprightness; of taking God's side against sin in our own lives and in the lives of others; of worshiping God in the Spirit as one serves him in the world; and of single-minded, whole-hearted, free and glad concentration on the business of pleasing God. It is the distinctive form and, so to speak, flavor of a life set apart for God that is now being inwardly renewed by his power.

Holiness is thus the demonstration of faith working by love. It is wholly supernatural in the sense of being God's gracious achievement within us, and wholly natural in the sense of being our own true humanness, lost through sin, misconceived through ignorance, and through listening too hard to current culture—but now in process of restoration through the redirecting and reintegrating energy of new creation in Christ through the Holy Spirit. Oswald Chambers called God's gift of holiness "our brilliant heritage." The phrase was well chosen. *Brilliant*—bright, shining, precious, glorious—is the word that fits.

6

Attention and Obedience

W. E. Sangster

Never taken to a place of worship for the first eight years of his life, W. E. Sangster (1900-1960) found his way into an inner-city London Methodist mission, where he attended Sunday school for several years. When he was twelve years of age, a sensitive teacher gently asked him if he wanted to become a disciple of Jesus Christ. "I sputtered out my little prayer," he wrote years later. "It had one merit. I meant it."

Years later, the outbreak of World War II found Sangster as the senior minister at Westminster Central Hall, the "cathedral" of British Methodism. The sanctuary, seating three thousand, was full Sunday mornings and evenings for sixteen years.

In 1949 Sangster was elected president of the Methodist Conference of Great Britain. He knew that while the Spirit alone ultimately brings people to faith in Jesus Christ, the witness of men and women is always the context of the Spirit's activity. He coveted for his people a "whole-souled, self-oblivious, horizon-filling immersion in the depth of God and in the suffering of their neighbors."

⟳⟳

People talk about "the secret of the saints" but, insofar as the phrase has any meaning at all, it must be an open secret. Surveying the nineteen centuries of Christian history and remembering again—despite the high distinctiveness which identified them—the wide variety of the saints, it is impossible to believe that their secret has anything of the occult or esoteric. It must be in the New Testament and known, in a sense, to all.

Reduced to a minimum, and put in the plainest words, it comes to this:

they *attend* and *obey*. These two principles underlie all Christian sanctity. Examine holiness wherever it is found in Christendom, and seek what is elemental in the methods employed, and it will bring you to attention and obedience. But, observe! It is *absorbing* attention and *utter* obedience. By this docility on the part of the saints, the Holy Spirit enters and the work is done.

Let us look at each of these principles in turn.

Attention. The saints attend to God. How mild the word seems for the absorbing, adoring, passionate gaze they fix upon Him, but that is the essence of it and their absorption and fixity grew as they grew in grace. They *attend to God.*

They attend to God, of course, in prayer. There is no instance of one great in sanctity who was not great in prayer.

The "secret" of St. John Bosco turns out to be the secret of prayer. In nineteen hours a day he never lost conscious communion with God.[1] St. Aloysius Gonzaga could not tear himself away from prayer.[2] To the fixed prayer-pattern of his days, Fletcher of Madeley spent two whole nights a week in prayer.[3] With St. Francis of Assisi, all life was prayer.[4] Alexander Grant called prayer his "Fourth Dimension."[5] Thomas Collins was wrapped in God for hours on end, and would wander in the country for a day of prayer.[6] They said of St. Gerard Majella that "for him, everything was prayer."[7] Everything was prayer, also, for the Sadhu Sundar Singh, though within two or three years of his conversion, he had ceased to pray for things and prayed only for God.[8] St. Thérèse of Lisieux found a similar development in her absorbing prayer. She said: "I am no longer able to ask eagerly for anything save the perfect accomplishment of God's designs on my soul."[9] All progress with Catherine Booth was progress in prayer. "Oh to live in the spirit of prayer!" she cries. "I feel it is the real secret of religion."[10] Lost in prayer at times, Henry Martyn "knew not how to leave off."[11] David Hill spent whole nights on his knees and—overcome by nature—was sometimes found asleep upon them in the morning.[12] It was in prayer that John Woolman found renewal from all the toils and trials of the day.[13] Jeremy Taylor laid it down that "he that is cold and tame in his prayers hath not tasted of the deliciousness of religion."[14] James Fraser of Brea, that master of prayer, urges a correspondent: "Be not discouraged by your repugnance to prayer.

It is your fallen nature to feel that repugnance. But you must do yourself violence in that matter . . ."[15]

It must, of course, be conceded that the word "prayer" is too wide for our immediate purpose. Some things are included in prayer which are alien to the spirit of the saint who fixes his gaze on God alone. Prayer is not so holy an occupation that it cannot be demeaned by sad misuse. The prayers of some people are entirely for themselves.

A few years ago Mr. J. E. O'Leary, the chief librarian at Dagenham, discovered among the papers of John Ward, M.P., this prayer: "O Lord, Thou knowest I have mine estates in the City of London and likewise that I have lately purchased an estate in fee-simple in the County of Essex. I beseech Thee to preserve the two counties of Middlesex and Essex from fire and earthquake, and, as I have a mortgage in Hertfordshire, I beg Thee likewise to have an eye of compassion on that county: for the rest of the counties. Thou mayest deal with them as Thou art pleased . . ."[16]

But the misuse of prayer is not always as crude as that. Deeper insight shows that there is something crude in the use of prayer at all. A saint does not *use* prayer. To gaze fixedly on God is an end in itself. God uses the prayer to shape His image in the soul of the saint and impart His will to that adoring heart but, for a mortal to use prayer, is dangerously near to using God, and opens the door to all explanation of the efficacy of prayer on grounds of auto-suggestion or as a means to stimulating oneself in moral effort.

Let it be said clearly that this is not prayer as the saint knows it. Personal petition—as we have seen—often disappears from his prayer altogether. Intercession for others keeps its place. But thanksgiving, praise, and worship comprise most of his praying. And chiefly worship! Sheer adoration! He just gazes on God in love and longing, and can think of no bliss in eternity which will exceed the bliss of gazing still. He says with Faber:

Father of Jesus, love's reward,
What rapture will it be
Prostrate before Thy throne to lie,
And ever gaze on Thee!

In this adoring contemplation of God, we come to the heart of anything that can be called "the secret of the saints." They are not weighing, probing, seeking, asking. They are not even trying to understand. They are just looking in love and longing on God as revealed in Jesus. They only want to

. . . gaze transported at the sight
Through all eternity.

All their holiness is a byproduct of this. They look at God, and He looks at them. They grow in holiness as they grow in the steadiness and fixity of their gazing. Though the most mature saints complain at times of mind-wandering in adoration, their self-accusations must be understood only by their own high standards. Normally, they lose all sense of time in their holy attending. Hours slip away as moments. Even the most egocentric person, reducing all prayer to personal petition, grows weary of saying "Give me . . . Give me" for thirty minutes. But who that sees God—however dimly—could grow weary of gazing on Him? At times, the saint is in a coma of contemplation: rapture and ecstasy may come to him and transport him into "the third heaven." He may indeed, with Paul, hear "unspeakable words which it is not lawful for a man to utter."

And, all the time, by the blessed agency of the Holy Spirit, and all unaware of it himself, that dedicated mortal is being made a saint. He asks for nothing. He only looks on God in Jesus. But it is enough! God uses his steady gazing and gives him Himself. The Holy Spirit effects that blessed byproduct and a saint is made.

Perhaps no picture puts it more clearly than a metaphor of St. Paul. He speaks of "reflecting as a mirror the glory of the Lord."[17] That is what the saint does. Gazing on his Lord, he becomes a mirror in which the likeness of Jesus is more and more clearly seen. Yet it is more than *reflection*. Under the necessity of truth, St. Paul mixes his metaphors and says that it is a *transformation*, as though the mirror were changed by the reflection that falls on it. The saint is "transformed into the same image." He has held himself steadily where his Lord's reflection could fall. That has been his one concern. All his mind has been given to Jesus. He has practiced His presence, studied and copied His deeds, and kept His living image before his eyes. And the reflection has become a transformation. They said of St. Francis of Assisi that he was "The Mirror of Perfection" and—allowing for the idiosyncrasy of personality in all the saints—something similar could be said of them all. They *reflect* perfection.

Not that the saints are aware how clearly they reflect their Lord. The mirror cannot see the lovely image on its surface. The whole task of the mirror is to keep still before its object. Keeping still before the Lord is half, at least, of the secret of the saints. They keep still in adoring worship before the "Great Object of their growing love"—the Holy Spirit does the rest.

With the primacy of worship clearly in mind, it is now possible to see why holiness can never be an aim in itself. Many students of sanctity write of the "aims" and "achievements" of the saints, as though the saints set out with a deliberate aim for holiness (like a business magnate might set out to make a fortune) but the saints do not *normally* write that way themselves. They do not set out for ethical perfection. They set out for God. They gaze on God in love and longing, and the Holy Spirit makes them holy as they gaze. They are normally unaware of holiness themselves. Indeed, it is more usual for them to grow in self-abasement the nearer they come to the eternal throne. Seen from the human side, sanctity is a by-product. It is given by God to those who want nothing but Himself, and who know no higher bliss than just to be with Him.

Nor is it hard to understand why this should be so. To set out for holiness, and make it the prime aim, sets self right in the center of the picture. It is what *I* want. Its self-regarding nature is not altered because the end is virtue and not vice. Indeed, in some ways it is more perilous. If I achieve ethical perfection, I shall be in awful danger of spiritual pride. If I fail to achieve it, I shall be plunged into spiritual despair. Either way, I shall be terribly preoccupied with myself. In a fine and memorable phrase, Henri Bremond (quoting Father Lemonnyer) speaks of the power of worship to "disinfect us from egoism,"[18] and that phrase is pertinent here. One of the chief problems of all pursuit of holiness—some would think the chief problem of all—is how to secure ourselves from the insinuations of self at the very moment when we think we are free of it. Worship is the way. To adore God, and see all worth in Him, is to put Him at the centre of one's life, and no longer on the circumference. It is, indeed, truly to see our own worthlessness except as He gives us worth. In His pure presence, thoughts of our own holiness become almost a blasphemy and the self-regarding principle receives its fatal thrust.

But, while it is easy to see that holiness can never be an aim in itself without reintroducing the self-seeking principle, it is not so easy to see why *service* should not be an aim in itself, co-equal, if not superior, to worship. The complaint of the plain man against gazing on God is that it does nothing obvious in this evil world. The more one insists that we should gaze on God for God alone, the further one moves from the plain man's point of view. He could tolerate prayer—even as worship—if it were recognized as a means whereby the battery of moral effort and social reform were renewed, but to insist that this is only *using* prayer (and soiling it in the use) perplexes him, and drives him into opposition. Consequently, talk of contemplative orders of monks bewilders and exasperates many people. 'What good do they do?' they ask rhetorically. The only saints likely to win renown in the world are those whose guided path led them into social reform or deeds of charity. "The idea of a holy working man is grotesque," says a socialist writer."[19]

Nor can perplexity so widespread and so deep be lightly turned aside. This is the problem of the contemplative and activist all over again. It would be folly—and worse—to deny the selflessness of many lovely lives spent prodigally in the service of others. It would be dishonoring to heaven to dissociate God from the beautiful work of those who, without any obvious thought of themselves, have poured out their lives for the love of humanity. God, doubtless, had more to do with their work than they knew, but it cannot be forgotten that some have served and suffered for their fellows without reward in this world, or any faith for it in a world hereafter.

Nevertheless, even of service, as of the pursuit of personal holiness, we may say again with Bremond that worship "disinfects us from egoism."

It cannot be without significance that our Lord always put the love of God before the love of our fellows and it is more than a priority. It is a superiority as well.

Moreover, seeing that it always belongs to our nature to identify ourselves with any cause we take up, the danger of the return of the self-regarding principle is always present where service and not worship is made the ideal. Service is not *more* unselfish than worship. It is always possible for those with the ideal of service to say that those who worship, worship because they want to—and expose themselves to the rejoinder that those who serve their fellows serve because they want to also. But into the sterile exchanges of psychological hedonism no earnest seeker wants to go.

Let the appeal be made to experience. Is it not a known fact by all who make service the ideal that self has—and takes—many opportunities of insinuating itself into the central place again? Identification with the cause involves self: one battles for one's point of view, comes to live on gratitude (or to miss it, when it is not there), and feels a terrible temptation to abandon the cause because of the stupidity or cupidity of other men.

One is insulated from that when worship is first. God is one's whole reward. He may direct his willing servant to many tasks in the service of others, but they are all subservient to God's will, and they are done for God's sake. If men are ungrateful for service rendered them at God's bidding, their ingratitude is a trifle. Certainly, it cannot tempt one to abandon a task which God has set. Experience would seem to show that for purity of motive, tenacity of purpose, indifference to reward and self-effacement in service, nothing equals those who serve their fellows as a consequence of their worship of God—much as we honor those who serve humanity for humanity alone. Again, worship disinfects from egoism.

If it is said that some of those who worship God seem never to be busy in His practical service, one can only reply that God has many services to do. Many invalids have been glad that God has accepted their life of prayer. Conceivably, that is God's will for some who are not invalids too. What the will of God is for any life is more likely to be known by the person concerned than by a stranger, and far more likely to be known by that person if he is a worshipping soul than by the stranger who may know nothing of God at all.

Our task, in short, is not to judge others, but to obey God within the orbit of our own life, and that brings us to the second principle underlying all sanctity: namely, to obedience.

Obedience. Not only do the saints attend to God. They obey Him—utterly, instantly, gladly. Edwin Hatch looked on to the time when he would "will *one* will" with God. That time came for the saints while yet on earth. No longer did they try to persuade, or cajole, or dragoon their wills into harmony with the will of God. They willed *one* will with Him. They were so disciplined in obedience that the discipline itself seemed to drop out. As they became aware of it, their wills moved with the will of God.

Saints make no assertion of themselves over against God. They seek only identity with Him. It is common even for good men to need to conform their wills to the will of God. A ripe saint has passed beyond that need of dutiful conformity. He is in a state of glad obedience.

Not only do the saints make no assertion of themselves as over against God; they are not worried when they do not understand the reasons for His will. They obey it just the same. The scorn the saints sometimes heap upon the understanding perplexes philosophers, but many saints come to look upon human reason (at its best) as an inadequate guide, and (at its worst) a serious obstacle in obedience to God. The reason wants to know why. The saint only wants to know what. Saints have come to regard the desire to understand why God commands this and not that as insulting to the majesty of heaven. "Do not consult me," they say in effect: "Command me!" The idea that it is consonant with human dignity (and, indeed, a duty of our race) to understand the meaning of any command before it is obeyed, they reject *in toto*. "How can a mortal 'check' the Mighty God?" they ask. The only legitimate spheres they see for the use of human reason is, first (in times of perplexity) to make *sure* what God's will is and, then, in how best to carry out the commands which He has given. But to sit in judgment on the commands themselves is, they would say, blasphemous effrontery and certain to lead to sin.

When tragedy overtakes them—or overtakes the community—they are assured that it is only blessing in disguise. With Whittier, they would all say:

No harm from Him can come to me
On ocean or on shore.

They are certain that God is on the throne of the universe. All things are in His loving hands. He permits things to happen which we humans call disasters but—because it is His universe and no other's—He does not even *permit* anything to happen out of which He cannot bring good. To every event, therefore, the saint says with the divine Son: "Even so. Father, for so it seemed good in Thy sight."

Now and then, brooding on the mystery of existence, the saint sometimes glimpses the divine plan behind the seeming contradictions of earth, as when St. Paul perceived that the sad rejection of the Savior by his own nation had served God's loving purposes for a wider world: "O the depth of the riches," he cried, "both of the wisdom and knowledge of God!"

But when he *cannot* see it, the saint still trusts—and, trusting, he obeys.

St. Francis de Sales taught his people to greet God's will in all events—even the bitterest—with "Yes, Father. Yes and always Yes." And that glad cry was not, I need hardly say, a cry of stoical endurance. There are people today who grimly boast in the face of calamity, "I can take it," but that is not the spirit St. Francis taught. He *welcomed* the will of God. He saw it always, as St. Paul saw it, as "the *good* and *acceptable* and *perfect* will of God."

Being equal, in God, to unexpected tragedy, saints are equal in God to life's normal demands. Everything that happens, they hold, is a means God uses to work out His wise ends. The span of life, and the cycle of life, and every stage in life, are serving His purposes: childhood, adolescence, the middle years and old age. Mrs. Howard Taylor, of the China Inland Mission, felt something of the pain of waning powers, but took comfort, as her sight dimmed, and as door after door of opportunity closed upon her, knowing that this also was God's will. These changes, as she came to see, were the Maker's finishing touches, perfecting the soul in patience, humility and love. And who would want to hinder the Master in finishing His work?

The better to understand this glad obedience of the saint, let us look at a little devotional classic which sets out this principle of obedience in moving terms. I refer to Father J. P. de Caussade's *Self-Abandonment to Divine Providence*. The teaching has two sources—St. Francis de Sales and St. John of the Cross—and not only weaves together in its deep simplicity the Dominican and Carmelite Schools, but overleaps denominational barriers and has been welcomed in most branches of Christendom.

Observe the name: *Self-Abandonment!* The translator could hardly hope to find so good a word in English to express that joyful obedience to the will of God which we have distinguished as the second principle beneath all sanctity.

Caussade lays it down that "holiness may be reduced to one point only: fidelity to the Order of God." Active fidelity he sees as obedience to the laws of God and the Church, and passive fidelity is the loving acceptance of all that God sends us in each instant of time."[20] He insists—he is speaking to disciplined souls—that it is easy to attain eminent sanctity.[21] He denies that holiness is for the few.[22] It is for all, and there is no secret in it.[23] He says that human intelligence must be reduced, "like a dangerous slave," to the last place.[24]

Everything that happens, he holds, happens by the will of God. He enters into no distinctions between what God *does* and what God *permits*. The distinction, though important, is not relevant to his purpose. When the event reaches the individual, it is just "the will of God." It is to be embraced. "Sanctity consists in willing whatever happens to us by God's ordering, a simple 'Be it so,' the simple disposition of the will in conformity with the Will of God."

Caussade believed that this glad obedience which belongs to eminent sanctity accepts life in every moment as it comes.[25] It is a day-by-day, even a moment-by-moment, response to the God who does all things well. The wise do not preoccupy themselves with the past or the future. Here and now they have God. Realize "the divine plenitude of the present moment!" Everything you meet with God leads to union with Him. "Everything [so met] perfects you."[26]

He traces the blessed work of sanctification to the Holy Spirit[27] and summarizes the whole of spirituality in this:

> We should abandon ourselves purely and entirely to the Order of God and when we are in that Order we should, with a complete self-forgetfulness, be eternally busied with loving and obeying Him, without all these fears, reflections, returns on ourselves, and disquietude which sometimes result from the care of our own salvation and perfection. Since God offers to manage our affairs for us, let us once for all hand them over to His infinite wisdom, in order to occupy ourselves only with Himself and what belongs to Him.[28]

To some who read of saintly obedience in the terms of Caussade, it will seem too *simple*. When he says, for instance, that self-abandonment delivers us from the "low and feverish methods so necessary to human prudence" (and illustrates it in Herod) whereas all we have to do is to follow the star like the Magi,[29] some will protest that finding the will of God is not always so easy as that.

And they will be right. To Caussade, uncertainty of the will of God seems never to arise and his contempt of reason almost obscures the divine command that we are to love the Lord our God with all our mind. Experience of God does not lead us to say that He normally issues His commands as an army officer might address a private soldier whose business is "not to think but to obey." A father is often glad to explain himself to his child.

It must be borne in mind, however, that Caussade assumes every serious pilgrim on the path to perfection to be under the eye of a wise human counsellor, as well as the divine Spirit, and is receiving help in those ways.[30]

But his simplicity has many merits too. Too many who have essayed the heights of spirituality have been bewildered by the complexity of method and the multitude of counsel. Learning that one obscure saint made a practice of offering a certain prayer at a certain hour of the night, they have felt an inward constraint to do the same.

Of another saint they learn something else . . . and something else, also, from another and another. So life becomes a prison. The efficacy of prayer is almost measured by the hours one puts in and it has been inferred that holiness is possible only to those who can achieve so many hours a day in 'pure adoration'. The joyous freedom of the gospel is lost, and a Christian may find himself back in a slavery of devotional "law" almost as imprisoning as the Jewish Law from which St. Paul was so glad to be released.

It will be said that a wise spiritual guide would not allow the aspiring soul to get into this tangle, but not all have a guide and not all guides are wise. One of the merits of Caussade's teaching is the simplicity he brings into this practice of obedience. He holds that certain disciplines necessary to beginners are no longer necessary to the advanced.[31] Throw them aside! He even discourages searching in many books, and heartily disapproves feverishness over one's progress.[32] Let God have His way. The whole thing is in His hands. Meet Him in each passing moment and embrace His will as it comes.

So far from finding the teaching too simple, others find it too *hard*. If this instant, complete, and glad obedience be the second basic principle of sanctity, they are inclined to believe that a man is a saint before he gets there. What mastery of human nature, they protest, any man must possess who can give an instant, complete, and glad obedience to something which might cut right athwart his natural desires. How advanced and disciplined in virtue is that soul who, in the face of crushing calamity, can say from the heart: "Yes, Father! Yes!—and always Yes!" Not its simplicity, but its difficulty, is the problem to many who ponder on obedience as the second key to holiness.

But this teaching is not for beginners. It presupposes a high seriousness (as it justly may) in any who essay the heights of holiness, and it presupposes also an apprenticeship already served in the school of God. How faith is strengthened, and how the self is chained, has still to engage our attention. At the moment it is enough to insist that after absorbing attention to God comes this utter obedience.

Ready for all Thy perfect will,
My acts of faith and love repeat,
Till death Thy endless mercies seal,
And make the sacrifice complete.

Still others find this stress on obedience—and especially in the accent of Caussade—too passive. No direct instruction is given in this teaching on *Self-Abandonment to Divine Providence* to a man in a perplexing situation in which it is hard to be sure of the will of God; or in an iniquitous situation which clearly calls for rebellion rather than for acquiescence. Whether Caussade himself would ever have thought it right to raise the standard of rebellion against the settled order anywhere may be doubted, but it cannot be doubted that he would expect the saint to protest against iniquity wherever he met it, and compromise with evil would be impossible in anyone who followed his teaching.

Instant obedience to God does call for much passivity on the part of mortals. Charles Wesley sang:

Mould as Thou wilt Thy passive clay.

But active obedience is called for also.[33] Think of the massive service of the saints. Obedience to the will of God, even in the modern world, might lead in some lands to prison and to death.

The deep answer to this question is in the saint's utter faith that God has all things in His hands. Loyalty to the will of God in any situation might lead the obedient servant to loss of property, limb, and life. This he quite understands and gladly accepts. Obedience to God might connect the saint—with all his passivity—in some widespreading revolution. He would not be seeking this deliberately, because all his deliberations in any moment are to do the will of God, but, if those consequences came, he would accept this also as God's will.

But it is hard to suppose that the saint would ever lift the standard of some bloody rebellion and initiate, even in a good cause, the slaughter of his fellowmen. Brave to endure the most awful sufferings that might come upon him personally, he would be loth to inflict any pain upon others. Some will accuse his passivity here of supineness but he must bear the accusation.

Yet, he would be a bold man who spoke slightingly of what God has done, even in the affairs of this world, through the ready and unhesitating obedience of His saints. What God could do in this world, even now, if those who gave Him instant obedience were multiplied, moves the mind to adoring wonder and the heart to longing hope. Well, those are the two basic principles of sanctity as we make them out: attention and obedience. To those who were looking for something hidden and mysterious, they will seem simple to the point of absurdity. To those who say "We knew it all the time," it will be enough to ask, "How are you getting on in the practice of them?"

The saint on his knees: his mind all adoration.
The saint on his feet: his aim all obedience.

It is as simple and as profound as that.

7

Counsels and Warnings

Horatius Bonar

One of eleven children, Horatius Bonar (1808-1889) was born and educated in Edinburgh, Scotland. He came from a long line of ministers who have served a total of 364 years in the Church of Scotland. He and two of his brothers, John and Andrew, were closely involved with Thomas Chalmers, William C. Burns, and Robert Murray M'Cheyne in the revivals of their day, revivals which impacted thousands in Scotland in the 1830s and 1840s.

It was his awareness of the great blessings that God had brought to pass in his day, that caused Bonar to write in 1843, "No one who passed through them would wish either to forget or underestimate the privilege of having been one of the labourers in the reaping of that blessed harvest."

In his hymns, books, and pastoral and revival ministries, Bonar's desire was to give God all the glory and praise that "Christ must increase, but I must decrease."

That which among men so frequently takes the name of holiness is very unlike the Bible reality. Whether used in connection with the hardness of a lifeless orthodoxy, or the genialities of a fond idealism, or the smooth regularities of a mechanical devotion, or the religiousness of pictorial superstition, or the austerities of self-righteous mortification, or the sentimentalisms of liberalized theology, or the warm dreams of an earnest pantheism, the words "holy" and "holiness" and "spirituality" have become misnomers or ciphers, as ambiguous in meaning and profane in use, as would have been

Aaron's ephod upon the shoulders of a priest of Baal. This retention of Bible formulas and a Bible terminology after the expulsion or perversion of Bible meaning is one of the sacrilegious dishonesties of the age, which are so uncomfortably offensive to a straight-forward student of the Word.

Holiness may be called *spiritual* perfection, as righteousness is *legal* completeness, and both are exhibited in Christ. He is the representation, the illustration, the model. Likeness to Him is holiness. He that is holy is conformed to His image. Every other ideal is vanity. We must learn from the four Gospels what living holiness is, and for a doctrinal exposition of it we must turn to the Epistles. Thus we shall understand both what it is not and what it is.

"Abide in Me," "learn of Me," "follow Me," are the contents and summing-up of the Christian statute-book, constituting our true directory and guide in the pursuit of holiness.

The Life

From the Prince of Life the new life comes to us, even out of His death and tomb, for "we are planted together in the likeness of His death, that we may be also in that of His resurrection" (Rom. 6:5); "we are dead (have died), and our life is hid with Christ in God" (Col. 3:3). Thus we are "alive unto righteousness"; we live, and yet not we, but Christ in us. We come to Him for life, or rather, first of all, He comes to us with life; we "apprehend Him," or rather, first of all, "we are apprehended of Him"; and the "abiding in Him" is but a continuance of the first act of "coming," a doing the same thing all our life which we did at first. Thus we live. Thus life increases by a daily influx, and as yesterday's sunshine will not do for today, nor today's for tomorrow, so must there be the constant communication of heavenly life, else there will be immediate relapse into death and darkness. Because He liveth, we live, and shall live for ever. His life is ours, and our Christianity must be (like its Fountain-head) a thing of vitality, and power, and joy; our life the most genial, earnest, and useful of all lives, "out of us flowing rivers of living water" (John 7:38).

The Scholarship

"*Learn of Me.*" His is the school of heaven, the school of light. Here there is all truth and no error. The Tutor is as perfect as He is "meek and lowly."

He is at once the teacher and the lesson. With Him is the perfection of training and discipline and wisdom. There is no flaw, no failure, no incompleteness in the education which He imparts. He teaches to know, to love, to act, to endure, to rejoice, and to be sorrowful, "to be full and to suffer want." The range of scholarship enjoyed by His disciples is only to be measured by His divine stores: His "treasures of wisdom and knowledge." And the end of His instruction and discipline is to make us holy men, conformed to His likeness, and imitators of His heavenly perfection.

The Walk

"Follow Me." It is not merely a life to which we are called, but a walk (a "walking about," as the Greek implies); not a sitting alone; not a private enjoying of religion, but a walk—a walk in which we are visible on all sides, a walk which fixes many eyes upon us, a walk in which we are "made a spectacle" to heaven, earth and hell. It is no motionless resting or retirement from our fellows, but a moving about in the midst of them, a coming into contact with friends and foes, a going to and fro upon the highways and byways of earth. As was the Master so must the servant be. On His way to the cross He looked round and said, "Follow Me" (John 12:26); on His way to the throne, after He had passed the cross, He said the same (John 21:22). To the cross, then, and to the crown alike, we are to follow Him. It is one way to both.

He then that would be holy must be like Christ, and he that would be like Christ must be "filled with the Spirit." He that would have in him the mind of Christ must have the same "anointing" as He had, the same indwelling and inworking Spirit, the Spirit of "adoption," of life, faith, truth, liberty, strength, and holy joy. It is through this mighty Quickener that we are quickened; it is through "sanctification of the Spirit" that we are sanctified (2 Thess. 2:13; 1 Peter 1:2). It is as our Guest that He does His work, not working without dwelling, nor dwelling without working (2 Tim. 1:14), not exerting a mere influence, like that of music on the ruffled soul, but coming into us and abiding with us; so that being "filled with His company," as well as pervaded by His power, we are thoroughly "transformed." He does not merely ply us with arguments, nor affect us with "moral suasion," but impresses us with the irresistible touch of His divine hand, and penetrates us with His own vital energy; nay, He impregnates us with His own purity and life, inspite of desperate resistance and unteachableness and unbelief on our part, all the days of our life.

He that would be like Christ, moreover, must study Him. We cannot make ourselves holy by merely trying to be so, any more than we can make ourselves believe and love by simple energy of endeavor. No force can effect this. Men try to be holy, and they fail. They cannot by direct effort work themselves into holiness. They must gaze upon a holy object and so be changed into its likeness "from glory to glory" (2 Cor. 3:18). They must have a holy Being for their bosom friend. Companionship with Jesus, like that of John, can alone make us to resemble either the disciple or the Master.

He that would be holy must steep himself in the Word. He must bask in the sunshine which radiates from each page of revelation. It is through the truth that we are sanctified (John 17:17). Exposing our souls constantly to this light, we become more thoroughly "children of the light," and

Like the stain'd web that whitens in the sun,
Grow pure by being purely shone upon.

For, against evil, divine truth is quick and powerful. It acts like some chemical ingredient, that precipitates all impurities, and leaves the water clear. It works like a spell of disenchantment against the evil one, casting him out, and casting him down. It is "the sword of the Spirit," with whose keen edge we cut our way through hostile thousands. It is the rod of Moses, by which we divide the Red Sea, and defeat Amalek, and bring water from the desert rock. What evil, what enemy, within or without, is there that can withstand this unconquered and unconquerable Word? Satan's object at present is to undermine that Word, and to disparage its perfection. Let us the more magnify it, and the more make constant use of it. It is indeed only a fragment of man's language, made up of human letters and syllables, but it is furnished with superhuman virtue. That rod in the hand of Moses, what was it? A piece of common wood. Yet it cut the Red Sea in twain. That serpent on the pole, what was it? A bit of brass. Yet it healed thousands.

Why all this? Because that wood and that brass were connected with omnipotence, conductors of the heavenly electricity. So let the Bible be to us the book of all books, for wounding, healing, quickening, strengthening, comforting, and purifying.

Yet, he that would be holy must fight. He must war a good warfare (1 Tim. 1:18); fight the good fight of faith (1 Tim. 6:12), though not with carnal weapons (2 Cor. 10:4). He must fight upon his knees, being sober, and watching unto prayer (1 Peter 4:7). He must wrestle with principalities and powers, being strong in the Lord and the power of His might, having put on the whole armor of God: girdle, breastplate, shield, helmet and sword (Eph. 6:13-17). This battle is not to the strong (Eccles. 9:11), but to the weak; it is fought in weakness, and the victory is to them that have no might; for in this conflict time and chance do not happen to all; but we count upon victory from the first onset, being made more than conquerors through Him that loved us, and are cheered with the anticipation of the sevenfold reward "to him that overcometh" (Rev. 2:7). Though, in this our earthly course and combat, we have the hostility of demons, we have the ministry of angels in aid (Heb. 1:14), as well as the power of the Holy Ghost (Eph. 1:13).

He that would be holy must watch. "Watch thou in all things" (2 Tim. 4:5); "watch ye, stand fast in the faith, quit you like men, be strong" (1 Cor. 16:13). Let the sons of night sleep or stumble in the darkness, but let us, who are of the day, be sober, lest temptation overtake us, and we be ensnared in the wiles of the devil, or the seductions of this wanton world. "Blessed is he that watcheth" (Rev. 16:15). In watching let us witness a good confession (1 Tim. 6:13), not ashamed of Him whose badge we bear; let us run a swift and patient race; "let us lay aside every weight, and the sin [unbelief] which doth so easily beset us" (Heb. 12:1) and "follow after righteousness, godliness, faith, love, patience, meekness" (1 Tim. 6:11), having our eye upon the coming and the kingdom of our Lord Jesus.

He that would be holy must feel his responsibility for being so, both as a member of Christ's body and a partaker of the Holy Ghost. The thought that perfection is not to be reached here ought not to weaken that sense of responsibility, nor lead us to give way to aught that would "grieve the Holy Spirit of

God whereby we are sealed unto the day of redemption." The sevenfold fullness of the risen Christ (Rev. 2:1), and the sevenfold fullness of the Holy Ghost (Rev. 5:6), these are the church's birthright, and for no mess of pottage is she to sell it; nay, for the personal possession of that fullness, insofar as vessels such as ours can contain it, each saint is responsible. We are *sanctified by the blood* (Heb. 13:12), that we may be *sanctified by the Holy Ghost* (1 Cor. 6:11), be led by the Spirit (Gal 5:18), be temples of the Holy Ghost, even in our bodies (1 Cor. 6:19), walking in the Spirit (Gal. 5:16), speaking by the Spirit (1 Cor. 12:3), living in the Spirit (Gal. 5:25), and having the communion of the Holy Ghost (2 Cor. 13:14).

The doctrine of the personality and energy of the Holy Spirit was not more offensive to the cold infidelity of the last century than it is to the more earnest and plausible idealism of the present day. It is set aside as savoring of superstition, and at variance with human liberty and self-power. Energies from beneath or from above are either denied, or recognized only as "principles" or "sensations," or developments of natural law, not connected with personalities in either case. Supernatural personalities are exploded relics of superstition! The thought that there was one perfect and superhuman book, in this world of imperfect literature, used to be cheering; but if modern theories of inspiration be true, this consolation is gone, and the world is left thoroughly disconsolate, without one fragment of the superhuman or the perfect in the midst of it.

The Christian man must not trifle with sin under any pretense; least of all on the plea that he is not "under the Law." The apostolic precepts and warnings are quite as explicit as the Mosaic, and much more numerous. He that thinks himself free from the latter will have no difficulty in persuading himself that he may set aside the former; and he who reckons it bondage to listen to the Sinaitic statute, "Thou shalt not kill," will think it equal bondage to hearken to the Pauline commandment: "Be not drunk with wine," or "Owe no man anything," or "Let him that stole steal no more."

As possessors of the Spirit of love, we must be loving, laying aside all malice, and guile, and hypocrisies, and evil-speaking, discharging daily the one debt that is never to be paid (Rom. 13:8). For the indwelling Spirit is not idle nor barren, but produces fruit, divine fruit in human hearts, heavenly fruit on earthly soil, fruit which indicates its inner source, and tells of the glorious Guest within; "for the fruit of the Spirit is love, joy, peace, long-suffering, gentleness, goodness, faith, meekness, temperance: against such there is no law" (Gal. 5:22,23).

As those whose feet have found the rock, let us be stable, not carried about with every wind of doctrine, not vacillating nor undecided nor compromising. As those who have been "delivered from a present evil world," let us, like the saints of old, be separate from it, standing aloof from its gaieties, as men who have no time for such things, even were they harmless, keeping our raiment undefiled. Let us be suspicious of its foolish talking and jesting, jealous of its light literature, which "eats as doth a canker," vitiating the taste, and enervating the soul. Let us maintain unblunted the edge of our relish for prayer and fellowship with God, as the great preservative against the seductions of the age; for only intimacy with God can keep us from intimacy with the world. . . .

Let us be on our guard against *old self* in every form, whether it be indolence, or temper, or coldness, or rudeness, or inconveniences, or slovenliness, or shabbiness, or covetousness, or flippancy, or self-conceit, or pride, or cunning, or obstinacy, or sourness, or levity, or foolishness, or love of preeminence. Let us cultivate a tender conscience, avoiding old notions and conceits; yet watching against the commission of little sins, and the omission of little duties; redeeming the time, yet never in a hurry; calm, cheerful, frank, happy, genial, generous, disinterested, thoughtful of others. Seeing we must protest against the world on so many important points, let us try to differ from it as little as possible on things indifferent, always showing love to those we meet with, however irreligious and unlovable, especially avoiding a contemptuous spirit or an air of superiority.

As disciples of Christ, let our discipleship be complete and consistent, our connection with Him exhibiting itself in conformity to His likeness, our life a comprehensive creed, our walk the embodiment of all that is honest, and lovely, and of good report. Christ's truth sanctifies as well as liberates; His wisdom purifies as well as quickens. Let us beware of accepting the liberty without the holiness, the wisdom without the purity, the peace without the zeal and love.

Let us be *true men*, in the best sense of the word: true to ourselves, true to our new birth and our new name, true to the church of God, true to the indwelling Spirit, true to Christ and to the doctrine concerning Him, true to that book of which He is the sum and the burden. Let us be true to truth, loving it, not because it is pleasant or picturesque or ancient, but because it is true and divine. On it let us feed, with appetite new-whetted every day; so shall we add, not one, but many cubits to our stature, growing in grace and in the knowledge of our Lord Jesus Christ.

There is such a thing in the church as poverty of blood. Hence the blotches that discolor her. For the removal of these, not mere medicine is needed, but a more generous diet. That diet is only to be found in the Word, which is as nourishing (Jer. 15:16) as it is healing and purifying to the blood, being truly what old Tyndale calls it, "the word of our soul's health." There is needed, too, the infusion of richer blood, to be brought about by a second Pentecost, in which the existing life will be greatly intensified, and large additions made by conversions of a deeper kind than heretofore. So shall our leanness of faith, of love, of life, of zeal, of joy be efficaciously and abidingly cured. So shall we "come behind in no gift; waiting for the coming of our Lord Jesus Christ" (1 Cor. 1:7).

Our spiritual constitution must be *braced*, not only that we may be strong for work or fight, but that we may be proof against the infection of the times, against the poison with which the god of this world, "the prince of the power of the air," has impregnated our atmosphere. For this we need not only the "strong meat" recommended by the apostle (Heb. 5:12-14), but the keen fresh mountain air of trial, vicissitude, and hardship, by means of which we shall be made hardy in constitution and robust in frame, impervious to the contagion around, . . . impregnable against the assaults of Satan the Pharisee, or Satan the Sadducee. . . .

In a time of uncertainty, skepticism, speculation, false progress, we need to recognize the full meaning of the apostolic "we know" (1 John 5:13-20), "we believe" (2 Cor. 4:13), "we are confident" (2 Cor. 5:6), "we are persuaded" (2 Tim. 1:12). For that which is divine must be true; that which is revealed must be certain, and that which is thus divinely true and certain must be immortal. Like the results of the exact sciences, it is fixed, not varying with men and ages. That which was true, is true, and shall be true for ever. It is the more needful to recognize all this, because the ground underneath us has been thoroughly mined and is very largely hollow; a process of skeptical decomposition and disintegration has been going on, the extent of which will soon be manifest when the treacherous crust gives way. . . .

At the same time let us beware, in the details of personal religion, merely of repeating the past, or getting up an imitation of religion. The genuine in life does not thus repeat itself; nor does it need to do so. The living face of man is of a certain type; yet each face varies from its fellow. The Holy Spirit's work is not to form mere statues. He produces life, and life is always varied. It is death that repeats itself. As silence is always the same, so is it with death. The presence of life is the security against tame monotony. The larger the infusion of life, the greater the diversity, not of gifts merely, but of beauty, and fruit, and power. Let us not then seek the living among the dead, not try to revivify old forms. Let us place ourselves simply in the hands of the quickening Spirit. He will pour into us the fullness of a diversified, fruitful, healthful life. The evil in us is too strong for any power save omnipotence. The resistance of a human will is too powerful for philosophy or logic, or poetry or eloquence. The Holy One alone can make us holy.

Life is not one battle but many. It is made up, too, of defeats as well as victories. Let us not be unduly troubled or grow moody when a battle is lost. There is always time to win another, and such a thing as flight or demoralization should be unknown in the army of the living God. It is the lost battles of the world (like Thermopylae) that have told most on a nation's history. "If God be for us, who can be against us?" "Thou hast girded me with strength unto the battle" (Ps. 18:39).

The Christian life is a great thing, one of the greatest things on earth. Made up of daily *littles*, it is yet in itself not a little thing, but insofar as it is truly lived, whether by poor or rich, by child or full-grown man, is noble throughout, a part of that great whole, in which and by which is to be made known to the principalities and powers in heavenly places . . . the manifold wisdom of God (Eph. 3:10). It does not need to be a long life; a short one may be as true and holy as a long one. A short one is not a failure. John the Baptist had perhaps the shortest ministry in the church, yet it was no failure; it was one of the greatest successes. He was a burning and a shining light. We do not need to say profanely, "Whom the gods love die young," but we may say that it does not need the threescore years and ten to unfold the beauties of holiness.

If the new life were the mere rubbing off the rust of the old, if the sweetening of the Marah well of our corrupt nature were but a common, non-miraculous process, if all goodness be within the easy reach of any earnest man, if a refined literature and a liberalized theology, and the cultivation of the beautiful, and social science, and a wider range of genial recreation, be the cure for all the evil that is in us and in our age, then there has been much ado about trifles, the Bible is an exaggeration, and the gift of the Holy Spirit a superfluous exhibition of power. If sin be but a common scar or wrinkle, to be erased from the soul's surface by a few simple touches, if pardon be a mere figure of speech, meaning God's wide benevolence or good-natured indifference to evil, why tell of wrath, and fire, and judgment, the never-dying worm and the ever-rising smoke? Does God love to torment His creatures by harsh words, or fill their imaginations with images of woe which He does not intend to realize? Or why did the Son of God suffer and weep, and grieve? If error be but a trifle, a foible, a freak at worst, or if it be a display of honest purpose and the inevitable result of free thought, why is the "strong delusion" (literally, "the energy of error") spoken of so awfully, "that they all might be damned who believed not the truth" (2 Thess. 2:12), and why did the Lord Himself say, once and again, in reference to false doctrine, "which thing I hate"?

As the strongest yet calmest thing in the world is light, so should a Christian life be the strongest and greatest, as well as the calmest and brightest. As the only perfectly straight line is a ray of light, and as the only pure substance is sunshine, so ought our course to be, and so should we seek to shine as lights in the world, reflections of Him who is its light, the one straight, pure thing of earth.

Let us then shine! Stars indeed, not suns; but still stars, not tapers nor meteors. Let us shine! Giving perhaps slender light, but that light certain and pure; enough to say to men "It is night," lest they mistake, but not enough bring day; enough to guide the seeking or the erring in the true direction, but not enough to illuminate the world. The sun alone can do that. It is the sun that shows us the landscape; stars show but themselves. Let us then show ourselves beyond mistake. The day when all things shall be seen in full warm light is the day of the great sun-rising.

8

The Indwelling Christ

J. Gregory Mantle

J. Gregory Mantle (1853-1925) had a wide and varied ministry in Great Britain, America, and around the world. For many years he was the well-loved superintendent of the flourishing Central Hall in Deptford, England, as well as a popular speaker at Keswick Conferences and other large conventions for the deepening of spiritual life. He spent the last twelve years of his life in America, where he was associated with A. B. Simpson and the Christian & Missionary Alliance. He traveled extensively, conducting missions, teaching, and speaking in conventions all over the United States. He was an avid supporter of foreign missions throughout his entire career.

Mantle edited a missionary paper and wrote several books, including *Better Things*, a commentary on the Epistle to the Hebrews, and *The Way of the Cross*.

The *abiding* indwelling of Jesus Christ in the heart of the believer is an experience more to be coveted than any other. It constitutes the crown and climax of the Christian life. God not only pardons our guilt and saves us from its consequences; He not only forgives, saying: "Go in peace and sin no more"; He not only gives us a new nature, one that loves to do right and hates to do wrong; He not only comes to our aid in temptation and trial, and interposes His strength and succor; but, above all this, He comes to live His own wonderful life in us in the person of His Son, Jesus Christ, and says to work out your own salvation with fear and trembling, "for it is God who worketh in you both to will and to work, for his good pleasure" (Phil. 2:12-13 RV).

Our union with our risen Lord is of such a character that we become partakers of His very nature; drawing our spiritual life from His Spirit; our mental vigor from His mind; our physical strength from His risen body; and our power for service from His omnipotence. He is already in us, the dawn of the coming day. We are in vital contact with our destiny, that marvelous destiny of companionship with God throughout the ages. We have in this experience the hope of it. Christ is in us the hope of the glory yet to be revealed.

Blessed are the sons of God,
They are bought with Christ's own blood;
One with God, with Jesus one;
Glory is in them begun.

Dr. A. B. Simpson said that the two prominent advantages of this secret are its simplicity and its universality. It is not a complicated mass of petty rites, ceremonies or enactments but one simple and comprehensive prescription, covering everything, and needing only to be habitually applied; namely, Christ for everything. And as it is so simple, so it is universal in its application. There is no side of human nature to which it does not apply, whether the inner life of the soul, the needs of the body, the circumstances of life, or the exigencies of duty and work.

But this life has its conditions, and these we will now consider.

Detachment

"I do not say that I have already won the race or have already reached perfection; but I am pressing on, striving to lay hold of the prize for which also Christ has laid hold of me. Brethren, I do not imagine that I have yet laid hold of it; but this one thing I do—forgetting everything which is past and stretching forward to what lies in front of me, with my eyes fixed on the goal I push on to secure the prize of God's heavenward call in Christ Jesus" (Phil. 3:12-14 Weymouth).

H. C. G. Moule, the Bishop of Durham's comment on this passage is so wise and luminous that I venture to reproduce it:

The apostle's complete repose in Christ as the righteousness of God *for* him, and then his deep nearness to his Lord as the power of God *in* him, alike seem not so much to banish as utterly to preclude any thought about himself but that of his own imperfection. He writes as one whose very last feeling is that of complacency in his spiritual condition. His spiritual *position*, in Christ, as he is "found in Him," fills him with much more than complacency; it is his glory and his boast. But when he comes to speak of his spiritual *condition*, the possessing thought is that all is imperfect and progressive. He has a perfect blessing; but he is an imperfect recipient of it; he has "not attained." He is deeply happy, but he is thoroughly humble. He has had a vision of absolute holiness which has completely guarded him from the delusion of thinking that he is himself absolutely holy, even in the fullest state of grace.

Unless we are prepared to detach ourselves, not only from things sinful, but also from things inexpedient, we shall never know this experience in all its fullness and glory. I have read of a clever oculist who was also a clever cricketer. He was passionately fond of cricket, but a few days of cricket always unfitted him for his delicate professional work. His hand was not as steady as before the excitement of the cricket match. He had, at last, to make his choice between being a great oculist or a great cricketer. He decided on the former, and detached himself from cricket that he might the more perfectly exercise his ministry of healing.

We must, like Paul, forget everything that is behind us, refusing to allow the dead hand of the past to be laid upon our present or future, and turn a deaf ear to the Satanic suggestion that the past, with its failures, and imperfectly realized ideals, is only the prophecy of the future. Detached from everything that would hinder our progress, we must continually stretch forth to what lies in front of us, remembering that in this life there is no such thing as finality. "There is no commoner cause of declension in Church life," says one, "than the settling down upon second bests."

What a picture there is here, not only of detachment but of intensity. Who that has ever seen the racer stretching forward "toward the goal," that he may not lose the slightest advantage, can fail to see the force of the apostle's figure. Is our life characterized by any such intensity?

81

Dethronement

"We thus judge, that one died for all, therefore all died; and he died for all, that they that live should no longer live unto themselves, but unto him who for their sakes died and rose again" (2 Cor. 5:14-15 RV). The question in every life is, Who is on the throne? The power ruling within determines the character of the life manifested, for a throne implies a king.

Are we living unto ourselves, or unto Him Who for our sakes died and rose again? If we are living to Self we shall find that Self is "the long, low, ugly tap-root" out of which all that is hateful springs. If the power of the Holy Spirit has been claimed against Self for its dethronement, we shall find out in daily experience the truth of Charles Wesley's words:

> *More of Thy life and more I have,*
> *As the old Adam dies;*
> *Bury me, Saviour, in Thy grave,*
> *That I with Thee may rise.*

Romaine, writing on *The Inward Cross*, says: "If Christ be not all in all, Self must still be looked upon as something great, and there will be food left for the pride of self-importance and self-sufficiency. Seek for the death of sin where thou wilt, it is not to be found but in His death. Dethroned in the life by the power of the Cross of Jesus . . . sin is put to a lingering death, kept upon the Cross, dying daily."

Self as a personality is not destroyed but displaced. Christ takes His place on the throne, and the outcome is no longer the Self-life but the Christ-life. We are never meant to be our own centers, and we are eccentric until we find our true center, which is Christ. When Self vacates the throne, and Christ becomes the center of our personality, then everything is adjusted to His sovereign will.

Weymouth's translation of Paul's words is very luminous: "The love of Christ overmasters us, the conclusion at which we have arrived being this— that One having died for all, His death was their death, and that He died for all in order that the living may no longer live to themselves, but to Him who died for them and rose again."

This is Paul's explanation of the overmastering love of Christ. So fully had the apostle entered into the purpose of his Saviour's death and resurrection; so absolutely was Christ enthroned in his life, that Self had no place whatever in it. He could say, "no more I." There are multitudes who never differentiate, in their prayers and utterances, between Jesus as Saviour and Jesus as Lord and King. He must be absolute Ruler, else the inexpressible possibilities of the Christian calling can never become actualities. There must be no more living to ourselves. "I was quite willing," said one, "that Jesus Christ should be King, so long as He allowed me to be Prime Minister." In other words, I want to be permitted, now and again, to assert my independence; there are certain matters which I wish to decide on my own account. There is certain business in the kingdom of my being that I want to transact. But that can never be. Jesus can never be Lord at all unless He is allowed to become Lord of all.

I very much question whether the change, from absolute selfishness to absolute selflessness, has ever been more effectively described than by Theodore Monod in his well-known hymn.

The first verse describes Self enthroned as Sovereign:

Oh! the bitter shame and sorrow,
That a time could ever be,
When I let the Saviour's pity
Plead in vain, and proudly answer'd,
"All of Self and none of Thee."

The second verse describes the beginning of Love's conquest, and the shaking of the dominion of Self:

Yet He found me; I beheld Him
Bleeding on the accursed tree:
Heard Him pray, "Forgive them, Father,"
And my wistful heart said faintly,
"Some of Self and some of Thee."

The third verse describes the anxiety of Self to be retained as Prime Minister, if not as King:

Day by day His tender mercy,
Healing, helping, full and free,

Sweet and strong, and ah! so patient,
Brought me lower, while I whispered,
"Less of Self, and more of Thee."

The last verse describes the complete subjugation of Self by the Christ of Calvary, and the enthronement of Jesus as King:

Higher than the highest heavens,
Deeper than the deepest sea,
Lord, Thy love at last has conquered;
Grant me now my supplication,
"None of Self and all of Thee."

That great disciple of William Law, Dr. Alexander Whyte declared:

Let me henceforth seat Christ, my Redeemer and my King, on the very throne of my heart, and then keep every gate of my body and every avenue of my mind as all not any more mine but His. Let me open my eye, my ear, and my mouth, and all my members, as if, in all that, I were opening Christ's eye, Christ's ear, and Christ's mouth; and let me thrust nothing on Him, as He dwells within me, that will make Him ashamed or grieved, or that will defile or pollute Him. Yes, O Paul, I shall henceforth hold with thee that my body is the temple of Christ, and that I am not my own, but that I am bought with a paralyzing price, and must therefore, do nothing less than glorify God in my body and in my spirit, which are God's.

Dependence

"I can of my own self do nothing" (John 5:30).

In other words, Jesus took the place of dependence which Adam refused to take. The words in Psalm 40:6 (RV margin) are applied to Him in the Hebrews letter: "thou hast no delight in; mine ears hast thou pierced for me." The reference here is to Exodus 21:5-6, where the love-slave, refusing his proffered freedom, had his ears pierced, and was for a few moments held by an awl, through those pierced ears, to the door post of his master's house. "I love my master," he said, "I will not go out free"; and the ears fastened to the door post indicated this willing bondage and identity of interest with those of his master.

Even so, Jesus refused to allow any of His powers for a single instant to go out free (see Phil. 2:5-11). That would have been an assertion of His independence, with its consequent penalty of death for His own sin. Satan tried again and again to tempt Him to assert His own powers. Let your powers go out free," he said; "make these stones into bread to satisfy your hunger" (Matt. 4:3). But Jesus disowned all power of a self-originating life. He never tried to act independently. He just hung on His Father, and said: "As the living Father sent me, and I live because of the Father; so he that eateth me, he also shall live because of me" (John 6:57 RV). What a suggestive study this is as revealed in the Gospel of John:

> nothing of Himself (John 5:19; 5:30; 8:28);
> never spoke of Himself (John 7:16; 8:38; 12:49);
> never wrought a miracle of Himself (John 5:36; 10:37-38);
> was ever the Sent One (John 4:34; 5:24; 5:30; 9:4; 11:42; 12:44-45);
> never used human judgment (John 5:30).

Not in the emergencies, not in the great crises, but in everything, we must cultivate the habit of dependence on Christ. Habitually recognize that He has undertaken the business of your life in all its departments; that there is not a difficulty that crops up but He has undertaken to carry you through it. He has become responsible, and only waits for you to use Him.

"To have Him and make use of Him," says Bishop Moule, "is peace, and power, and purity. To do without Him is impossible; it is death. To use Him only partially is perpetual unrest and disappointment. He must be 'all things in all things'; then there shall be a great calm within, and a great strength and great holiness with it, and at last an 'appearing with Him in glory,' to crown the process, and give it its development forever."

Devotion

The question which Judas (not Iscariot) asked the Master proves that he held a low place among the apostles (see John 14:21, 24). It seems pretty certain that the groups of fours, into which the apostles were divided, were arranged according to their spiritual nearness to the Saviour. In all the lists Judas is in one of the last groups. A few days earlier Jesus seemed to have begun to do what they always wanted Him to do, manifest Himself to the world. Judas (son of James) now thinks something has happened to make the Master go back to the old plan of a secret communication. So he says in effect "Lord! *What has come to pass* to induce You to falter upon the course on which we entered, when, amid the hosannas of the multitude, You rode triumphantly into Jerusalem?" (see Matt. 21:1-11).

It was the old expectation of Messianic glory displayed in some still more ostentatious and pompous way. Jesus quietly tells Judas and the others the positive conditions and the negative qualifications for His manifestation. We therefore have in one of these verses, as a great expositor says, "what brings Christ and what Christ brings; and in the other, what keeps away Christ and all His gifts."

"If a man love me, he will keep my Word" (not words, as in the Authorized Version; John 14:23). It is an expression that includes all His teaching. His sayings constitute one organic whole, and we dare not pick and choose, saying in our hearts, "This I will keep and this I will reject." Remember that every word of His teaching has in it the imperativeness of His manifested will. And His Word must become the law of our lives. Are we as willing to come to Him for law as we are to come to Him for life?

How, then, can we show our devotion to Christ? There is only one way; it is by loving Him and keeping His Word. Let us listen to that spiritual teacher, George Bowen:

> Christ represented the Father, and as men treated Christ they revealed their sentiments toward the Father. The Word of Christ represents Christ, and *our sentiments toward Christ are revealed by our treatment of His Word.* How many are laboring to settle the question whether they love Christ or not? It would wonderfully help them in the solution of this if they would first seek to ascertain *whether they love the Word of Christ or not.* The Christian is one who keeps the Word of Christ. He that keeps not the Word of Christ, but suffers the Adversary to take it away from him as often as it is given him, is not a Christian.

Are you longing to show your devotion to Jesus Christ? There is a simple way of showing it quite within your reach. Begin to treat the Word of Christ as you would treat Christ Jesus Himself, and remember that all assurances of devotion that do not find expression in this way are valueless.

Listen again: "If a man love me, my Father will love him." So the Father identifies all love to Jesus as love to Himself, and, in wonderful language, the Master says: "*We* will come and make our mansion with him." Our heart is His permanent abode (qualitatively) only so long as we fulfill the conditions. If Self-will is indulged, and is allowed to reassert itself in the heart, Christ's (manifested) presence vanishes. We can only keep Him enthroned as the King of our life by perpetual acts of loving obedience, and we can only lovingly obey as we yield to the pressure and power of the Holy Spirit.

Discipline

"Every competitor in an athletic contest practices abstemiousness [self-discipline] in all directions. They indeed do this for the sake of securing a perishable wreath, but we for the sake of securing one that will not perish. That is how I run, not being in any doubt as to my goal. I am a boxer who does not inflict blows on the air, but I hit hard and straight at my own body, and lead it off into slavery, lest possibly, after I have been a herald to others, I should myself be rejected" (Weymouth's translation of I Cor. 9:25-27).

Paul tells us that he exercises constant discipline lest, after being a herald to others, and telling them how to win the prize, he should lose it himself.

The word translated "a castaway" in the Authorized Version is *adokimos,* and means disapproved, just as *dokimos* in 1 Corinthians 11:19 means approved. A man may be a child of God, and yet disapproved as a servant of God. To be approved, to reach the maximum of our spiritual privileges, involves constant self-judgment, self-denial, self-crucifixion. Many are accustomed to think that the question of their personal security is the only question of any moment. That is a great mistake, for by careless living, by giving lodgment to Self in any of its forms, whether hateful or beautiful; by carelessness and unwatchfulness; by neglect of communion; by failing to keep the Master's sayings, we forfeit the highest possible service to the world that of manifesting, in our life, the loveliness of Jesus Christ.

If we are to know the blessed secret of making use of Jesus as He reigns enthroned in our life, we must take care to do always the things that please Him. Will He be pleased if we spend our early morning leisure moments over the newspaper to the neglect of His Word? One of the greatest preachers of the age resolutely refuses to look at his newspaper until the afternoon. He does this as a matter of discipline, because he found that the reading of the news encroached upon time needed for the study of God's Word. The tongue must be disciplined, for the temptations to superficiality and shallowness through over-much talk were never greater than today. The mind must be disciplined, and its loins girded up, to use Peter's figure, otherwise there will be great mental slackness in all directions. So easily do we turn aside and grieve our gracious Guest, if we neglect self-discipline.

"Want of self-control," says one,

makes one a poor slave—slave of his impulses, slave of his passions, slave of his surroundings: disqualifies him for great and noble uses in this life (2 Tim. 2:20-21). It was not Paul's life, it was Christ's life in Paul—a great, real, divine thing that had caught Paul in its current and was bearing him on, flowing through him soul and body, and reducing him daily to its own heavenly complexion. Every believing man knows that. He knows that he is perfect master of himself only in the proportion in which Christ is Master of him, and he knows that Christ is Master of him in proportion as he shrinks from sin, and puts Self-seeking and Self-indulgence under his feet. The Christian man is bound to call into solemn review every sinless enjoyment and every innocent habit which he finds to be encroaching on his reserve of moral power, and lessening in him that moral enthusiasm which is the spring of all moral attainment.

This is true Christian discipline.

A Prayer

My omnipotent Lord, enable me to do what, apart from Your enabling, is impossible. Yet since it is Your will I can ask in the utmost confidence. I would be detached from everything that would hinder me, and therefore hinder You, in the accomplishment of Your purpose.

Let me be willing that Self should be completely dethroned in my life. When I have sometimes thought the victory was won, I have found to my humiliation that I was still in bondage to my old enemy. He is too strong and subtle for me. Do, therefore, cleanse the temple of my being as You did in the days of Your flesh. Drive out all the buyers and sellers, and make my heart a house of prayer.

Teach me the life of absolute dependence upon You. I am so prone to creaturely activity and creaturely self-assertion. I have so often failed to realize that apart from You I can do nothing.

My Master, lead me to Thy door;
Pierce this now willing ear once more:
Thy bonds are freedom; let me stay
With Thee, to toil, endure, obey.

May I show my devotion to You by my love of Your Word, and by my glad and quick obedience to Your sayings. May I never pick and choose among Your commands, but regard every Word of Yours as binding upon me. To this end help me patiently and diligently to study Your precepts; to be as glad to come to You for law as for life; and to remember that Your commandments are not grievous.

Let me never through carelessness or self-indulgence be disapproved; but, submitting to the discipline of the Holy Spirit, may I lay aside every weight; run the heavenly race; and at last finish the course and win the crown. I ask this in the name of Jesus my Saviour and King. Amen.

9

The Rest

Andrew Murray

Andrew Murray (1828-1917) was raised in what was considered then the most remote corner of the world—Graaff-Reinet (near the Cape), South Africa. It was here, after his formal education in Scotland and three years of theological study in college in Holland, that Andrew Murray returned as a missionary and minister. He would eventually author many books

As a preacher, he consistently drew large crowds and led many to trust Christ as their Savior. But Murray came to realize there was a definite lack in his heart and ministry: "I had never learnt with all my theology that obedience was possible," writes Murray. "My justification was as clear as noonday. I knew the hour in which I received from God the joy of pardon. I remember in my little room at Bloemfontein how I used to sit and think, What is the matter? Here I am, knowing that God has justified me in the blood of Christ, but I have no power for service. My thoughts, my words, my actions, my unfaithfulness—everything troubled me." He eventually was led to the answer.

Murray often prayed, "May not a single moment of my life be spent outside the light, love, and joy of God's presence, and may not a moment without the entire surrender of myself as a vessel for Him to fill full of His Spirit and His love."

The Rest of Faith (Hebrews 4:1-3)

After Israel's deliverance from Egypt, there were two stages. The one, the life in the wilderness, with its wanderings and its wants, its unbelief and its murmurings, its provocation of God and its exclusion from the promised rest. The other, the land of promise, with rest instead of the desert wanderings, with abundance instead of want, and the victory over every enemy instead of defeat: symbols of the two stages in the Christian life. The one in which we only know the Lord as the Saviour from Egypt, in His work on the cross for atonement and pardon. The other, where He is known and welcomed as the glorified Priest-King in heaven, who, in the power of the endless life, sanctifies and saves completely, writes God's laws in the heart, and leads us to find our home in the holiest of God's presence. The aim of the writer in this whole section is to warn us not to rest content with the former, the preparatory stage, but to show all diligence to reach the second, and enter the promised rest of complete deliverance. *"Let us fear therefore, lest haply, a promise being left of entering into His rest, any of you should come short of it."*

Some think that the rest of Canaan is the type of heaven. This cannot be, because the great mark of the Canaan life was that the land had to be conquered and that God gave such glorious victory over enemies. The rest of Canaan was for victory and through victory. And so it is in the life of faith, when a soul learns to trust God for victory over sin, and yields itself entirely, as to its circumstances and duties, to live just where and how He wills, that it enters the rest. It lives in the promise, in the will, in the power of God. This is the rest into which it enters, not through death, but through faith, or rather, not through the death of the body, but the death to self in the death of Christ through faith. For indeed we have *"had good tidings preached unto us, even as also they: but the word of hearing did not profit them, because it was not united by faith with those that heard."*

The one reason why they did not enter Canaan was their unbelief. The land was waiting: the rest was provided; God Himself would bring them in and give them rest. One thing was lacking; they did not believe, and so did not yield themselves to God to do it for them what He had promised. Unbelief closes the heart against God, withdraws the life from God's power; in the very nature of things unbelief renders the word of promise of none effect. A gospel of rest is preached to us as it was to them. We have in Scripture the most precious assurances of a rest for the soul to be found under the yoke of Jesus, of a peace of God which passeth all understanding, of a peace and a joy in the soul which nothing can take away. But when they are not believed they cannot be enjoyed: faith is in its very nature a resting in the promise and the *Promiser* until He fulfil it in us. Only faith can enter into rest. The fullness of faith enters into the full rest.

"For we which have believed do enter into rest." It is not, shall enter. No. Today, even as the Holy Ghost saith, "Today," now and here, we which have believed do enter into rest. It is with the rest of faith here as with what we heard of being partakers of Christ—the blessing is enjoyed, *"if we hold fast the beginning of our confidence firm unto the end."* The initial faith, that passes out of Egypt through the Red Sea, must be held fast firm, then it comes to the fullness of faith that passes through Jordan into the land.

Let every student of this Epistle realize how intensely personal its tone is, and with what urgency it appeals to us for faith, as the one thing needful in our dealings with the word of God. Without this the word cannot profit us. We may seek by thought and study to enter into the meaning of the promise—God has sworn that we never shall enter into its possession, or into His rest, but by faith. The one thing God asks in our intercourse with Him and His word is the habit of faith, that ever keeps the heart open towards God, and longs to enter in and abide in His rest. It is the soul that thirsts for God, for the living God, that will have the spiritual capacity for receiving the revelation of how Jesus, the High Priest, brings us into God's presence. What is to be taught us later on of our entering into the Holiest of All is nothing but the clearer unfolding of what is here called entering into rest. Let us in studying the Epistle above everything have faith.

Would you enter into the rest? Remember what has been taught us of the two stages. They are represented by Moses and Joshua. Moses the leader, Joshua the perfecter or finisher of the faith of Israel. Moses brought the people out; Joshua brought them in. Accept Jesus as your Joshua. Let past failure and wandering and sin not cause either despair or contentment with what you are. Trust Jesus who, through the sprinkling of the blood, brought you out of Egypt, to bring you as definitely into the rest. Faith is always repose in what another will do for me. Faith ceases to seek help in itself or its efforts, to be troubled with its need or its weakness; it rests in the sufficiency of the all-sufficient One who has undertaken all. Trust Jesus. Give up and forsake the wilderness. Follow Him fully; He is the rest.

Let no one imagine that this life in the rest of faith is something that is meant only for a favored few. I cannot too earnestly press it upon every reader: God calls you—yes *you*, to enter the rest. He calls you to a life of entire consecration. If you rest content with the thought of having been converted, it may be at the peril of your soul: with Israel you may perish in the wilderness: "I have sworn in my wrath: they shall not enter into my rest."

If God be indeed the fountain of all goodness and blessedness, it follows that the nearer we are to Him, and the more we have of Him, the deeper and the fuller our joy will be. Has not the soul, who is not willing at all costs to yield to Christ when He offers to bring us into the rest of God, reason to fear that all its religion is simply the selfishness that seeks escape from punishment, and is content with as little of God here as may suffice to secure heaven hereafter?

The Rest of God (Hebrews 4:4-8)

We speak, with Scripture, of the rest of faith. Faith, however, only gives rest because it rests in God; it rests because it allows God to do all; the rest is in God Himself. It is His own divine rest into which we enter by faith. When the Holy Ghost says, *My rest, His rest, God rested*, it teaches us that it is God's own rest into which we enter, and which we partake of. It is as faith sees that the creature was destined to find its rest nowhere but in the Creator, and that in the entire surrender to Him, to His will and His working, it may have perfect rest, that it dares to cast itself upon God, and have no care. It sees that God, the cause of all movement and change, is Himself the immovable and unchangeable One, and that His blessed rest can never be disturbed by what is done either by Himself or by others. Hearkening to the loving offer, it forsakes all to find its dwelling-place in God and His love. Faith sees what the rest of God is; faith believes that it may come and share in it; faith enters in and rests, it yields itself to Jesus to lead it in and make it partaker. Because it honours God and counts Him all, God honours it; He opens the door, and the soul is brought in to rest in Him.

This faith is faith in Jesus. It is the insight into His finished work, the complete salvation He bestows, the perfection which was wrought in Him personally, and in which we share as *"partakers of Christ."* The connection between the finishing of a work and the rest that follows is clearly seen in what is said of creation. *"God rested on the seventh day from all His works. He that is entered into His rest, hath himself also rested from his work, as God did from His."* The rest of God was His glad complacency in what He had finished in Creation, the beginning of His blessed work of Providence to care for and bring on to perfection what He had wrought. And so it is the finished work of Jesus that is ever set before us in the Epistle as the ground of our faith, the call for us in fullness of faith to draw nigh and enter in and rest. Because Christ has put away sin, has rent the veil, and is set down on the right hand of the throne—because all is finished and perfected, and we have received the Holy Spirit from heaven in our hearts to make us the partakers of that glorified Christ, we may with confidence, with boldness, rest in Him to maintain and perfect His work in us. And, resting in Him, He becomes our Joshua, perfecting our faith, bringing us in, and giving us a home in the rest of God with Himself, now to go no more out forever.

And if you would know why so few Christians enjoy this rest, it is *because they do not know Jesus as their Joshua.* We shall see later how Aaron was only a type of Christ in His work on earth. Melchizedek is needed as a type of His work in heaven, in the power and joy of the heavenly life. Moses and Aaron both shadow-forth the beginning of Christ's work—His work on earth; Melchizedek and Joshua His work in heaven. They show us clearly how, as in the type God ordained, so in reality there are two stages in Christian knowledge and experience.

All the feebleness of our Christian life is owing to one thing: we do not know Jesus in heaven; we do not know that Jesus has *entered* in for us (6:20; 9:12, 14), and that this secures to us *boldness* and *the power of entrance* into a heavenly state of life; that He there sits upon the throne as our High Priest in power, maintaining in us His own heavenly life; keeping us in personal fellowship with the living Father, so that in Him we too enter the rest of God. It is because we do not know Jesus in His heavenly life and power that our life is feeble; if we learn to know Him as He is to be revealed in this Epistle, as our heavenly Joshua, actually bringing us and our inmost nature into the rest of God, we cannot but enter into that rest. When Joshua went before, the people followed at once in fellowship with him. Entering the rest of God is a personal practical experience of the soul that receives the word in living faith, because in it it receives Jesus on the throne.

Let us do what Israel did in crossing Jordan; they allowed Joshua to bring them in; they followed him. Let us follow Jesus in the path He trod. In heaven God's will is all. On earth Jesus made that will all. He lived in the will of God, in suffering and doing, in meeting trial, in waiting for the Father's guidance; in giving up everything to it, He proved that God's will was His path. Follow Him. Yield yourself, in the death to self, to the will of

God; have faith in Jesus on the throne, as your Head and life, that He has brought you in and will make it true in your experience; trust Jesus, as being partaker of His nature and life, to work all in you that the Father seeks; and you shall know how blessed it is to enter the rest of God.

Deep restfulness, even amid outward activity, is one of the most beautiful marks and aids of the life of faith. Cultivate that holy stillness that seeks to abide in Gods presence, and does not yield too much to things around.

This rest is Gods rest; it is found in His fellowship. Think of all He sees, of all He feels, and has to bear; think of the divine peace and patience with which He guides all; and learn to be patient and trustful, and to rest in Him. Believe in Him, as the one God who works all in all, and works in you that which is well pleasing in His sight, and you shall have perfect rest in letting Him do all for you and in you.

God is a supernatural, incomprehensible Being; we must learn to know Him in a way that is above reason and sense. That way is the adoration of faith, and the deep humility of obedience. Through these the Holy Spirit will work the work of God in us.

All entering in means a coming out from the place we were in before. Forsake all, and follow Jesus into God's presence.

O my soul, listen to this word of the great God, and let His unspeakable love draw you—Today, enter into My rest.

Rest from Works (Hebrews 4:9-10)

"There remaineth therefore a sabbath rest for the people of God." Taken in connection with what precedes about the seventh day or Sabbath, the rest is here called a sabbatism or sabbath rest. It is spoken of as *remaining,* with reference to the rest in Canaan. That was but a shadow and symbol; the real sabbath rest remained, waiting its time, till Christ the true Joshua should come, and open it to us by Himself entering it.

In verse 10 we have here another proof that the rest does not refer to heaven. How needless it would be in that case to say of those who have died, *"For he that hath entered into his rest, hath himself also rested from his works, as God did from His."* The remark would have no point. But what force it has in connection with the rest of faith in this life, pointing us to what is the great secret of this entrance into rest—the ceasing from works, as God did from His.

96

In God we see, as it were, two distinct stages in His relation to His work. The first was that of creation—until He had finished all His work which He created and made. The second, His rest when creation was finished, and He rejoiced in what He had made, now to begin the higher work of watching the development of the life He had entrusted the creature with, and securing its sanctification and perfection. It is a rest from work which is now finished, for higher work now to be carried on. Even so there are the two stages in the Christian life. The one in which, after conversion, a believer seeks to work what God would have him do. The second, in which, after many a painful failure, he ceases from his works, and enters the rest of God, there to find the power for work in allowing God to work in him.

It is this resting from their own work which many Christians cannot understand. They think of it as a state of passive and selfish enjoyment, of still contemplation which leads to the neglect of the duties of life, and unfits for that watchfulness and warfare to which Scripture calls. What an entire misunderstanding of God's call to rest. As the Almighty, God is the only source of power. In nature He works all. In grace He waits to work all too, if man will but consent and allow. Truly to rest in God is to yield oneself up to the highest activity. We work, because He works in us to will and to do. As Paul says of himself, "I labor, striving according to His working who worketh in me with might" (lit., "agonizing according to His energy who energizes in me with might"). Entering the rest of God is the ceasing from self-effort, and the yielding up oneself in the full surrender of faith to God's working.

How many Christians are there who need nothing so much as rightly to apprehend this word. Their life is one of earnest effort and ceaseless struggling. They do long to do God's will, and to live to His glory. Continued failure and bitter disappointment is their too frequent experience. Very often as the result they give themselves up to a feeling of hopelessness; it never will be otherwise. Theirs is truly the wilderness life—they have not entered into God's rest. Would that God might open their eyes, and show them Jesus as our Joshua, who has entered into God's presence, who sits upon the throne as High Priest, bringing us in living union with Himself into that place of rest and of love, and, by His Spirit within us, making that life of heaven a reality and an experience.

"He that is entered into rest, hath himself also rested from his works, as God

did from His." And how does one rest and cease from his works? It is by ceasing from self. It is the old self-life that always insists upon proving its goodness and its strength, and presses forward to do the works of God. It is only in death that we rest from our works. Jesus entered His rest through death; each one whom He leads into it must pass through death. "Reckon yourself to be indeed dead unto sin, and alive unto God in Christ Jesus our Lord." Believe that the death of Christ, as an accomplished fact, with all that it means and has effected, is working in you in all its power. You are dead with Him and in Him. Consent to this, and cease from dead works. "Blessed are the dead that die in the Lord. Yea, saith the Spirit, for they do rest from their labors." That is as true of spiritual dying with Christ as of the death in the body. To sinful nature there is no rest from work but through death.

"He that is entered into rest hath rested from his works." The ceasing from our works and the entering the rest of God go together. Read the first chapter of Joshua, and hear God's words of strength and encouragement to everyone who would enter. Exchange the wilderness life with your own works for the *rest-life* in which God works. Fear not to believe that Jesus came to give it, and that it is for you.

"Not I, but Christ." This is the rest of faith in which a man rests from his works. With the unconverted man it is, "Not Christ, but I." With the feeble and slothful Christian, "I and Christ"—I first, and Christ to fill up what is lacking. With increasing earnestness it becomes, "Christ and I"—Christ first, but still "I" second. With the man who dies with Christ it is, "Not I, but Christ"—Christ alone and Christ all. He has ceased from his work: Christ lives in him. This is the rest of faith.

God says of His dwelling among His people, "This is My rest; here will I dwell." Fear not to say this too. It is the rest of God in His delight and pleasure in the work of His Son, in His love to Jesus and all who belong to Him. It is the rest of Jesus in His finished work, sitting on the throne, resting in the Father's love. It is the rest of our faith and love in Jesus, in God, in His love.

Give Diligence to Enter into the Rest (Hebrews 4:11)

Our Epistle is intensely practical. How it detains and holds us fast in hope of persuading us not to be content with the knowledge or the admiration of its teaching, but personally to listen to the message it brings from God by the Holy Ghost, and indeed do the thing God would have us do—enter into His rest. *"Let us give diligence to enter into that rest."*

"Let us give diligence." The word means, "make haste, be in earnest, put your whole heart into it, see that you do it"—enter into the rest. *"That no man fall after the same example of disobedience."* The danger is imminent—the loss will be terrible. God has sworn in His wrath that unless we hearken and obey, we shall not enter His rest. Let us give diligence to enter in. All the wonderful teaching the Epistle contains further on, as to the Holiest that is opened for us as the place where God wants to receive us into His rest and live, as to the great High Priest who has opened the way and entered in and lives as our Joshua to bring us in, will profit us nothing, unless there be the earnest desire, the willing readiness, the firm resolve, to enter in. It is this disposition alone that can fit a man spiritually to apprehend the heavenly mysteries the Epistle opens up.

And surely it ought not to be needful to press the motives that should urge us to obedience. Ought not the one motive to suffice—the unspeakable privilege God offers me in opening to me the entrance into His own rest? No words can express the inconceivable greatness of the gift. God speaks to me in His Son as one who was created in His image, capable of fellowship with Himself; as one whom He has redeemed out of the awful captivity of sin and death, because He longs to have me living with Him in His love. As one for whom He has made it possible to live the outer life in the flesh, with the inner life in Christ, lifted up, kept safe in the Holiest of All, in God's own rest—oh, can it be that anyone believes this and does not respond? No, let each heart say, "Blessed be God, into this rest would I enter, here would I dwell."

We are so accustomed to the wilderness life of stumbling and sinning, we have so learnt to take the words God speaks of that life (3:10), "They do always err in their heart," as descriptive of what must be daily Christian experience, that we hardly count it a practical possibility to enter into the rest. And even when the desire has been awakened, the path appears so dark and unknown. Let me for the sake of such once again gather up what has been said as to the way to enter in: it may be God, of His great mercy, may help some to take the step. The instructions need be very simple.

First, settle it in your mind, *believe with your whole heart that there is such a rest, and that Today.* It is God's rest, in which He lives; into which Jesus, as your Joshua, has entered. It is your rest, prepared for you; your land of promise; the spiritual state of life which is as surely yours as Jesus is; into which Jesus will bring you, and where He will keep you. It is the rest in which you can live every hour, free from care and anxiety, free from weariness and wanderings, always resting in the rest that trusts God for all. Believe this.

Then *cease from your own works.* Not as if you had to attain this perfectly before entering into God's rest. No, but consent, yield, be willing that all self-working should come to an end. Cease from self. Where there is life there is action; the self-life will seek to work, except you give up self into the death of Christ; with Him you are buried, in Him you live. As Christ said, "Hate your own life, lose it." Cease from your own works, and bow in deep humility and helplessness of all good, as nothing before God.

Trust Jesus as your Joshua, who brings you in, even now. Israel had simply to trust and obey and follow Joshua. Set your heart on Him who has entered the heavens to appear before God for us. Claim Jesus as yours, not only in His cross and death and resurrection, but above all in His heavenliness, in His possession of the rest of heaven. Claim Him, and leave Him to do His blessed work. You need not understand all. Your feelings may not be what you would wish. Trust Him, who has done all for you in earth and heaven, to do all in your heart too.

And then be *a follower of them who through faith and patience have inherited the promises.* Israel passed in one day through Jordan into Canaan, but did not in one day come to the perfect rest. It is at the end of the life of Joshua we read, "The Lord gave them rest round about." Enter today into the rest. Though all may not be bright at once, look to Jesus, your Joshua, and leave all in His hands. Come away out of self, and live in Him. Rest in God whatever happens. Think of His Rest, and Jesus who has entered it in your name, and out of it fills you with its Spirit, and fear not. *Today*, if you hear His voice, enter in.

Jesus said, *"Take My yoke upon you, and learn of Me, for I am meek and lowly in heart, and ye shall find rest unto your souls."* It was through meekness and lowliness of heart that Jesus found His rest in God. He allowed God to be all, trusted God for all—the rest of God was His abode. He invites us to share His rest, and tells us the secret in the meekness and lowliness of Jesus is the way to the rest.

Israel did not enter Canaan. And why? It is twice said because of diso-bedience, and thrice because of unbelief. The two things always go togeth-er. Yield yourself in everything to obey. This will strengthen you to trust for everything He has promised to do.

The rest includes victory: *"The Lord will give thee rest from all thy enemies round about, and thou shalt dwell in safety." "And the Lord gave them rest round about, all their enemies gave He into their hand."*

10

The Letter and the Spirit

D. Martyn Lloyd-Jones

Dr. Martyn Lloyd-Jones (1899-1981) was brought up in Welsh Calvinistic Methodism, first as a boy in Wales and then as a teenager and student in London. Pursing a future in medicine, he completed his academic education and training in London, and by the age of 26, he also became a Member of the Royal College of Physicians. With a brilliant and lucrative career in front of him, however, God had plans for Lloyd-Jones to be a physician of souls rather than of bodies. Though raised in church, it wasn't until he was a young doctor that Lloyd-Jones came to a saving knowledge of the Lord Jesus Christ. Some time later he was called of God to preach and took his first pastorate in Wales.

It was as the pastor of Westminster Chapel, London, (1938-1968) where "The Doctor," as he came to be affectionately called, his ministry eventually reached a global audience through his published sermons and writings. His consuming desire was to live and minister to the glory of God; his passionate love for Christ, and his keen sensitivity to the ministry of the Holy Spirit pervaded his spoken and written ministries.

It is characteristic of human nature that we always prefer to have things cut and dried rather than have them in the form of principles. That is why certain forms of religion are always popular.

The natural man likes to be given a definite list; then he feels that, as long as he conforms to the things stated in the list, all will be well. But that is not possible with the gospel. That was partly the position under the Old Dispensation, and even there it was carried too far by the Pharisees and scribes. But it is not at all like that under the New Testament dispensation. However, we still tend to like this sort of thing. It is very much easier, is it not, to think of holiness in terms of observing Lent for six weeks or so during the year, rather than to be living with a principle which demands and insists upon application day by day.

We always like to have a set of routine rules and regulations. That is why I am pressing this point. If you take the Sermon on the Mount with these six detailed statements (Matt. 5:21, 27, 31, 33, 38, 43) and say, "As long as I do not commit adultery—and so on—I am all right," you have entirely missed our Lord's point. It is not a code of ethics. He is out to delineate a certain order and quality of life, and He says in effect: "Look, I am illustrating this kind of life. It means this type of behaviour." So we must hold on to the principle without turning the particular illustration into a law.

Let me put it again in this form. Any man in the ministry has to spend a good deal of his time answering the questions of people who come and want him to make particular pronouncements upon particular questions. There are certain problems which face us all in life, and there are people who always seem to want some kind of detailed statement so that when they are confronted by any particular problem, all they have to do is to turn up their textbook and there they find the answer. Catholic types of religion are prepared to meet such people. The casuists of the Middle Ages, . . . those so-called doctors of the Church, had thought-out and discussed together the various moral and ethical problems likely to confront Christian people in this world, and they codified them and drew up their rules and regulations. When you were faced with a difficulty you immediately turned up your authority and found the appropriate answer.

There are people who are always anxious for something like that in the spiritual realm. The final answer to them in terms of this Sermon can be put in this form: the gospel of Jesus Christ does not treat us like that; it does not treat us as children. It is not another law, but something which gives us life. It lays down certain principles and asks us to apply them. Its essential teaching is that we are given a new outlook and understanding which we must apply with respect to every detail of our lives. That is why the Christian, in a sense, is a man who is always walking on a kind of knife edge. He has no set regulations; instead he applies this central principle to every situation that may arise.

All this must be said in order to emphasize this point. If we take these six statements made by our Lord in terms of the formula "Ye have heard" and "I say unto you," we shall find that the principle He uses is exactly the same in each case. In one He is dealing with sex-morality, in the next with murder and in the next with divorce. But every single time the principle is the same. Our Lord as a great Teacher knew the importance of illustrating a principle, so here He gives six illustrations of the one truth.

Let us now deal with this common principle which is to be found in the six, so that when we come to work each one out we shall always be holding this central principle in our minds. Our Lord's chief desire was to show the true meaning and intent of the law, and to correct the erroneous conclusions which had been drawn from it by the Pharisees and scribes and all the false notions which they had founded upon it. These, I suggest, are the principles.

First Principle

First, it is the spirit of the law that matters primarily, not the letter only. The law was not meant to be mechanical, but living. The whole trouble with the Pharisees and the scribes was that they concentrated only on the letter, and they did so to the exclusion of the spirit. It is a great subject—this relationship between form and content. Spirit is always something that must be embodied in form, and that is where the difficulty arises.

Man will ever concentrate on the form rather than on the content, upon the letter rather than upon the spirit. You remember that the apostle Paul stresses this in 2 Corinthians where he says: "The letter killeth, but the spirit giveth life," and his whole emphasis in that chapter is that Israel was so constantly thinking of the letter that they lost the spirit. The whole purpose of the letter is to give body to the spirit; and the spirit is the thing that really matters, not the mere letter.

Take, for example, this question of murder. As long as the Pharisees and scribes did not actually murder a man they thought they had kept the law perfectly. But they were missing the whole point and spirit of the law, which is not merely that I should literally not commit murder, but that my attitude towards my fellow men should be a right and loving one. Likewise with all these other illustrations. The mere fact that you do not commit adultery in an actual physical sense does not mean that you have kept the law. What is your spirit? What is your desire as you look, and so on? It is the spirit, not the letter, that counts.

It is clear, then, that if we rely only upon the letter we shall completely misunderstand the law. Let me emphasize that this applies not only to the law of Moses, but still more, in a sense, to this very Sermon on the Mount. There are people today who so look at the letter of the Sermon on the Mount as to miss its spirit. When we come to details we shall see that in practice. Take for instance the attitude of the Quakers with regard to taking the oath. They have taken the letter here literally, and, it seems to me, have not only denied the spirit, but have even made our Lord's statement almost ridiculous.

There are people who do exactly the same with turning the other cheek, and giving to those who ask gifts of us, bringing the whole teaching in to ridicule because they are constantly living on the letter, whereas our Lord's whole emphasis was upon the primary importance of the spirit. That does not mean of course that the letter does not matter; but it does mean that we must put the spirit before it and interpret the letter according to the spirit.

Second Principle

Now take a second principle, which is really another way of putting the first. Conformity to the law must not be thought of in terms of actions only. Thoughts, motives and desires are equally important.

The law of God is concerned as much with what leads to the action as it is with the action itself. Again, it does not mean that the action does not matter; but it does mean very definitely that it is not the action only that is important. This should be an obvious principle.

The scribes and Pharisees were concerned only about the act of adultery or the act of murder. But our Lord was at pains to emphasize to them that it is the desire in man's heart and mind to do these things that is really and ultimately reprehensible in the sight of God. How often He said in this connection that it is out of the heart that evil thoughts and actions come. It is the heart of man that matters.

So we must not think of this law of God and of pleasing God merely in terms of what we do or do not do; it is the inward condition and attitude that God is always observing. "Ye are they which justify yourselves before men; but God knoweth your hearts: for that which is highly esteemed among men is abomination in the sight of God" (Lk. 16:15).

Third Principle

The next principle we can put in this form. The law must be thought of not only in a negative manner, but also positively. The ultimate purpose of the law is not merely to prevent our doing certain things that are wrong; its real object is to lead us positively, not only to do that which is right, but also to love it. Here again is something which comes out clearly in these six illustrations.

The whole Jewish conception of the law was a negative one. I must not commit adultery, I must not commit murder, and so on. But our Lord emphasizes all along that what God is really concerned about is that we should be lovers of righteousness. We should be hungering and thirsting after righteousness, not merely negatively avoiding that which is evil.

It is surely unnecessary that I should turn aside to show the practical relevance of each one of these points to our present condition. Alas, there are still people who seem to think of holiness and sanctification in this purely mechanical manner. They think that, as long as they are not guilty of drinking, gambling or going to theatres and cinemas, all is well. Their attitude is purely negative. It does not seem to matter if you are jealous, envious and spiteful. The fact that you are full of the pride of life seems to be of no account as long as you do not do certain things. That was the whole trouble with the scribes and Pharisees who perverted the law of God by regarding it purely in a negative manner.

Fourth Principle

The fourth principle is that the purpose of the law as expounded by Christ is not to keep us in a state of obedience to oppressive rules, but to promote the free development of our spiritual character. This is vitally important. We must not think of the holy life as something hard and grievous which puts us into a state of servitude. Not at all.

The glorious possibility that is offered us by the gospel of Christ is development as children of God and growing "unto the measure of the stature of the fullness of Christ." "His commandments," says John in his first Epistle, "are not grievous." So if you and I regard the ethical teaching of the New Testament as something that cramps us, if we think of it as something narrow and restrictive, it means we have never understood it. The whole purpose of the gospel is to bring us into "the glorious liberty of the children of God," and these special injunctions are simply particular illustrations of how we may arrive at that and enjoy it.

Fifth Principle

That, in turn, brings us to the fifth principle which is that the law of God, and all these ethical instructions of the Bible, must never be regarded as an end in themselves. We must never think of them as something to which we just have to try to conform.

The ultimate objective of all this teaching is that you and I might come to know God. Now these Pharisees and scribes (and the apostle Paul said it was true of him, too, before he was truly converted) put, as it were, the Ten Commandments and the moral law on the wall, and having viewed them in this negative, restricted manner said: "Well, now, I am not guilty of these various things, therefore I am all right. I am righteous, and all is well between me and God." You see they viewed the law as something in and of itself. They codified it in this way, and as long as they kept to that code they said all was well.

According to our Lord that is an utterly fallacious view of the law. The one test which you must always apply to yourself is this: "What is my relationship to God? Do I know Him? Am I pleasing Him?" In other words, as you examine yourself before you go to bed, you do not just ask yourself if you have committed murder or adultery, or whether you have been guilty of this or that, and if you have not, thank God that all is well. No. You ask yourself rather, "Has God been supreme in my life today? Have I lived to the glory and the honour of God? Do I know Him better? Have I a zeal for His honour and glory? Has there been anything in me that has been unlike Christ—thoughts, imaginations, desires, impulses?' That is the way. In other words, you examine yourself in the light of a living Person and not merely in terms of a mechanical code of rules and regulations.

And as the law must not be thought of as an end in itself, neither must the Sermon on the Mount. These are simply agencies which are meant to bring us into that true and living relationship with God. We must always be very careful, therefore, lest we do with the Sermon on the Mount what the Pharisees and the scribes had been doing with the old moral law. These six examples chosen by our Lord are nothing but illustrations of principles. It is the spirit not the letter that matters; it is the intent, object and purpose that are important. The one thing we have to avoid above everything else in our Christian lives is this fatal tendency to live the Christian life apart from a direct, living, and true relationship to God.

Finally, we can illustrate it like this. Discipline in the Christian life is a good and essential thing. But if your main object and intent is to conform to the discipline that you have set for yourself it may very well be the greatest danger to your soul. Fasting and prayer are good things; but if you fast twice a week or pray at a particular hour every day merely in order to carry out your discipline, then you have missed the whole object of fasting and praying. There is no point in either of them, or in observing Lent, or in anything else that is meant to be an aid to the spiritual life, unless they bring us into a deeper relationship to God. I may stop smoking, I may stop drinking or gambling during these six weeks or at any other period. But if during that time my poverty of spirit is not greater, my sense of weakness is not deepened, my hunger and thirst after God and righteousness is not greatly increased, then I might just as well not have done it at all. Indeed, I would say it would be very much better for me if I had not done it.

All this is the fatal danger of making these things ends in themselves. We can be guilty of the same thing with public worship. If public worship becomes an end in itself, if my sole object in a pulpit is to preach a sermon and not to try to explain the blessed gospel of God that you and I, and all of us, may come to know and love Him better, my preaching is vain and it may be the thing that will damn my soul. These things are meant to be aids to help us, and illustrations of the Word. God forbid that we should turn them into a religion. "The letter kills, but the Spirit giveth life."

11

Christ's Ideal of Character

J. Oswald Sanders

J. Oswald Sanders (1902-1992) was the general director of Overseas Missionary Fellowship (then known as China Inland Mission) in the 1950s and 1960s. He authored more than forty books on the Christian life. He became an elder statesman and worldwide conference speaker from his retirement until his death.

Sanders was born in Invercargill, New Zealand, and gained a law degree in 1922. He attended the Bible Training Institute in Auckland and joined its staff in 1926. He left a promising law practice in his native New Zealand to serve as an instructor and administrator at the Bible College of New Zealand.

In 1954 Sanders became general director of the China Inland Mission and led the reorganization of the CIM into the Overseas Missionary Fellowship. He was instrumental in beginning many new missions projects throughout East Asia. Upon his retirement in 1969, he continued to teach worldwide and to write prolifically.

In striking contrast to the thunderings and threatenings of the law, the manifesto of Christ's kingdom (Matt. 5:1-11) commences with a benediction. *Blessedness* is the keynote. And yet the pathway to this blessedness leads His followers through strange and unexpected territory. In a few concise and vivid word pictures Jesus outlines the ideal life, an ideal which was a reflection of the supremely attractive life He lived among men. He was the embodiment and example of His own lofty teaching in this pungent and penetrating sermon.

Jesus was an authority on blessedness. He was the blessed man depicted in Psalm 1 and was therefore qualified to reveal the qualities and attitudes of which this blessedness was the reward. How different they are from what one would expect—poverty, mourning, hunger, thirst, reviling, persecution. There must surely be some mistake, for how can these bring blessedness? It is a common idea that blessedness flows from the possession of wealth, the absence of sorrow, the gratification of appetite, being well spoken of and kindly treated. Christ's teaching cut right across this popular concept of happiness and indicated that the very experiences we are eager to avoid are the ones conducive to the deepest joy and most to be coveted.

"Blessed" is a word which has been ennobled by its use in the New Testament. It is derived from the Greek "to speak well of," and is akin to our word "happy," which in English etymology goes back to hap, chance, good luck. Originally it was used of Greek gods and men, but connoted largely outward prosperity. Jesus invested the word with a new dimension, giving it the sense of spiritual prosperity which is the outcome of pure character and a correct sense of values. It has been variously translated as "to be envied, to be congratulated, to be superlatively happy, to be spiritually prosperous, to be enviably fortunate, to be radiantly joyous."

Of the eight characteristics with their compensations which He listed, the first four relate *to our attitude to God* and the last four *to our attitude to our fellow-men*. The first group are passive personal qualities, the second active social qualities. In his relations with his God, the superlatively happy man is conscious of a sense of inadequacy.

A sense of Inadequacy

"Blessed are the poor in spirit, for theirs is the kingdom of heaven." Note, poor in spirit, not poor-spirited. Not merely diffident, but renounced in spirit. He is emptied of self-reliance. There is no hint of self-sufficiency. He considers himself insignificant. With Paul he confesses, " I know that in me . . . dwelleth no good thing."

It was the habit of Principal Cairns, the Scottish theologian, to say, "You first, I follow." Once, on approaching the platform a great burst of applause greeted him. He stood aside and let the man behind him go first and began himself to applaud. He never dreamed the applause could be for him! Such is the blessed man.

It is significant that there are two words translated "poor." One refers to a laborer who is poor by reason of his circumstances, the other to a beggar who is poor by choice. The laborer has nothing superfluous; the beggar has nothing at all. It is the latter word, suggesting spiritual destitution, which is employed here. To be a beggar in spirit, to be bankrupt on the grace of God is an attitude to covet. The man of the world is proud of his independence and self-reliance. The blessed man like his Master confesses, "I can of mine own self do nothing." The typical attitude of the beggar is seen in Acts 3:5: "He gave heed unto them, *expecting to receive something of them.*" This man is broken pride, and his sense of inadequacy for the demands of his consciousness of having empty hands, throws him back on the illimitable resources of God. His attitude is the complete antithesis of that of the Laodiceans who boasted, "I am rich and increased with goods and have need of nothing." Such poverty inevitably leads to spiritual affluence. Though himself poor, the blessed man makes many rich. He may not be a success by earthly standards but he enjoys the kingdom of Heaven.

A Sense of Contrition

"Blessed are they that mourn, for they shall be comforted." It is not the sorrow itself that is a blessed thing, but rather the comfort which God ministers to the sorrowing. There can be no comfort where there is no grief. "The man who knows nothing of sorrow is incomplete. One side of his nature has not been developed," wrote Archbishop Harrington Lees. "The happiness of the Gospel message is that it alone professedly deals with the common lot of sorrow, and gives the oil of joy for mourning. This is its initial undertaking: its final guarantee is 'no sorrow, nor crying.'"

The word "mourn" indicates a sorrow which begins in the heart, takes possession of the whole person, and is outwardly manifested. The special form of sorrow envisaged in this word is sorrow over spiritual failure or actual sin. The sense of spiritual poverty, of lukewarmness toward God, of distance from Him, of unlikeness to Christ inevitably leads to regret and contrition. The boasting and self-sufficient Pharisee did not mourn or beat his breast like the penitent publican, nor did he enjoy the experience of justification. The prodigal first recognized his abject poverty: "I perish with hunger"; then in true contrition he acknowledged his sin: "Father, I have sinned." It was only when Job had a vision of God that he said in deep self-abasement, "I abhor myself and repent in dust and ashes." He mourned over what might have been had he not been self-satisfied.

The paradoxical thing about this mourning is that it is not incompatible with rejoicing. Paul claimed to be sorrowful, yet always rejoicing. The enjoyment of the comfort which God imparts to the contrite spirit is another of the ingredients of the superlatively happy life.

A Sense of Modesty

"Blessed are the meek, for they shall inherit the earth." Meekness is not an invertebrate virtue, says one writer. It is not weakness or mere mildness of disposition, for our Lord claimed it as an element of His character, to be emulated by His disciples. Moses was meek (Num. 12:3) but he certainly was not weak. It is the gentleness of strength in reserve, not of effeminacy. Meekness can fight with strength and vigor when the glory of God or the interests of the kingdom are at stake. It was the meek and lowly Jesus who with upraised whip of cords expelled the mercenary traders from His Fathers house. Nor is meekness mere good-naturedness which will take anything from anybody. Essentially it is that attitude of mind which does not insist on its own rights and is always ready to waive its privileges in the interests of others. It is always ready to renounce its own plans and to joyously embrace God's plans. Nietzsche preached that the world is ours if we can get it. Jesus preached that the world is ours if we renounce it; it is the meek, not the aggressive, who inherit the earth.

Of all qualities of character, meekness is probably the one least coveted. But Jesus extols it as a grace highly esteemed by God. "The ornament of a meek and quiet spirit, which is in the sight of God of great price" (1 Peter 3:4). The meek person is generally regarded as too good to make his way or count for much. Jesus refutes this concept by stating that it is he who inherits the earth. He is characterized too by a willingness to yield to others when principle is not at stake. He claims nothing, but the whole earth is his.

A Sense of Desire

"Blessed are they which do hunger and thirst after righteousness: for they shall be filled." One version renders it, "Blessed are they that are starving for righteousness, for they shall be crammed full." Jesus uses these elemental human instincts to illustrate the passionate desire for holiness and likeness to Christ which commands the full response of God. These are the most intense and agonizing human appetites when denied satisfaction. When Sir Ernest Shackleton and his party were left without food for some time during one of their journeys in the Antarctic, he said it was extremely difficult to think of anything else but food. The person who has an unquenchable thirst, an insatiable hunger, for a holy life, is one to be envied. Blessed starvation!

> *As pants the hart for cooling streams*
> *When heated in the chase,*
> *So pants my soul for Thee, my God,*
> *And Thy redeeming grace.*

It is noteworthy that the beatitude does not speak of hungering and thirsting after *happiness*. Happiness is the object of pursuit of the vast bulk of mankind but generally it proves only an elusive mirage. Jesus teaches here that when a man makes the primary object of his pursuit not happiness but righteousness—a right relationship with God—he obtains superlative happiness to boot. "They shall be filled"—to repletion, both here and hereafter. "He satisfieth the longing soul, and filleth the hungry soul with goodness" (Ps. 107:9).

From indicating the ideal attitude of the subjects of His kingdom toward God, Jesus turns to his social relationships with his fellows. The man who is spiritually prosperous exhibits a fourfold disposition in testing circumstances—"strength with weakness at its mercy, purity in contact with defiling company, love which sees others at variance, rectitude suffering at the hands of tormentors. Each has its own beatitude, the fruit of a work of divine grace."

A Compassionate Spirit

"Blessed are the merciful: for they shall obtain mercy." This beatitude has been correctly described as a self-acting law of the moral world. It is the man who shows mercy who receives mercy. We reap what we sow. It is possible for a man to hunger and thirst after righteousness, but for his righteousness to be hard and exacting. That quaint evangelist, Sam Jones, used to say that righteousness without mercy results in the indigestion countenance.

Like meekness, mercy is a distinctively Christian virtue and was little known among non-Christian people. It has its source in a compassionate feeling and is expressed in the compassionate act. Mercy is shown to those who have no claim on it. If they have a claim to mercy, then it is only justice they receive. The man of a compassionate spirit is always ready to make allowances for those who have failed, or to put the best construction on ambiguous behavior. He does not judge harshly, remembering that he is not in possession of all the facts. We do well to bear in mind that our experience is only the rebound of our attitude. Mercy knows no retaliation.

A Clean Heart

"Blessed are the pure in heart: for they shall see God." The beatific vision is vouchsafed on earth only to those of pure heart. Purity here is an inclusive term employed in its widest meaning—purity of thought, imagination, motive, act. It signifies moral holiness or integrity, and refers especially to one who is without guile. Jesus bypassed mere external and ceremonial purity and enforced the absolute necessity of inner purity. Outward conformity to ceremonial requirements satisfies the heart of neither God nor man.

"Create in me a clean heart, O my God," pleaded David in contrition, deeply conscious of his impurity and sin against his fellow-men. The psalmist connected clean hands with a pure heart, recognizing his responsibility in human attitudes and relationships. There is no such thing as clearness of vision where there is not cleanness of heart. Too many are satisfied with outward presentability. They do not mind minor deviations from the path of moral rectitude so long as they can evade "losing face" with their own circle. The divine dictum is, "Without holiness no man shall see the Lord." There is a daily need of self-examination and appropriation of the cleansing of the blood of Christ.

To see God involves moral not physical vision, for God is Spirit. Sin beclouds the heart and obscures the face of God. To see God is to know God, to enjoy intimate fellowship with Him. Hypocrisy and insincerity are ruled out if one is to see God in this sense. With Christ in the heart as the indwelling fountain of purity, the maintenance of a clean heart becomes a glorious possibility. When this is experienced, it is possible to anticipate here on earth the day when we shall see Him face to face.

A Conciliatory Ministry

"Blessed are the peacemakers: for they shall be called the children of God." This beatitude is often read as though it referred to peacekeepers—keepers of a peace which was already in existence—or to peaceable men. Instead it refers to the one who makes peace in a situation where that peace has been broken. It is not a virtue, but an activity which is in view. Making peace is a much more costly ministry than maintaining peace. Our Lord "made peace by the blood of his cross." We can make peace only by allowing our own peace to be broken. There is always a cross in this ministry. In the presence of such a person, quarrels and discord die away. It was said of a noted British statesman, that when he came into the House, no matter how bitter the debate or wrangling, it always withered away in his presence. And why? He lived in the presence of God. No matter how late the House sat, he always spent two hours in prayer and devotion before embarking on the work of the day. He carried the peace of God with him and radiated it wherever he went. This is a ministry which calls for uncommon courage and insight and tact. But what a ministry it is to bring together those who have been estranged. Paul used all his skill and tact in his endeavor to heal the breach between Euodias and Syntyche, as recorded in his Philippian letter (4:2).

The reward for the peacemaker is not to *become* a child of God but to *be called* a child of God. He is already a child of God. It is not his pedigree but his reputation that is in view. As people see him going about his costly ministry of bringing peace, they see in him the image of his Master and recognize the family likeness.

A Courageous Loyalty

"Blessed are they that are persecuted for righteousness' sake . . . when men shall revile you, and persecute you, and say all manner of evil against you falsely, for my sake. Rejoice, and be exceeding glad: for great is your reward in heaven." Even a peacemaker is not immune from the assaults and persecutions of his fellow-men. The sinless Jesus Christ was not exempt from persecution and reviling. But note that the blessedness does not lie in the persecution or reviling. It is they that *have been persecuted*—for this is the correct tense—who *are* superlatively happy. It is the "afterward" of chastening. The blessedness consists in the joy of the special nearness of Christ in the time of trial. The man who is enviably fortunate, like the three young men in the burning fiery furnace, discovers that in the midst of the fierce fires of persecution, the Son of God walks with him and the fire does not kindle on him.

It must be observed, however, that all persecution does not bring this blessedness. There are three qualifying conditions. It must be . . .

Persecution "for righteousness' sake" (v. 10), not because of our own angularity or unwisdom. Many Christians bring unnecessary opprobrium upon themselves and the cause of Christ by their aggressive tactlessness. The persecution in view here comes upon us because we will do right at all costs, even if it results in social ostracism.

Reviling falsely based (v. 11), not which has been deserved. It is reviling which has no justification in either our words or actions which brings blessedness.

Persecution and reviling "for my sake" (v. 11). Ill-treatment which arises from our loyalty to Christ and His righteousness will bring its own magnificent reward. The sharing of His sufferings is deeply appreciated by our Master. "Be glad and supremely joyful, for your reward in Heaven is strong, intense." This must have been a strikingly new concept to the Jews, who generally considered suffering and persecution as a curse from God.

Such is our Lord's lofty concept of ideal Christian character. Is it ours? Is it too high? God knows no standard but the character of His Son. He purposes that we should all be conformed to the image of His Son, and it is the delight of the Holy Spirit to bring this about.

12

Transfiguration of Character

J. Sidlow Baxter

J. Sidlow Baxter (1903-1999) was born in Sidney, Australia, and grew up in Lancashire, England. He trained for the ministry at Spurgeon's College, London, where the foundations were laid for a life of fruitful ministry; he was a pastor in Scotland and England. He later moved to the United States, where he eventually retired and died. His ecclesiastical roots were in the Calvinistic Methodist Church.

Dr. Baxter was not only a preacher of outstanding ability, but first and foremost he was a Bible teacher. He was in great demand as a speaker at conferences and conventions. Among Baxter's best-known books are *Awake My Heart, Divine Healing of the Body, The Strategic Grasp of the Bible*, and *Rethinking Our Priorities*. His most popular work is *Explore the Book*, a 1760-page tome that analyzes and summarizes each book of the Bible. He also authored a superb trilogy on the doctrine of sanctification: *A New Call to Holiness, His Deeper Work in Us*, and *Our High Calling*, which were later published as one volume. His writings are some of the most winsome on the doctrine of holiness—most likely because he was himself a very winsome person!

Whatever other issues may be involved in this subject of scriptural holiness, never for one moment must we forget that the supreme purpose of the Holy Spirit's deeper work in the believer is the *transfiguration of character*. However often we may fight it down, there is a reassertive tendency in most of us to think that the infilling of the Holy Spirit is mainly an emotional experience. Perhaps this misunderstanding is the more persistent because of our knowing that sudden envelopments by the Holy Spirit have not infrequent-ly been *accompanied* by an eruption of ecstatic emotion. It is important that we distinguish between the purposive and the merely associative.

The human mind is usually conceived of as having three main areas or centers of activity: (1) intellect, or reason, (2) volition, or free-will, (3) emotion, or feeling. Which is the true order of precedence? The intellect is meant to be king; with the will as prime minister, or executive of the crown; and the emotions as obedient subjects. When that order is violated, and especially when the emotions run amok, we are soon in trouble, either physically or psychopathically, or both. We live in an age of suspense and nervous tension. Emotional behavior patterns and disturbances are receiving more attention than ever. We dare not understate the importance of the emotions. Yet when we have said the most and the last about them it still remains true that they are comparatively the *least* important. They are the most volatile, the most variable, the most unpredictable, the most *superficial* part of us.

Is it thinkable, then, that the Holy Spirit comes to do His deepest work in the least substantial part of us? No; whatever emotional accidence there may or may not be, that major invasion by the Holy Spirit . . . designs a renovation in the deepest depths of the human personality. It is meant to effect such a purification and refinement within the moral nature that there shall be a transfiguration of *character*.

I have made a distinction between "nature" and "character." Nature is the raw material, so to speak. Character is what we make out of it. In the final consummation, we shall all be presented "faultless" in our nature; but does that mean we shall all be equal in *character*? No; for as "one star differeth from another star in glory" (1 Cor. 15:41) so will there be greater and lesser resplendencies of character, developed by our voluntary reactions while living on earth in the mortal body. (Oh, how important is this present span on earth!). In that gracious suffusion by the Holy Spirit which effects inwrought holiness, the divine purpose is not only even the correcting of wrong bias, and the cleansing of impure impulse, and the refining of desire; it is that *nature*, being thus renewed, may be developed into holy *character*.

In other words, inwrought holiness is not only negative; it is both negative and positive. Wonderful as are the aspects of it which we have already mentioned, those more negative features (i.e. cleansing, correcting, renewing, refining) are the clearing away of obstructions, so that all those traits and qualities which are most natively human, "after the image of God," may be unimpededly developed, even sublimated, in the transfiguration of character. Holiness is not only a reclamation of the garden of weeds, but a filling of it with fragrant flowers. It is not only (negatively) a clearing away of obnoxious undergrowths from the orchard, but (positively) a producing of gracious fruit, even "the fruit of the Spirit . . . love, joy, peace, longsuffering, kindness, goodness, faithfulness, meekness, godly self-control" (Gal. 5:22-23), and all manner of "good works which God afore prepared that we should walk in them" (Eph. 2:10).

The kind of character-beauty which true holiness begets is not that of elegant marble statuary, charming in profile, graceful in silhouette, yet cold and hard to the touch, voiceless, uncommunicative, and locked up in itself. Any kind of holiness which turns the inner life into a mental monastery, and the outer life into a walled-off enclosure, is not holiness according to Christ. One of the loveliest traits of character engendered by true holiness is a self-forgetting otherism. Instead of a continually in-looking self-culture, there is an out-looking diffusion of goodness to others.

Genesis 1:11 tells how God caused the earth to bring forth herb and fruit tree "whose seed is in itself." The miracle of herb and fruit self-propagation has been since, and it always happens at the point of full development or ripeness. Similarly, holiness in full development or ripeness expresses itself in an outreaching graciousness of character which propagates goodness and moral beauty everywhere. Except where there is Satanic resistance or Pharisaic hypocrisy, it gently "provokes to love and good works" (Heb. 10:24) in other hearts and lives. It is never self-advertising, yet neither can it conceal itself. It continually reaches out in soul-winning activity, and atmospheres evangelism in the very love of God. It is full of effort, yet somehow it is effort with ease. Its hands are full of "good works." It produces character which visibly incarnates those words of the Apostolic benediction, "the grace of the Lord Jesus Christ, and the love of God, and the fellowship of the Holy Spirit."

Inward Metamorphosis

Now of course there are many New Testament verses which bear on this matter of Christian character; but I here call special attention to two, because of their using a certain Greek verb, i.e. *metamorphoo*, which, incidentally, seems to have found new vogue today in our rather modem word, "metamorphosis." Both in the Greek and in the English the meaning is *to transform*. That Paul should speak about a *character-metamorphosis* through inward renewal is, to say the least, arresting. In Romans 12:1-2, he writes,

> I beseech you therefore, brethren, by the mercies of God, to present your bodies a living sacrifice, holy, acceptable to God, which is your reasonable service. And be not fashioned according to this world; but be ye transformed [*metamorphosed*] by the renewing of your mind, that ye may prove what is the good and acceptable and perfect will of God.

It is interesting to see how different translators try to bring out the full force of the meaning in these two verses. From a dozen or so, I pick out the rendering given by Weymouth's *New Testament in Modern Speech*.

> I plead with you therefore, brethren, by the compassion of God, to present all your faculties to Him as a living and holy sacrifice to Him—a spiritual mode of worship. And do not conform to the present age, but be TRANSFORMED BY THE ENTIRE RENEWAL OF YOUR MINDS, so that you may learn by experience what God's will is, namely, all that is good and acceptable to Him, and perfect.

This metamorphosis is here connected with certain factors which immediately catch the eye. (1) *Separation* from the world: "Do not conform to the present age." Our Lord could transfigure a Stephen, but never a Demas who "loved this present age." (2) *Consecration* to God: "Present all your faculties to Him as a living and holy sacrifice." Our Lord may bless others in many ways, but it is only the completely yielded whom He transfigures. (3) *Renovation* inside the human personality: "the entire renewal of your minds." Nothing less than this can really transfigure character. (4) *Realization* of the divine will by new perception and in actual experience: "that you may learn by experience what God's will is . . ."

All these well merit separate consideration, but the central and vital thing to grasp is that this character-transformation is wrought by "ENTIRE RENEWAL OF THE MIND." If anything could unanswerably show to us how astray both the eradication theory and the conventional counteraction theory [of the doctrine of sanctification] are, this second verse in Romans 12 does. If, as eradicationism says, the Second Blessing completely extirpates the so-called "*old* nature," leaving only the "*new* nature," then Paul's exhortation here, in Romans 12:1-2, must be to that "*new* nature," which, however, makes the exhortation a useless redundance. For if the so-called "new nature" is (according to theory) sinless, why need Paul exhort *it* to separation from the world, and consecration to God, and inward renewal? On the other hand, if, as says the "counteraction" idea, the "old nature" must persist within us as an inerradicable evil entity to our dying day, how could Paul exhort us to "ENTIRE RENEWAL OF THE MIND"!

How long must some of us continue to sponsor such exegetically untenable concepts in the name of scriptural holiness? How long must unsuspicious audiences be a prey to such misguidance and its hurtful after-effects? How long are we to let well-meant theory, venerated names and tenacious *shibboleths* blindfold us to the true, precious teaching of our New Testament? With such clear guidance flowing to us through Apostolic pens, why are we so slow to see the real truth about regeneration and sanctification? Regeneration, other than being merely the superinducement of a (suppositionary) "new nature" which is not the human "I" or "me", is the Holy Spirit's transfusing of a new spiritual *life* into our human nature itself And, through *further* work in us, this new life may fill, may interpenetrate, may "renew" our whole moral and spiritual nature—not to a static ethical absoluteness but to moral and spiritual *fullness of health* in which inward purity, at last, has the upper hand over all animal appetites, over all temptations injected from without, and over every wrong response from within. *That* is the true New Testament teaching as to regeneration, inward renewal, inwrought holiness, and transfiguration of character.

Yes, that is the central, vital thing: true Christian character-transformation issues from this "entire renewal of the mind." Our Lord said of John the Baptist, "He was a burning and a shining light" (John 5:35). The burning was inward. The shinning was outward. There would have been no outward shining without the inward burning. The inward burning was sanctification through the infilling Holy Spirit (Luke 1:15). The outward shining was that of transfigured character. It is *still* true that there cannot be a true outward "shining" without the same inward "burning." Many of us are needing to learn that more deeply. So, then, let us briefly analyze this character-transfiguration in its inwrought and outwrought features.

Transformation of the Mind

First there is transformation of the *mind*. The word which Paul uses in Romans 12: 2 (*metamorphose*) is used of our Lord's mountain-top transfiguration: "He was transfigured before them" (Matt. 17:2, Mark 9: 2). Luke's verbal variation of it is, "the fashion of His countenance was altered" (Luke 9:29); it was the same face, yet not the same. Correspondently, there can be such a transfiguration of the mind, by the Holy Spirit, that the very "fashion" of its thinking is changed; so that although it remains the same mind as to personal identity, it is no longer the same in its deepest impulses and responses. It means that all the thoughts, imaginations, emotions, motives, ambitions, yearnings, joys and loves of the heart and mind are made to become radiant with "the joy of the Lord." I myself have known persons who have given every convincing evidence, under widely varied testings, of this fundamental refashioning of the mind.

Transfiguration of the Personality

Resultantly, there is transfiguration of the *personality*. This is the very opposite of self-decoration. It is also quite different from a prepossessing natural charm, which in its own way, of course, can be quite delightful. It is no mere exterior impressiveness of figure or feature, nor is it any kind of personal force which is self-achieved. It is an inner radiance which somehow shines through the personality, not in *any* way because of natural appearance or engaging gifts, but, as often as not, despite the *absence* of them. It is an indefinable but unmistakable glow which tinges and lusters one's way of saying and doing things. It is utterly unconscious of itself, yet it *atmospheres* the whole personality, expressing itself most often through the most ordinary activities of the most ordinary days. It shows itself distinctly to the public through the ministry of public men, but it shows itself most clearly to those who live nearest to it and observe it continually in private life.

I remember reading about a man who once went to breakfast with the saintly John Fletcher (whom John Wesley described as "the holiest man in England"). The breakfast was very plain fare, in itself, but the visitor afterwards described the meal in this way: "Do you know, taking breakfast with John Fletcher was like taking the Sacrament!" This transfiguration of the personality is a lovely fulfillment of that prayer in Psalm 90:17, "Let the beauty of the Lord our God be upon us."

Transformation of the Countenance

We may go further and say, with all due cautiousness, that this "entire renewal" of the mind often gradually transfigures *the face*. This may not be one of its most solidly important effects, but it is one of its most appealing adjuncts. It must have been transfixing to the gathered members of the Jewish Sanhedrin when they saw Stephen's face become "as the face of an angel" (Acts 6:15). Of course, it still remained the same human face, but some unearthly sheen must have shown through it.

I never thought I would ever see anything on earth near enough to that to remind me of it, but I did, a few years ago. My dear wife and I were travelling through what was then the Belgian Congo. On the occasion of which I now speak, I was addressing a crowd of between twelve and fifteen hundred negro men and women of varying ages, from several different tribes, many of whom had come, in larger or smaller contingents, two or even three days' trek through the jungles in order to be present at our conference. I had asked beforehand for guidance as to my type of message, and had been told, "They will go as deep in the Word as you can take them"—which proved to be true. I believe that many of those beaming-faced African brothers and sisters in the Lord knew more about implicit trust in the Word, and about deeply experienced sanctification, than I did myself. My subject was: "Out of Egypt and into Canaan"—and oh, how they listened, even though it had to be through two interpreters, because of different tribal languages.

Because of needing to preach through *two* interpreters, I practiced, as closely as possible, one complete thought to each complete sentence. Next to me, on my left, a lady missionary interpreted, and next further left was a negro interpreter. In that way the main two groups of languages were covered. I could not help noticing how the people looked at that negro interpreter. Maybe *they* could not help noticing how I kept looking at him. I became so absorbed in watching his face that sometimes when it was time for me to add my next bit, I had momentarily forgotten the thread of my discourse!

Oh, that face! I have seen many beautiful faces in my time, but never one quite like that. I have seen eyes shine and features beam, but never elsewhere quite like that. Using the word in its finest, uttermost sense, that negro's face was *radiant*. If ever I saw the "spiritual glow," I saw it there. As evidently as anything could be, it was the outshining of an inward purity. In scriptural phraseology, it was "the *beauty* of holiness." I learned afterward that the beauty of his character matched the radiance of his face.

That was not the only thing which we learned afterward. On our way back from the meeting to the missionary's dwelling, we passed a group of naked natives—six or seven men, squatting at the base of a great tree. Never before in our travels had we seen human beings so facially ugly, or with such prominent suggestion of the ape. I suddenly realized how easy it would be, if we had no authentic guidance from the written Word of God, to believe in human evolution from the anthropoid apes. One of those men was so strange-looking, so gorilla-like, it was disturbing to look at him, yet we could scarce turn away our gaze. As soon as we were past them, our missionary friend said, "I know what you were thinking. We missionaries have thought the same at one time or another. You were shocked at the appearance of that big one, with the coarse hair and ugly gorilla face. Well, he is the brother of the man who interpreted your sermon just now; and your radiant-faced interpreter was even *uglier than that* before his conversion to Christ!" For the moment we were dumb-struck. The contrast between the two was so great that such a transformation seemed incredible; but the missionary assured us that similar transfigurations had occurred in tens of hundreds of lives. When, despite their crudeness, those dark-minded people are brought to the point of simple yet vital faith in the Savior, and become truly regenerated contrast between their new life in Christ and what they were before, in their pre-conversion mental darkness and animalism, that the gracious shock of it causes wonderful *facial* transfigurations.

In a gentler, less vivid, yet equally real way, I have seen transfigured character and transfigured faces in England and America. Pure-hearted Christian saints; I think of them now, and my memory of the gentle light shining through some of those dear faces tempts me to fill pages here, telling about them and the gracious witness for Christ which they diffused. But I must forbear. I would only say that those faces, some masculine, some feminine, some younger though perhaps the more of them rather older, some naturally well-featured, others rather peculiar or else of the plain Jane type, have all had a radiance, a light, an expressive something which transfigured whatever kind of natural cast or feature they had. There was that Shekinah light within which tinges with beauty *whatever* it shines through.

Transfiguration of Disposition and Behavior

Then again, going with this inward renewal and transfiguration of character, there is always transfiguration of *disposition and behavior*. "Entire renewal of the mind" inevitably registers itself in refined and tempered attitudes. Hasty verdicts and drastic reactions drop away. The way of looking at things and dealing with things is modified. There is a new interest in others, a new tolerance of others, a new warmth of kindliness toward others. In matters of faith and conviction there is a new firmness which is the more Christlike because it is firmness without fierceness. The very manner of doing things is changed, even in the commonplace duties, chores, and contacts of everyday living; the way of answering questions, the way of conversing, the exhibiting of charitableness to those who differ—oh, in so many ways, transfigured character communicates itself through transformed disposition and behavior.

Have we not seen such transformation of character, of personality, of countenance, of disposition and behavior? It sheds abroad the most winsome of all influence for Christ. It is the most magnetic of all apologetics for the Christian faith. It generally shines out with its most victorious splendor amid life's darkest experiences. With heaven-reflecting eyes it smiles upon us even through sickness, and somehow gives the thin, wan face of the wearied invalid a soft, gentle light and beauty which transfigure even the mystery of permitted pain. It is indeed the transfiguration which comes from the Holy Spirit's deeper work in the entirely sanctified believer. It is the inner glory-light of inwrought holiness, gleaming through the outer windows of the consecrated personality. Or, in those words of Romans 12:2, it is "entire renewal of the mind" expressing itself through a metamorphosis of character.

Progressive Christlikeness

This brings us to a point where we ought to glance at the other place where Paul uses the verb, *metamorphose* in connection with transfiguration of character. It is Second Corinthians 3:17-18,

> But we all, with unveiled face, beholding [or, possibly, 'reflecting'] as in a mirror the glory of the Lord, are transformed [*metamorphosed*] into the same image, from glory to glory, even as from the Lord, the Spirit.

There is some doubt as to whether Paul here means (1) that we are the reflecting mirror, or (2) that our Lord Jesus is the mirror, reflecting "the glory of the LORD" i.e. of Yahweh, or (3) that the Gospel, as the "new covenant" (see verses 6-11) is the mirror, reflecting the glory of Christ. Perhaps number three best fits the context, but, yes or no, the central idea remains the same, namely, that we, by beholding with "unveiled face," our glorious Lord, are "transformed into the same image".

It is a striking figure, and flashes with meaning for us. Like Romans 12:2, it certainly teaches a transfiguration (*metamorphosis*) of character. The phrase, here, "with unveiled face", means with unveiled eyes of the mind. With our outer, physical eyes, we cannot see our Lord at all, for the present; but, with unveiled inward vision, we may see Him as being luminously ever-present to the mind. Let us be quick to notice the four aspects of this character-transfiguration which are here indicated and blended.

1. *It is transfiguration through communion.* The participle clause, "beholding-as-in-a-mirror" is all one word in the Greek (*katoptrizonienoi*), meaning a beholding or mirroring which is contemporaneous and *going on*. One of the things which we never dare forget, especially in teaching inwrought holiness through consecration and faith, is, that no matter what crisis we may experience or what spiritual elevation may come to us, *no* blessing of the Christian life ever continues with us unless there is continuous communion with Christ. Moreover, this "beholding" or "reflecting" is that kind of communion which we call *adoring contemplation*—of which, in this age of inane rush, there is so little that we are spiritually poverty-stricken.

2. *This transfiguration is progressive.* The verb is in the present tense:

"*being* transfigured." In these chapters we have emphasized that in no sense is inwrought holiness our reaching a fixed point of static sanctity. No, this deeper renewal within us marks a crisis-point of new departure into a *progressive* transfiguration of character. Heart-holiness is never a reservoir, but, in Frances Ridley Havergal's words, a "river glorious."

3. *This transfiguration is inwrought by the Holy Spirit.* It is "from the Lord, the Spirit," that is, it is a result from His activity in the mind. The noteworthy thing is that He effects His transfiguring work through the believer's adoring contemplation of "the glory of the Lord." In Romans 12:2, the transfiguration begins with "entire renewal of the mind." Here, in 2 Corinthians 3:18, it is developed through communion; through an adoring contemplation, which absorbs into itself the very impress of that beloved heavenly Lord.

4. *This transfiguration is approximating likeness to Christ—*"transformed into the same image." Yes, that is the supreme goal of true, Christian sanctification: to become ever-increasingly conformed in character to the sublime character of Christ, "the Altogether Lovely." Let it be reiterated yet again: entire sanctification, or restoration to holiness, *is not*, according to the New Testament, either a man-achieved or God-inwrought ethical top-level, an accomplished *goal* of moral perfectness; it is restoration from moral and spiritual disease to fullness of health, making possible there from an ever-developing likeness to the character and beauty of the Lord Jesus, who is the ineffable moral loveliness of God Himself in visible embodiment.

Inwrought holiness through "entire renewal of the mind" certainly *is* both restoration to moral fullness of health and an elevation to a new high plane impossible of attainment by merely human struggling; but instead of its being a high level from which we look *down*, conscious of an exalted superiority, it humbles us with a prostration deeper than any ever caused by the heartbreaking repentance of a prodigal returning from his wallowing in the mire. Why? Because, on that higher level of holiness through "entire renewal of the mind," we see as never before, "with unveiled face," the "heavenly vision" of the ineffable, all-holiness and all-loveliness of Jesus; the very "glory of God in the face of Jesus Christ" (2 Cor. 4:6); the one, ultimate attraction of all holy heart-longing; the solitary, absolute all-perfection in the universe; the one-and-only, all-eclipsing, ever-alluring GOAL which ever, fills the gaze of all the truly sanctified. When once, through inwrought holiness, we have seen that exquisite Goal, we never again talk about our own holiness, much less of "perfection"!—for the nearer we get to that beatific Goal, so the more do we realize how far we are from it. The more truly we approximate to that perfection, the less conscious of it we are, and the more humblingly conscious are we of our own *im*perfection. That which lifts us highest brings us lowest.

Is not that the reason why, in this matter of "Christian perfection," John Wesley is far safer as an example than as teacher? However insistently he may have preached and urged "Christian perfection," he never once claimed it. Nay, he *disclaimed* it. In a letter to Dr. William Dodd, he writes, "I tell you flat, I have not attained the character I draw." As time went on, the Wesley teaching of Christian "perfection" became so pared and trimmed that in reality it was no more than a self-contradictory concept of *im*perfect perfection.

So, then, to summarize. The supreme purpose of the Holy Spirit's deeper work in us is transfiguration of character. That inward transfiguration begins through "entire renewal of the mind," or inwrought holiness, and is revealed outwardly through transfigured personality, facial expression, disposition, attitude, and behavior. It develops especially through communion with God. It is not suppositionary ethical immaculateness of the religious perfectionist, but a growing *likeness to Christ*.

Oh, for a deeper knowing of such character-transfiguration through "entire sanctification"! Is not this inwrought holiness, the "perfect love" which "casteth out fear"? (1 John 4:18)—and is not this character-transfiguration that which John means when he says, "AS HE IS, even so are we in this world"? (4:17)—and is not the most thrilling prospect of the coming Rapture just this: "When He shall appear, we shall be LIKE HIM"?

Now, O my King above,
  Now, even more.
Thee for Thyself I love.
  Thee I adore;
For 'tis the glorious
  loveliness Thou art

Which captures and subdues
  my wondering heart.

Now, all my prayer is this:
  More, more of Thee.
Thou art the perfect bliss;
  Live, live through me.
Let me Thy life absorb,
  diffuse, express,
Till heaven itself unveils
  Thy loveliness.

13

Francis of Assisi: Re-formed by Love

Samuel L. Brengle

Samuel L. Brengle (1860-1936) was converted as a child at age 13. When he was 15, he was leading a Bible class as well as the Sunday school superintendent in his home church. He was a graduate of both Depaw University and Boston Theological Seminary. As a young man he had gained a reputation of being a gifted speaker, and had political ambitions until called by God into vocational ministry.

While a student at Boston Theological Seminary, Brengle experienced his "personal Pentecost," having been influenced by the teaching and life of Dr. Daniel Steele, a foremost Methodist scholar. Soon afterward, he refused the flattering offer of the pastorate of one of the largest and wealthiest Methodist churches of the day, choosing instead to identify with the Salvation Army, where he spent the rest of his life as a traveling evangelist, writer, and eventually commissioner. Among the several books Samuel Brengle authored are *Helps to Holiness, Love-Slaves, and The Soul-Winner's Secret.*

Most of the Ten Commandments can be made into laws of the land by legislative enactment, but not so the Sermon on the Mount. It is not only a sin, it is a crime, a breach of law, to murder and steal. But no statesman has ever yet passed a law compelling men to be poor in spirit, meek, merciful, pure of heart, loving to enemies, and glad when lied about and persecuted. A man may be restrained by the strong hand of the law from stealing or committing murder; but he can be constrained only by grace to be meek and lowly in heart, to bless them that curse him, to pray for them that despitefully use him, and to love them that hate him.

"The law was given by Moses, but grace and truth came by Jesus Christ" (John 1:17). Christ was "full of grace and truth" (John 1:14). When His heart broke on Calvary it was like the breaking of Mary's alabaster box of ointment. And when He poured out the Holy Spirit at Pentecost, rivers of grace and truth began to stream forth to every land, to all people.

The nature-religions and philosophies of the Gentile world, and the religion of the Scribes and Pharisees, sunk into legal forms and ceremonies, were powerless to give peace to troubled consciences, strength to slaves of vice and corruption, or life to souls dead in trespasses and sin. But this is just what the grace of God in Christ did. It met and fitted the moral and spiritual needs of men as light meets the eye, as the skin fits the hand.

When Paul went to luxurious, licentious Corinth and preached Christ to the reveling populace, lo! fornicators, idolaters, adulterers, sodomites, thieves, covetous people, drunkards and revelers became saints. Their eyes were opened, their darkness vanished, their chains fell off, and they received "beauty for ashes, the oil of joy for mourning, the garment of praise for the spirit of heaviness" (Isa. 61:3). Christ made them free. They loved each other. They lived in close association with each other, but they did not shut themselves away from their unsaved neighbors. They went everywhere declaring the good news of redeeming love and uttermost salvation in Christ.

But not all who named the name of Christ departed from iniquity. Heresies crept in. Persecutions arose. The awful corruptions and subtle philosophies of the heathen world undermined the morals, weakened the courage, and dimmed or destroyed the faith of many. The whole social and political order of the ancient world began to crumble. The Roman empire fell before the assaults of northern barbarians, and the Dark Ages supervened. The secret of salvation and sanctification by faith, which made Paul's converts in Corinth victorious over the proud and putrid world in which they lived, the flesh which had enslaved them and the Devil who had deceived them, was largely if not wholly lost.

Earnest souls, sick of sin, weary of strife, and ignorant of the way of victorious faith in an indwelling Christ, fled to the desert and wilderness to escape temptation. Many of them became hermits, living solitary lives on pillars in the desert and in dens and caves of the earth, while others formed monastic communities of monks and nuns. They harked back to the grim austerity and asceticism of Elijah and John the Baptist, and lost the sweet reasonableness and holy naturalness of Jesus. In the solitude of desert dens and the darkness of wilderness caves and on the tops of lonely pillars, they kept painful vigil and fought bitter battles with devils. With prolonged fastings and flagellations they struggled to overcome the unsanctified passions of the flesh.

There were saints among these seekers, who found God and kept sacred learning and faith alive. It was the hermit St. Jerome who translated the Scriptures into the common language, giving us the version known as the Vulgate. It was the monk Thomas a' Kempis who wrote *The Imitation of Christ*. And some of the sweetest and most stirring hymns of Christendom leaped forth from glad and loving hearts in monasteries of the Dark Ages. Those ages were dark, but not wholly dark.

As the iron empire of Rome, corroded and rusted by luxury and utterly corrupt vices, began to crumble and fall before the fierce, barbaric hordes of the north, feudalism sprang up and the great mass of men became serfs who tilled the fields and fought the wars of petty lords who lived in castles overlooking the towns and villages that dotted the plains. Towns and cities torn and reddened by internal factional strife made war on each other. The baron made war on his enemy, the rich abbot, and endowed and adorned his castle and church with spoils of his petty warfare. The clergy were generally greedy and corrupt. Poverty, illiteracy, filth and disease were universal. Brigands infested the forests and mountains, and pitiful, loathsome lepers begged for alms along the highways.

It was at the end of a thousand years of such dimness and darkness, when was breaking a new dawn which he was greatly to hasten, that St. Francis of Assisi appeared. He was the son of a prosperous Italian cloth merchant and of a gentle and devout French lady who probably sprang from the nobility. A beautiful, courteous lad, with flashing eyes and equally flashing spirit, who sang the songs of the troubadours in his mother's native tongue, delighted in the sports and revelry and dare-devil doings of the youth of the town—such was Francis Bernadone. Little did he seem to have in him the stuff of a saint who should transform the Christendom of his day and hold the wondering and affectionate gaze of seven centuries.

His father was a tradesman, but he was rich and free-handed with his dashing and attractive son.

The boy was lavish with money, courteous and light-hearted in spirit, which made him the friend and companion of the young nobility who dwelt in castles. War broke out between Assisi and the city of Perugia, so Francis, burning with the pride of youth and the fires of patriotism, went forth with the young noblemen and their bands of serfs to fight the enemy. But the battle went against the Assisians, and a company of the leaders, with Francis, were captured and spent a year in prison.

The youthful aristocrats, deprived of liberty, languished, but Francis, whom they kept among them, never lost his spirit, but cheered them with his kindness, his gaiety, and his songs. He laughed and sang and made merry, and possibly half in jest but more in earnest, through some strange youthful premonition, he assured them that he would one day be a great prince, with his name on the lips of all men. Little did he or they suspect what kind of a prince he would be, or the nature of the acclaim with which men would greet him.

Months of sickness followed his imprisonment. He began to think on the things that are eternal, the things of the Spirit. Recovered from his illness, he went forth again on a fine steed, in glittering armor, to war. But, for some rather obscure reason, he returned and fell into strange meditative moods. His companions suspected that it was an affair of the heart, and asked him if he was dreaming of a lady-love. He admitted that he was—a fairer love than they had ever imagined: Lady Poverty! He was thinking of giving up all for Christ.

One day, while Francis was serving a customer in his father's shop, a beggar came in and asked for alms in the name of God. Francis, busy with his customer, sent him away empty-handed, but afterwards said to himself, "If he had asked in the name of some nobleman, how promptly and generously I should have responded. But he asked in the name of the Lord, and I sent him away with nothing!" Leaving the shop, he ran after the beggar and lavished money upon him, and from that day he was the unfailing friend of beggars and all the poor.

Lepers were peculiarly repulsive to him, and he stood in a kind of fear of them. One day when riding he met a leper, and a fear he would not have felt on a field of battle gripped him. He rode past the poor creature and then, ashamed of himself, he won a greater victory than ever was won by armed warriors on a field of blood. He wheeled his horse about and returned, and leaping down he kissed the leper and gave him all the money he had with him. Joy filled his heart, and ever after he was the friend, the benefactor and the frequent nurse and companion of lepers.

He was a creature of generous, self-sacrificing impulse, but once he yielded to the impulse it became a life-long principle, and he served it with unfailing devotion of a lover to his mistress. As yet, however, like little Samuel, he "did not . . . know the Lord, neither was the word of the Lord yet revealed unto him" (1 Sam. 3:7). But one day he was praying before the altar in a poor, half-ruined little church: "Great and glorious God, and Thou, Lord Jesus, I pray, shed abroad Thy light in the darkness of my mind. Be found of me, O Lord, so in all things I may act only in accordance with Thy Holy Will." His eyes were upon a crucifix as he prayed, and it seemed to him that the eyes of the Savior met his. The place suddenly became a holy place, and he was in the presence of the Lord and Savior as was Moses when he drew near the burning bush on Horeb.

The sacred *Victim* seemed alive, and as a Voice spoke to Moses from the bush, so a wondrous, sweet, ineffable Voice seemed to speak from the crucifix to the longing soul of Francis, bidding him repair the church that was falling into decay and ruin. From that day he was assured that Christ knew him, heard him, loved him, and wanted his service. He could say: "I am my Beloved's, and my Beloved is mine."

Francis was essentially a man of action rather than of contemplation, so instead of retiring to a hermit's lodge in the desert or a monastery on some hilltop, he sallied forth at once to repair the little church of St. Damien in which he had been praying and had heard the Voice. He begged stones and carried them himself, repairing the church with his own hands, and when that was completed he repaired yet another church. It had not yet dawned upon him that the Voice was calling him to repair, not the four walls of a church made with hands, but the spiritual Church with its living stones not built with hands.

His proud and disappointed father fell upon him, beat him, and imprisoned him in his home; but during the absence of his father his mother released him, and he returned to the church, where he lived with the priest, wearing, instead of his popular clothing, a hair shirt and a rough brown robe tied around him with a rope, which was later to become the uniform of the myriad brothers of the Franciscan Order. He worked or begged for his bread and in Assisi was looked upon as a madman. His father and brother cursed him when they saw him.

He publicly renounced all right to his patrimony and adopted utter poverty as one of the rules of his life. He made poverty one of the rules—indeed, the most distinctive rule of the order which he founded. And later, when the Bishop of Assisi gently reproved him and argued that he should not go to such an extreme, he silenced the bishop, who had trouble with his own riches, by shrewdly replying, "If we own property we must have laws and arms to defend them, and this will destroy love out of our hearts."

In a short time—as with a true Salvationist [a term identifying a Salvation Army officer], with any true Christian—the sincerity, the sweetness, the joy and devotion of his life began to disarm criticism, win approval, and cause searchings of heart in many of his fellow townsmen.

His first convert was a wealthy man who had been impressed by his joyous, simple life. He invited Francis to spend the night with him, and only simulated sleep that he might watch the young man. When Francis thought he was asleep, he knelt by his bedside and spent most of the night in prayer. Next morning Bernardo, who became one of the most noted and devout of the brothers, decided to sell all, give to the poor, and cast in his lot with Francis.

A third, named Pietro, joined himself to them, and the three went to church where, after praying and examining the Scriptures, they adopted as the rule of their new life the words of Jesus:

If thou wilt be perfect, go and sell that thou hast, and give to the poor, and thou shalt have treasure in heaven: and come and follow Me (Matt.19:21).

Jesus, having called the twelve, gave them power and authority over an devils, and to cure diseases. And He sent them to preach the Kingdom of God. . . . And He said unto them, Take nothing for your journey, neither staves, nor scrip, neither bread, neither money; neither have two coats apiece. And whatsoever house ye enter into, there abide, and thence depart. And whosoever will not receive you, when ye go out of that city, shake off the very dust from your feet for a testimony against them. And they departed, and went through the towns, preaching the gospel, and healing everywhere (Luke 9:1-6).

The literal strictness with which Francis and his early disciples followed and enforced the rule of utter poverty gave them great freedom from care, great freedom of movement, and much joy. But, later, this led to much strife and division in the Order, the beginnings of which in his lifetime saddened the last days of the saint.

The Pope sanctioned his Rule and granted him and the members of the Order the right to preach. Like the early disciples they went everywhere testifying, singing, preaching, laboring with their hands for food, and, when unable to get work, not hesitating to ask from door to door for bread.

At first they were scorned and often beaten, but they gloried in tribulation. "My brothers, commit yourselves to God with all your cares and He will care for you," said Francis, and they went with joy, strictly observing his instructions:

> Let us consider that God in His goodness has called us not merely for our own salvation, but also for that of many men, that we may go through all the world exhorting men, more by our example than by our words, to repent of their sins and keep the commandments. Be not fearful because we appear little and ignorant. Have faith in God, that His Spirit will speak in and by you.
>
> You will find men, full of faith, gentleness, and goodness, who will receive you and your words with joy; but you will find others, and in great numbers, faithless, proud, blasphemers, who will speak evil of you, resisting you and your words. Be resolute, then, to endure everything with patience and humility.
>
> Have no fear, for very soon many noble and learned men will come to you; they will be with you preaching to kings and princes and to a multitude of people. Many will be converted to the Lord all over the world, who will multiply and increase His family.

How like William Booth [founder of the Salvation Army with his wife Catherine] that sounds!

And what he preached, Francis practiced to the end. He died prematurely, surrounded by his first followers, exhausted, blind and, at his own request, stripped, but for a hair shirt, and laid upon the bare ground. His Rule, his Order, his life and example were a stern and mighty rebuke to the wealth, the greed and the laziness of the priests and the monks. But he exhorted his brethren not to judge others, not to condemn or be severe, but to honor them, give them all due respect and pray for them, remembering some whom they might think to be members of the Devil would yet become members of Christ.

Within a brief time five thousand friars in brown robes were going everywhere with their glad songs, their burning exhortations, their simple testimony and sacrificial lives, and all who met them met with a spiritual adventure not to be forgotten. In Spain some of them fell upon martyrdom. They went to Germany, France, and to far Scandinavia, where they built the great cathedral of Upsala. Francis himself went to the Holy Land with the crusaders, and at the risk of his life, with two of his brothers boldly entered the camp of the Saracens and sought to convert the Saracen leader and his host. In this he failed, but he made a deep impression on the followers of Mohammed.

Once he was called to preach before the Pope and the College of Cardinals. He carefully prepared his sermon, but when he attempted to deliver it he became confused, frankly confessed his confusion, forgot his prepared address, threw himself upon the Lord, and spoke from his heart as moved by the Spirit—spoke with such love and fire that he burned into all hearts and melted his august audience to many tears. Long before Hus and Luther appeared, thundering against the abuses of the Church, he wrought a great reformation by love, by simplicity, and self-sacrifice. He was a kindred spirit of George Fox and John Wesley and William Booth, and would have gloried in their fellowship.

After seven centuries his words are still as sweet as honey, as searching as fire, as penetrating and revealing as light. One winter's day, bitterly cold, he was journeying with a Brother Leo, when he said:

"May it please God that the Brothers Minor (the 'Little Brothers,' the name he adopted for the Franciscan Order) all over the world may give a great example of holiness and edification. But not in this is the perfect joy. If the Little Brothers gave sight to the blind, healed the sick, cast out demons, gave hearing to the deaf, or even raised the four-days' dead—not in this is the perfect joy.

"If a Brother Minor knew all languages, all science, and all scripture, if he could prophesy and reveal not only future things, but even the secret of consciences and of souls—not in this consists the perfect joy.

"If he could speak the language of angels, if he knew the courses of the stars and the virtues of plants, if all the treasures of earth were revealed to him, and he knew the qualities of birds, fishes, and all animals, of men, trees, rocks, roots, and waters—not in these is the perfect joy."

"Father, in God's name, I pray you," exclaimed Leo, "tell me in what consists the perfect joy."

"When we arrive at Santa Maria degli Angeli (soaked with rain, frozen with cold, covered with mud, dying of hunger)," said Francis, "and we knock, and the porter comes in a rage, saying 'Who are you?' and we answer, 'We are two of your brethren,' and he says, 'You lie; you are two lewd fellows who go up and down corrupting the world and stealing the alms of the poor. Go away!' and he does not open to us, but leaves us outside in the snow and rain, frozen, starved, all night—then, if thus maltreated and turned away we patiently endure all without murmuring against him; if we think with humility and charity that this porter really knows us truly and that God permits him to speak to us thus, in this is the perfect joy. Above all the graces and all the gifts which the Holy Spirit gives to His friends is the grace to conquer one's self, and willingly to suffer pain, outrages, disgrace, and evil treatment for the love of Christ."

It is a commentary on the words of Jesus: "A man's life consisteth not in the abundance of the things which he possesseth" (Luke 12:13), and on those other, often forgotten and neglected words: "Blessed are ye, when men shall revile you, and persecute you, and shall say all manner of evil against you falsely, for My sake. Rejoice, and be exceeding glad (Matt. 5:11-12).

This sounds very like echoes from the Sermon on the Mount and the Epistles and testimonies of Paul. It is a commentary upon Paul's Psalm of Love in the thirteenth chapter of First Corinthians, and on his testimony: "I take pleasure in infirmities, in reproaches, in necessities, in persecutions, in distresses for Christ's sake" (2 Cor. 12:10).

Francis had found the secret of joy, of power, of purity, and of that enduring influence which still stirs and draws out the hearts of men of faith, of simplicity, of a single eye. Across the centuries he speaks to us in a wooing, compelling message that humbles us at the feet of Jesus in contrition and adoring wonder and love.

He found hidden reservoirs of power in union with Christ; in following Christ; in counting all things loss for Christ; in meekly sharing the labors, the travail, the passion, and the Cross of Christ. Thus his life became creative instead of acquisitive. He became a builder, a fighter, a creator; he found his joy, his fadeless glory, his undying influence, not in possessing things, not in attaining rank and title and worldly pomp and power, but in building the spiritual house, the Kingdom of God — in fighting the battles of the Lord against the embattled hosts of sin and hate and selfishness.

This creative life he found in the way of sacrifice and service. He found his life by losing it. He laid down his life and found it again, found it multiplied a thousand-fold, found it being reproduced in myriads of other men.

And this I conceive to be the supreme lesson of the life of Francis for us of The Salvation Army, and for the whole Church of God today. For it remains eternally true, it is a law of the Spirit, it is the everlasting word of Jesus, that: "He that findeth his life shall lose it: and he that loseth his life for My sake shall find it" (Matt. 10:39).

O Lord I help me, help Thy people everywhere, help the greedy, grasping, stricken world, to learn what mean these words of the Master, and to put them to the test with the deathless, sacrificial ardor of the simple, selfless saint of Assisi!

I knew that Christ had given me birth
To brother all the souls of earth,
And every bird and every beast
Should share the crumbs broke at the feast. (John Masefield)

14

"Look Not to Your Own Interests"

Dennis F. Kinlaw

Dennis F. Kinlaw (b. 1922) was born in Lumberton, North Carolina. He is an ordained minister in the United Methodist Church, who has enjoyed a long and successful ministry as a pastor, scholar, educator, and evangelist. He is the founder of the Francis Asbury Society and former president of Asbury College; received his B.A. degree from Asbury College in 1943 and his M.Div. degree from Asbury Theological Seminary in 1946. He did further graduate study at Princeton Theological Seminary and at New College, The University of Edinburgh, Scotland. He received the M.A. degree from Brandeis University in 1963 and the Ph.D. degree from Brandeis in 1967. His area of concentration was in Mediterranean Studies.

Dr. Kinlaw has served as chairman of the Board of Trustees of OMS International, Inc., and as a member of the boards of Christianity Today and Wesley Biblical Seminary. Among the books he has authored are *Preaching in the Spirit, This Day With the Master,* and *The Mind of Christ.*

⌘⎯⎯⌘

Philippians 2:5-11 is the best-known passage of Scripture concerning the mind of Christ. Some modern translations render it in such a way that the word *mind* is not used; but Paul employs the same Greek verb that occurs in Mark 8, where Jesus tells Peter he does not think as God thinks. The Greek word (*phroneite*) literally means "to be minded"—in this case, to be minded as God is minded:

Let each of you look not to your own interests, but to the interests of others. Let the same mind be in you that was in Christ Jesus, who, though he was in the form of God, did not regard equality with God as something to be exploited, but emptied himself taking the form of a slave, being born in human likeness (vv. 5-7).

Most scholars deal with verses 5-11 as if they were a unit, an ancient Christian hymn to the Christ. Perhaps they were. But I believe Paul used these words to illustrate the message he wished to convey to the Philippians.

A state of conflict existed within the Philippian church, and Paul wrote out of his desire to see that conflict resolved. Any time people work together, tensions will develop. But unresolved tension brings reproach on the cause of Christ. Paul knew that this conflict could be resolved only if the Philippians had a change of heart—and a change of mind.

In chapter 1, Paul observes that some people preach Christ out of right motives, while others preach Christ out of contentiousness: "Some proclaim Christ from envy and rivalry, but others from goodwill. These proclaim Christ out of love, knowing that I have been put here for the defense of the gospel; the others proclaim Christ out of selfish ambition . . ." (1:15-17a). Here Paul uses the Greek word *eritheia*, which literally means "to strive." Paul condemns the tendency to contend for one's own way, which is at the heart of carnal thinking.

He introduces the second chapter with these words: "If then there is any encouragement in Christ, any consolation from love, any sharing in the Spirit, any compassion and sympathy, make my joy complete: be of the same mind, having the same love, being in full accord and of one mind" (2:1-2). The basic problem at Philippi was that the Christians had different "minds"; each one thought his own way. So if Paul was to heal their division, he had to deal with the mind. He describes the sort of mind they must have:

Do nothing from selfish ambition (Gk., *eritheia)* or conceit, but in humility regard others as better than yourselves. Let each of you look not to your own interests, but to the interest of others (2:3-4).

The first time I read that in the Greek, I thought. *Wait a minute. Where is the word "only"?* The King James Version put the word *only* in italics, which indicates it is not in the original Greek text. Try as I might, I couldn't find it in the Greek. So I went to our classical Greek specialist at the college, who has a Ph.D. in classical languages from St. Louis University, and I said, "Help me here." He cast about for awhile and then wrote me a note that said: "It isn't there, Kinlaw." I went to Bob Mulholland, who has a Ph.D. from Harvard in New Testament. I said, "Bob, I've got a question . . ." He pulled books down and looked all around his office. Finally, he said, "Kinlaw, it isn't there."

Now why is the word *only* inserted in that verse, in most modern translations of the Bible? Why do most versions read, "Let each of you look not *only* to your own interests, but *also* to the interests of others"? Because we twentieth-century Christians don't believe the Lord can deliver us from self-interest, so we insert our assumptions into Scripture.

Four Ungodly Characteristics

In verses 3 and 14, Paul lists four characteristics that should be alien to the Christian life. He says that every Christian should act (1) without self-interest; (2) without vain conceit; (3) without grumbling; and (4) without questioning.

Self-interest (v. 3) is the supreme characteristic of a sinful person. It has been said that sinfulness is to be "curved inward upon oneself."

Conversely, the purpose of the redemption offered by Christ is to undo our distorted orientation—to turn us outward, so that we are not interested in ourselves but in the well-being of others. When we understand sin in these terms, we begin to break down the traditional dichotomy between evangelism and Christian social action. After all, the Christian life is not an "either/or" proposition: "Either I enrich my own relationship with Christ, or I go out and show others who Christ is, through my selfless service." Outwardness is all there is to the gospel. The essence of Christian living is making oneself a servant as Christ is a servant.

It is no accident that John Wesley became a paragon of Christian social action. He engaged in prison reform, slave emancipation, hospital work, and other activities that modern evangelicals sometimes disparage as the concerns of "the social gospel" (as if it were different from the gospel of

Christ). These activities were a normal consequence of Wesley's message about the necessity of entering into the Christ-life.

Self-interest is well demonstrated by the question, "What's in it for me?" Jesus never strived to get something for himself. The Gospels relate no instance in which Jesus' self-interest was his first consideration.[1]

Imagine the scene when Jairus asked Jesus to heal his daughter. Suppose Jesus had said, "Yes, I could do that. I could go home with you and lay my hands on your daughter, and she would get well. *But what's in it for me?*" My mentioning such an idea must offend you, because that attitude is utterly antithetical to what Jesus represented. He came to lay down his life for his sheep (John 10:15). He did not come to protect himself; rather, he came to spend himself. The Old Testament lifestyle may have been expressed by the statement, "Love your neighbor as yourself" (Lev. 19:18). But Jesus expressed the New Testament lifestyle like this: "Love one another as I have loved you. No one has greater love than this, to lay down one's life for one's friends" (John 15:12-13). Jesus changed the pattern of personal priorities when he became the Shepherd who sacrificed himself for his sheep.

Conceit (v. 3) is the common English translation of the New Testament Greek term *kenodoxia,* which comes from the word *kenos,* meaning "empty." In other words, a Christian should be unconcerned about elevating his own status or doing things for the sake of appearance.

How often we fall short of doing God's will because we are overly concerned about appearance! I have noticed that at an annual conference of ministers, when someone asks, "What can you tell me about your church?" a fellow will quail or strut, depending on the position of his congregation in the "pecking order." I don't think I have ever heard a minister say, " I have the appointment of my life. There are dozens of people in that community who don't know Christ, and I have an opportunity to reach them." We think instead of our status and position.

Jesus exemplified a life unconcerned with appearance. He talked with a Samaritan woman; he touched lepers; he cared nothing about his appearances before his disciples or the public.

Murmuring (v. 14) is the self-pitying attitude that says, "I deserve better than this." Self-pity is another mark of our fallenness.

When Helen Roseveare graduated from Cambridge in the early 1960s, she went to an area of Zaire where two hundred thousand people lived without a doctor. She made that her mission field. As her medical work progressed, she decided to build a hospital. She wrote her mother, asking for a book about how to build a hospital; her mother was unable to find such a book, but sent her a book about how to make bricks. So Helen Roseveare found herself teaching the African natives how to make kiln-fired bricks.

As they were taking the first load from the kiln, and she began pulling the spines off of the new bricks, she realized that her fingers were wet. They were dripping blood where she had broken her fingernails. She thought. *Lord, I didn't come to Africa to make brick; I came here to be a surgeon. Surely there's someone in England who could come to do this.*

While she stood there feeling sorry for herself, a runner came from the hospital and said, "We have an emergency. Come! You must perform surgery immediately!"

She went to the infirmary and began to prepare for surgery. She gritted her teeth as she scrubbed her hands with a brush; then she let her assistant pour alcohol over them, and her protest became a scream.

A few weeks later, one of the African workers at the kiln said, "Doctor, when you are in the surgery you are like a god. You terrify us. But when you're at the brick kiln and your fingers drip blood like ours, you're our sister. We love you!" At that moment, she realized God had not sent her to Africa to be a surgeon; he had sent her there to show the love of Christ. What did she deserve? Merely an opportunity to show the love of Christ. And she could not do that if she got what she thought she deserved!

Arguing (v. 14) is the mentality that tries to bargain with God. It is the attitude that says, "Yes, Lord, but . . ." Or, "Isn't there a better way to do this, Lord?" It professes a willingness to obey, but it hedges.

Arguing is the attitude of a Christian girl who marries a fellow that she knows is not really God's choice. It is the attitude of a young man who is called to serve God overseas, but allows himself to get trapped by career or family obligations at home. Arguing rears its head in a thousand ways, as we compromise the will of God in our lives by placing conditions upon it.

Future Hope or Present Reality?

Can you imagine a person who is not characterized by self-interest? A person who is not a slave to appearances? A person who is not always feeling he deserves better? Or a person who does not answer God's will with conditions? That would be the sort of person God could use! That person would be a part of the answer, rather than a part of the problem of evangelizing the world.

The Philippians and Corinthians had made themselves part of the problem. So Paul exhorted them to have the same mind which was in Christ. Christ had the attitude of a humble, obedient servant—the opposite of one who strives to protect his own interests.

On the night before the cross, Jesus said, "Father, glorify your Son." How was he glorified? By the cross, not by the crown. Christians are to find their glory in the same way, by renouncing all that serves self and by pouring out their lives for others.

Is that sheer idealism? Is it a goal toward which many people strive, but which no one attains? Is it to be accomplished in another world? In another world, such a life would be far less valuable than it is here. In the new world where Christ will reign, everyone will be like that! But this world needs to see the grace of Christ now; the unsaved masses long to see people who can live like that right now.

Jesus said, "Whoever listens to you listens to me, and whoever rejects you rejects me, and whoever rejects me rejects the one who sent me" (Luke 10:16). Christians are Christ to the world. This is what Paul meant when he said, "to me, living is Christ" (Phil. 1:21). We usually interpret that verse to mean that Christ gave significance to his life. But it also means that Paul's life gave Christ significance to other people. The only way the world will know Christ is through us. Therefore, there must be a correspondence between our lives and the life of the One we represent. Otherwise the world will never know who he is.

One tragic night, Helen Roseveare was raped by a band of rebel soldiers. Amid the anguish and agony of that dark night, she wondered, *How can God let this happen to me?* Immediately, she sensed the Lord saying to her, "Thank you, Helen. Thank you for letting me use your body. They are not raping you; they are raping me."

Afterwards she was locked up with a Roman Catholic nun who had also been raped. The nun was emotionally shattered because her vow of chastity had been broken. Helen tried to comfort her. "You did not sin," Helen said. "Remember the Virgin Mary. Everyone in the community thought she was an adulteress because she was unmarried and pregnant."

The nun gasped in horror. "How could anyone call Mary an adulteress?" she asked.

"That is what the people in Nazareth thought," Helen continued. "Yet she was pure, and you are just as pure. And think of this: The fact that you were raped may have saved someone else from being raped." She shared with the nun what she had heard from the Lord: *They are not raping you; they are raping me.*

Christ has no way to take the wrath of the world upon himself, except through us. When people of the world heap ridicule and persecution upon us, they heap it upon him. His life must be seen in this world, not only in the next world.

Is it possible for any human being to be Christ in the present world? Philippians 2 says it is. Paul never says that there are a great many people like this; but he does say there are some. Paul himself is one. Timothy is another. In fact, Paul says Timothy's other-oriented life proves his fitness for Christian ministry: "I hope in the Lord Jesus to send Timothy to you soon. . . . I have no one like him who will be genuinely concerned for your welfare. All of them are seeking their own interests, not those of Jesus Christ" (Phil. 2:19-21).

The Philippians and Corinthians could also become examples of other-oriented living. How? Not by striving for it. Not by imitating Christ or emulating him. Notice how Paul says this can happen: "Therefore, my beloved, just as you have always obeyed me, not only in my presence, but much more now in my absence, work out your own salvation with fear and trembling; *for God is at work in you, enabling you both to will and to work for his good pleasure'* (Phil. 2:12-13, italics added). God has no pleasure in our self-interest; but he has great pleasure in our sacrificing ourselves for his sake. God has no pleasure in our proper appearances; but he does take pleasure in our humbling ourselves to serve him. God has no pleasure in our murmuring, for that denies his sovereignty and his goodness; but he takes great pleasure in our being content with the situation in which he has placed us. God has no pleasure in our arguing, for that obstructs our faithfulness to him; but he takes great pleasure in our obedience, even when obedience leads to death.

How We Can Have the Mind of Christ

Becoming like Christ is a work of grace. It occurs only as Christ lives within us, not as we strive to be like him. Is this possible? Of course it is! Christian history is brimming with examples of men and women who have responded to life as Christ responded. They did it because Christ lived within them.

During Samuel Brengle's senior year at Boston University, he was offered the pastorate of a wealthy congregation in South Bend, Indiana. He had an opportunity to begin his ministry at the top of the social roster. But he felt that God was calling him to join the Salvation Army, so he crossed the Atlantic and presented himself to General William Booth.

"We don't want you. You're dangerous," Booth said.

"Dangerous? What do you mean?" Brengle asked.

"You would not take orders."

"But you haven't given me a trial," Brengle pleaded.

"You have too much education. You would not be willing to subordinate yourself to one of the officers here. Converted drunks and prostitutes are the staff leaders."

"Please give me a chance," Brengle said. So General Booth sent him to one of his sons, Ballington Booth, who put him through a similar interrogation. When Brengle still insisted on trying the Army, Booth's son made him bootblack for the Central Salvation Army Corps in London. In an unfinished basement, on a dirt floor half-submerged in water, Brengle began cleaning mud off of the boots of converted street bums who were now soldiers in the Army. One day he seemed to hear a voice that said, "You're a fool!"

I am not! he thought.

"You're a sinner, too."

What do you mean?

"Remember the man who buried his talent in the earth?" the inner voice said. "What are you doing here? Think of all the training you've gotten. You're just throwing it away."

Brengle sank into a depression. After awhile he prayed, "Lord, have I failed you? Did I miss your leading?"

And the Lord replied, "Remember, Sam, I washed their feet!"

That muddy cellar became an anteroom to heaven, as Brengle sensed the reassuring presence of his Lord. From that day forward, Brengle knew that he was called, not to invest himself, but to spend himself for others. He realized that Christ is a servant who looks for others to serve with him.

The Holy Spirit makes this sacrificial thinking possible. Jesus' ministry began when the Holy Spirit descended upon him. His disciples' ministry began when the Holy Spirit came upon them at the day of Pentecost, empowering them to "turn the world upside down." Likewise, the Spirit of Christ must control us if we are to be conformed to the character of Christ and filled with his power.

Christ must be free to spend us. As long as we attempt to save our own lives, we shall lose them; but if we surrender our lives to be controlled by his Spirit, we shall live and bear fruit for him. The Bible says very little about self-enrichment; but it says a great deal about giving our lives for the enrichment of others.

Letting Go of the Strings

I recently got acquainted with Josef Tson, the pastor of a large Baptist church in western Romania. Until a few years ago, the Romanian Communist Party was one of the most brutal in the world. As a Christian pastor, Josef spoke out on some issues and angered the government. So they decided to destroy him. They came in and stripped his library of all his books. Two books were quite worn and had no jackets on them, so the soldiers left them behind. One was Martin Niemoller's account of his suffering under Adolf Hitler. The other was *Abundant Living,* a devotional book by E. Stanley Jones.

This Romanian pastor put Martin Niemoller's book on his night stand to give him strength through the night. He put E. Stanley Jones' book on the shelf in his study.

The government then sent the police to interrogate Josef five days a week, and up to seven hours a day. The intent was to destroy him. Oftentimes they would interrogate him with a loaded pistol on the table in front of the interrogator. One day, after a very grueling period of questioning, Josef went into the study, locked the door, and fell to the floor, sobbing. He said, "God, I can't take any more." He thought he heard a voice. The voice said, "Josef, get up. Read the book on the shelf."

Josef said there was no problem knowing which book to read; there was only one left! So he pulled down E. Stanley Jones' book and opened it. The devotional for that day was on "How to Live Above Your Circumstances." It was about Jesus' facing the cross. Stanley Jones said Jesus did not resist the cross. Jones said that Jesus embraced the cross instead of resisting it.

Josef said, "God, you surely don't mean I'm supposed to embrace my interrogators!"

"Yes," the Lord said, "that's exactly what I mean."

"Well, God, if you want me to do that, you must do something in my heart that you have never done before."

Josef said that's exactly what the Lord did. He walked back into the interrogation room, ready to embrace his trial. He said the change in the atmosphere was almost comical. Before that time, the pastor had been in trauma; but now the chief interrogator was in trauma because he had lost control of his subject! The chief interrogator was beside himself. He finally spun in anger on the pastor and said, "You are stupid. I guess we'll just have to go ahead and kill you.

Josef found himself saying, "I understand, sir. That's your ultimate weapon. When everything else has failed, you can always kill. But you know, I have an ultimate weapon too. And when you use your ultimate weapon, I get to use mine."

"And what's your 'ultimate weapon?'" the Communist angrily demanded.

"Your ultimate weapon is to kill," Josef said. "Mine is to die. When I die, I will be much better off. But your troubles will just be beginning. You see, every tape of every sermon that I have ever preached will be sprinkled with my blood. So you'll have much more trouble with me dead than you have with me alive!"

The Communist shouted, "Take him out!"

A few weeks later, the pastor heard through the grapevine that the Communists were saying Josef Tson was crazy because he wanted to be a martyr. "But we're no fools!" the Communists said. So they stopped interrogating him. Josef said he could not even argue them into killing him then.

"When I was pulling every string to try to save my life, I was at my wit's end," Josef told me. "But when I turned the strings loose and let Christ control my life completely, I was free."

15

How to Be a Living Sacrifice

James Montgomery Boice

James Montgomery Boice (1938-2000) was the pastor of Tenth Presbyterian Church in Philadelphia for 32 years. From 1969-2000 he was the teacher on The Bible Study Hour radio broadcast on over 238 stations, and was President of the program's parent organization, the Alliance of Confessing Evangelicals. Dr. Boice held degrees from Harvard University (A.B.), Princeton Theological Seminary (B.D.), the University of Basel, Switzerland (D. Theol.), and the Theological Seminary of the Reformed Episcopal Church (D.D.).

In addition to authoring numerous journal articles, Boice was a consulting editor for the *Expositor's Bible Commentary*. His books and commentaries include *Foundations of God's City* and the five-volume work *The Gospel of John*. A gifted pastor and leader, he turned down many attractive opportunities in order to build a sense of permanence and belonging. And he urged his parishioners to do the same.

～⚬～

It is of the body that the apostle here speaks, and it is not proper to extract out of his language more than it contains. . . . This shows the importance of serving God with the body as well as with the soul. —Robert Haldane

Not long ago I reread parts of Charles Dickins' wonderful historical novel *A Tale of Two Cities*. The cities are Paris and London, of course, and the story is set in the years of the French revolution, when thousands of innocent people were being executed on the guillotine by supporters of the revolution. As usual with Dickins' stories, the plot is complex, but it reaches a never-to-forgotten climax when Sydney Carton, a disreputable character in the story, substitutes himself for his friend Charles Darney, who was being held for execution in the Bastille. Darney, who has been condemned to die, goes free, and Carton goes to the scaffold for him, saying, "It is a far, far better thing I do, than I have ever done; it is far, far better rest I go to, than I have ever known." The tale is so well written that it still moves me to tears when I read it, even though I have read it several times.

Few things move us to hushed awe so much as a person's sacrifice of his or her life for someone else. It is the ultimate proof of true love.

If we love Jesus, we are to sacrifice ourselves for him. Jesus said, "Greater love has no one than this, that he lay down his life for his friends" (John 15:13), and he did that for us. He did it literally. The self-sacrifice of Sydney Carton for his friend Darney is only a story, albeit a moving one, but Jesus actually died on the cross for our salvation. Now, because he loved us and gave himself for us, we who love him are likewise to give ourselves to him as "living sacrifices."

But there is a tremendous difference between Jesus' sacrifice and ours. . . . Jesus died in our place, bearing the punishment of God for our sin so that we might not have to bear it. Our sacrifices are not like that. They are not an atonement for sin in any sense. But they are like Christ's in this at least, that we are the ones who make them and that the sacrifices we make are ourselves. It is what Paul is talking about when he writes, "Therefore, I urge you, brothers, in view of God's mercy, to offer your bodies as living sacrifices, holy and pleasing to God—this is your spiritual act of worship" (Rom. 12:1). . . .

In this study I want to explore the nature of sacrifice, asking: What exactly is meant by it and how we are to do it.

The first point is the obvious one: This is to be a living sacrifice rather than a dead one. That was quite a novel idea in Paul's day, of course, though we have lost this by becoming overly familiar with it.

In Paul's day, sacrifices were always killed. In Jewish religious practices particularly, the animal was brought to the priest, the sins of the person bringing the sacrifice were confessed over the animal, thereby transferring them to it symbolically. Then the animal was put to death. It was a vivid way of reminding everyone that "the wages of sin is death" (Rom. 6:23) and that the salvation of sinners is by substitution. In those sacrifices the animal died in place of the worshiper. It died so that the worshiper might not have to die. But now, with a burst of divinely inspired creativity, Paul reveals that the sacrifices we are to offer are to be *living*, not dead. We are to offer our lives to God so that, as a result, we might "no longer live for [ourselves] but for him who died for [us] and was raised again" (2 Cor. 5:15).

Living sacrifices, yes. But with what life? Certainly not our old sinful lives in which, when we lived in them, we were already dead. Rather, we offer the new spiritual lives that have been given to us by Christ.

Robert Smith Candlish was a Scottish pastor who lived over a hundred years ago (1806-1873) and who left us some marvelous studies of the Bible. One set of these studies is of Romans 12, and in it there is a paragraph in which he reflects on the nature of the life we are to offer God. "What life?" Candlish asks. "Not merely animal life, the life that is common to all sentient and moving creatures; not merely, in addition to that, intelligent life, the life that characterizes all beings capable of thought and voluntary choice; but spiritual life: life in the highest sense; the very life which those on whose behalf the sacrifice of atonement is presented lost, when they fell into that state which makes a sacrifice of atonement necessary."[1]

What this means, among other things, is that we must be believers if we are to give ourselves to God as he requires. Other people may give God their money or time or even take up a religious vocation, but only a Christian can give back to God that new spiritual life in Christ that he or she has first been given. Indeed, it is only *because* we have been made alive in Christ that we are able to do this or even want to.

Offering Our Bodies

The second thing we need to see about the nature of the sacrifice that God requires is that it involves the giving to God of our bodies. Some of the older commentators stress that offering our bodies really means to offer our total selves, all that we are. Calvin wrote, "By *bodies* he means not only our skin and bones, but the totality of which we are composed."[2] Although it is true that we are to offer God all that we are, most commentators today rightly refuse to pass over the word *bodies* quite this easily, because they recognize how much the Bible stresses the importance of our bodies.

For example, Leon Morris says, "Paul surely expected Christians to offer to God not only their bodies but their whole selves. . . . But we should bear in mind that the body is very important in the Christian understanding of things. Our bodies may be 'implements of righteousness' (6:13) and 'members of Christ' (1 Cor. 6:15). The body is a temple of the Holy Spirit (1 Cor. 6:19); Paul can speak of being 'holy both in body and in spirit' (1 Cor. 7:34). He knows that there are possibilities of evil in the body but that in the believer 'the body of sin' has been brought to nothing (6:6)."[3]

In a similar manner, Robert Haldane says, "It is of the body that the apostle here speaks, and it is not proper to extract out of his language more than it contains. . . . This shows the importance of serving God with the body as well as with the soul."[4]

Paul does not elaborate in Romans 12 upon what he means by presenting our bodies to God "as living sacrifices," but we are not left in the dark about his meaning since this is not a new idea, not even in Romans. It has already appeared in chapter 6. In that chapter Paul said, "Therefore do not let sin reign in your mortal body so that you obey its evil desires. Do not offer the parts of your body to sin, as instruments of wickedness, but rather offer yourselves to God, as those who have been brought from death to life; and offer the parts of your body to him as instruments of righteousness. For sin shall not be your master, because you are not under law, but under grace" (vv. 12-14). This is the point at which Paul first began to talk about sanctification, and the point he was making there is the same one he is making here, namely, that we are to serve God by offering him our bodies.

Sin can control us through our bodies, but this need not happen. So, rather than offering our bodies as instruments of sin, we are to offer God our bodies as instruments for doing his will. To be practical we need to think about this as involving specific parts of our bodies.

1. *Our minds.* I begin with the mind because, although we think of ourselves largely as our minds and thus separate our minds from our bodies, our minds actually are parts of our bodies and the victory we need to achieve begins here. In this study I will not say a great deal about presenting our minds to God, because I will be treating this more fully later when I talk about mind renewal. But I remind you that this is the point at which Paul himself begins in verse 2: "Do not conform any longer to the pattern of this world, but be transformed by *the renewing of your mind*" (emphasis mine).

Have you ever considered that what you do with your mind will determine a great deal of what you will become as a Christian? If you fill your mind only with the products of our secular culture, you will remain secular and sinful. If you fill your head with trashy "pop" novels, you will begin to live like the trashy characters *you* read about. If you do little else but watch television, *you* will begin to act like the scoundrels on the screen. On the other hand, if you feed your mind on the Bible and Christian books, train it by godly conversation, and discipline it to critique what you see and hear by applying biblical truths to the world's ideas, you will grow in godliness and become increasingly useful to God.

For every secular book you read, make it your goal also to read one good Christian book, a book that can stretch your mind spiritually.

2. *Our eyes and ears.* The mind is not the only part of our body by which we receive and filter impressions and which must therefore be offered to God as an instrument of righteousness. We also receive impressions through our eyes and ears, and these, too, must be surrendered to God.

Sociologists tell us that by the age of twenty-one the average young person has been bombarded by 300,000 commercial messages, all arguing from the assumption that personal gratification is the dominant goal in life.[5] Our modern means of communication put the acquisition of "things" before godliness. In fact, they never mention godliness at all. How are you going to grow in godliness if you are constantly watching television or reading printed ads or listening to secular radio?

I am not advocating an evangelical monasticism in which we retreat from the culture, though it is far better to retreat from it than perish in it. But somehow the secular input must be counterbalanced by the spiritual. Another simple goal might be for you to spend as many hours studying your Bible, praying, and going to church as watching television.

3. *Our tongues.* The tongue is also part of our body, and what we do with it is important either for good or evil. James, the Lord's brother, wrote, "The tongue also is a fire, a world of evil among the parts of the body. It corrupts the whole person, sets the whole course of his life on fire, and is itself set on fire by hell" (James 3:6). If your tongue is not given to God as an instrument of righteousness in his hands, this will be true of you. You do

not need to be a Hitler and plunge the world into armed conflict to do evil with your tongue. A little bit of gossip or slander will suffice.

What you need to do is use your tongue to praise and serve God. For one thing, you should learn how to recite Scripture with it. You probably know the words of many popular songs. Can you not also use your tongue to speak God's words? And how about worship? You should use your tongue to praise God by means of hymns and other Christian songs. Above all, you should use your tongue to witness to others about the person and work of Jesus Christ.

Here is another goal for you if you want to grow in godliness: Use your tongue as much to tell others about Jesus as for idle conversation.

4. *Our hands and feet.* There are several important biblical passages about our hands and feet. In 1 Thessalonians 4:11-12, Paul tells us to work with our hands so that we will be self-supporting and not have to rely on others: "Make it your ambition to lead a quiet life, to mind your own business and to work with your hands, just as we told you, so that your daily life may win the respect of outsiders and so that you will not be dependent on anybody." In Ephesians 4:28, he tells us also to work so that we will have something to give to others who are in need: "He who has been stealing must steal no longer, but must work, doing something useful with his own hands, that he might have something to share with those in need."

As far as our feet are concerned, Paul wrote in Romans 10 of the need that others have for the gospel, saying, "How can they hear without someone preaching to them? And how can they preach unless they are sent? As it is written, 'How beautiful are the feet of those who bring good news!' " (Rom. 10:14-15).

What do you do with *your* hands? Where do *your* feet take you? Do you allow them to take you to where Christ is denied or blasphemed? To where sin is openly practiced? Are you spending most of your free time loitering in the "hot" singles clubs or in other unsavory places? You will not grow in godliness there. On the contrary, you will fall from righteous conduct. Instead, let your feet carry you into the company of those who love and serve God. Or, as you go into the world, let it be to serve the world and witness to it in Christ's name. Use your feet and hands for him.

For every special secular function you attend, determine to attend a

Christian function also. And when you go to a secular function, do so as a witness by word and action for the Lord Jesus Christ.

Holiness, without Which . . .

The third word Paul uses to indicate the nature of the sacrifices we are to offer God is "holy." Any sacrifice we make must be holy. That is, it must be without spot or blemish and be consecrated entirely to God. Anything less is an insult to the great and holy God all people are to serve. But how much more must *we* be holy—we who have been purchased "not with perishable things such as silver or gold . . . but with the precious blood of Christ, a lamb without blemish or defect" (1 Peter 1:18-19). Peter explained, "But just as he who called you is holy, so be holy in all you do; for it is written: 'Be holy, because I am holy'" (vv. 15-16). The author of Hebrews said, "Without holiness no one will see the Lord" (Heb. 12:14).

This is the very heart of what we are talking about when we speak of living sacrifices, of course. Or, to put it in other language, holiness is the end of the matter. Or, to put it in still other language, it is the point to which the entire epistle of Romans has been heading. Romans is about salvation. But, as someone has wisely noted, salvation does not mean that Jesus died to save us *in* our sins but to save us *from* them.

Handley C. G. Moule expressed this well. "As we actually approach the rules of holiness now before us, let us once more recollect what we have seen all along in the Epistle, that holiness is the aim and issue of the entire Gospel. It is indeed an 'evidence of life,' infinitely weighty in the enquiry whether a man knows God indeed and is on the way to his heaven. But it is much more; it is the expression of life; it is the form and action in which life is intended to come out. . . . We who believe are 'chosen' and 'ordained' to 'bring forth fruit' (John 15:16), fruit much and lasting."[6]

Is there any subject that is more generally neglected among evangelicals in America in our day than holiness? I do not think so. Yet there was a time when holiness was a serious pursuit of anyone who called himself a Christian, and when how one lived and what one was inside was vitally important.

England's J. I. Packer has written a book called *Rediscovering Holiness* in which he calls attention to this matter. "The Puritans insisted that all life and relationships must become 'holiness to the Lord.' John Wesley told the world that God had raised up Methodism 'to spread scriptural holiness throughout the land.' Phoebe Palmer, Handley Moule, Andrew Murray, Jessie Penn-Lewis, F. B. Meyer, Oswald Chambers, Horatius Bonar, Amy Carmichael, and L. B. Maxwell are only a few of the leading figures in the 'holiness revival' that touched all evangelical Christendom between the mid-nineteenth and mid-twentieth centuries."[7]

But today? In our time, holiness is largely forgotten as an important quality for Christians. So we do not try to be holy. We hardly know what holiness means. And we do not look for holiness in others. The great parish minister and revival preacher Robert Murray McCheyne once said, "My people's greatest need is my personal holiness." But what pulpit committees look for holiness in a new pastor today? Hardly any. They look for winsome personality, good communication skills, administrative ability, and other secular things.

As for ourselves, we do not seek out books or tapes on holiness or attend seminars designed to draw us closer to God. We want information on "How to Be Happy," "How to Raise Children," "How to Have a Good Sex Life," "How to Succeed in Business," and so on.

Fortunately, this lack has begun to be noticed by some evangelical leaders who are disturbed by it and have begun to address the subject. I commend Packer's book, as well as a book written a few years ago by Jerry Bridges called *The Pursuit of Holiness*. There is also the older classic by the English Bishop John Charles Ryle on the same topic.[8]

"Pleasing to God"

The final words that Paul uses to describe the nature of our living sacrifices is "pleasing to God." But this is also a conclusion for what I have been saying so far in this study, since the point is that if we do what Paul has urged us to do—namely, to offer our "bodies as living sacrifices, holy . . . to God"—we will also find that what we have done is pleasing to him, or acceptable.

It is amazing to me that God could find anything we might be able to do to be pleasing. But it is so! Notice that the word *pleasing* occurs twice in this short paragraph. The first time, which is what we are looking at here, it indicates that our offering of ourselves to God pleases him. The second time, which occurs at the end of verse 2, it indicates that when we do this

we will find God's will for our lives to be pleasing as well as good and perfect. I understand that God's will for me should be pleasing—pleasing to
me, that is. How could it be otherwise if God is an all-wise and all-good
God? He must will what is good for me. But that my offering of myself to
him should somehow also please *him*—when I know myself to be sinful
and ignorant and halfhearted even in my best efforts—that is astonishing.

But so it is! The Bible tells me that at my best I am to think of myself as
an "unworthy" servant (Luke 17:10). But it also says that if I live for Jesus,
offering back to him what he has first given to me, then one day I will hear
him say, "Well done, good and faithful servant! . . . Come and share your
master's happiness!" (Matt. 25:21, 23).

16

Acceptable Candlesticks: Service

Helen Roseveare

Helen Roseveare (b. 1925) was born in England; she became a Christian as a medical student in Cambridge University in 1945. She built a combination hospital/training center in Ibambi, Congo, in the early 1950s, then relocated to in Nebobongo, Congo, living in an old leprosy camp, where she built another hospital. She returned to England in 1958. She returned to the Congo in 1960. In 1964 she was taken prisoner by rebel forces and she remained a prisoner for five months, enduring beatings and rapings. She left the Congo and headed back to England after her release but returned to the Congo in 1966 to assist in the rebuilding of the nation.

Dr. Roseveare helped establish a new medical school and hospital (the other hospitals that she built were destroyed) in the Congo and served there until she left in 1973. Since her return from Africa, she has had a worldwide ministry in speaking and writing. She is now retired and lives in Northern Ireland.

⚯

I was making a great effort to stay awake in the increasing heat, when I heard these words: "Can you boil a potato in a candlestick?"

I was suddenly wide awake, leaning forward in amazement. Had I really heard the preacher ask that question, or had I just imagined it?

"Well, can you?" I reasoned. "How stupid! Of course not!"

But what was the inference? Why ask the question? Where, oh where was the connection with the text?

As one of the four people asked to speak on the year's text, I had been studying it for six months. We were, in turn, to emphasize Christ in us, hating sin; Christ in us, loving God; Christ in us, obeying His will; and Christ in us, serving others. In preparation for the conference, I had sought to understand each of these four aspects of the truth of the text "Christ in you, the hope of glory"—in order to present the third aspect in relationship to the other three. The text had begun to take hold of me, so no wonder I was startled by this extraordinary phrase—"Can you boil a potato in a candlestick?"—wondering how on earth it could relate to the subject in hand. It seemed to have no bearing on the subject and was so wholly unexpected.

I'm not sure now that I ever worked out the relevance of the phrase to the text under discussion, but over the years, I have frequently returned to it with a wry sense of humor.

How frequently our lives are spoiled by an attitude of "if only . . ." "If only I were a saucepan instead of a candlestick . . . how much easier it would be to be useful to God!"

"If only I had his qualifications or her gifts. If only I lived in a different community or had a more satisfying job. If only I had not made that mistake years ago or missed that opportunity last week . . . how different might my life now be!"

Others of us may look out on the suffering world around us and be tempted to sigh, "If only God would raise up another John Wesley . . ." thinking that thus the masses might be reached with the Gospel of Redemption. I believe it was Watchman Nee who said that if God had wanted another John Wesley, He could easily have sent one! But He has not. He has sent you and me instead. And God knows His business: He does not make mistakes. If He wanted to boil a potato, He could send a saucepan! But if He wants to send the Light of Life to a needy world in its darkness, it is more reasonable to suppose that He will send a candlestick. And if God wants a candlestick of a certain size and color, to carry a particular Candle to a particular dark spot, He can doubtless make that candlestick exactly as He wants it.

I believe that is what He is busy doing with each one of us, His children—making or re-making each one of us into a candlestick that is according to the perfect pattern He has planned:

For He chose us in Him [Christ] before the creation of the world to be holy and blameless in His sight (Eph. 1 :4).

For we are God's workmanship, created in Christ Jesus to do good works, which God prepared in advance for us to do (Eph. 2:10).

God's business is creating and molding candlesticks to carry brightly burning Candles into places of darkness. Am I willing to be molded into one of God's candlesticks rather than saucepans? Am I willing to be made to fit a particular Candle, rather than demanding that God shapes the Candle to fit the candlestick? Am I prepared for God to prescribe the way I carry the Candle, rather than demanding my right to do so in the way I choose? Am I content that God should send me and my Candle into any dark spot that He chooses, without first asking my permission?

How patient God is, in the fulfilment of His strategy. I can look back now and marvel at His gracious dealing to prepare me for the job He had planned for me at Nyankunde. I am at heart a teacher, yet, for twelve years, God kept me at work in general medicine at Nebobongo. Often I was tempted to grumble and to ask, "Why, God?"

In 1966, following the great destruction caused by the rebellion in northeast Zaire, God sent me to help in the opening of medical services at Nyankunde. My part in the team for that inter-mission medical project was to be the training of national para-medical personnel—teaching! At that time, the newly appointed Minister of Health in the Kinshasa Government determined that only fully qualified doctors, with at least ten years' experience of medical practice in the country, would be eligible as directors of colleges for the training of national para-medical personnel.

In 1953, God had known that that decree would be passed in 1966, and He had patiently shaped a particular candlestick to carry the Candle in that particular spot at that particular moment in time. I may not have rejoiced in the training process, but I certainly learned that God never makes mistakes. We can trust Him absolutely and always.

God wants to fit us perfectly into His plan, if we will allow Him to do so. He is willing to bring all circumstances to bear to that end. Ephesians 2:10 tells us that God had already prepared, "before the creation of the world," the "good works" that He wants us to do, when He planned our salvation. He doesn't have to look around to see if He can find a job to fit my qualifications when I decide to apply to Him for employment! No. All is prepared. The only problem is my unwillingness to obey and take my part in the predetermined plan.

Look at Jonah. During the reign of Jeroboam II, somewhere between 793 and 753 BC, maybe fifty years before the fall of the northern kingdom of Israel, Jonah was born to Amittai in Gath Hepher, a few miles north of Nazareth in Galilee. He grew up in the knowledge of God.

The times in which he lived were not dissimilar to our own. To a large extent, men ignored God and went their own ways. Few acknowledged any absolute standards of righteousness. Idolatry abounded on all sides. Permissiveness was the order of the day, harlotry acceptable and evil considered right. To be godly in such a society was to be "peculiar" and to stick out like a sore thumb.

And there was Nineveh. Just to say the name of that city brought a reaction of hatred and of fear. The name summed up for the Israelite all that was most evil and sinister. It was a vast conglomerate of four cities, with a population of over two million, covering four hills and the intervening valleys. It was so wide flung that it would take three days to walk round the perimeter wall of this great capital of the heathen empire of Assyria. Legends were rife about the evil practiced within its walls, and of the barbaric cruelty meted out to its subjugated peoples.

Not only did the Israelites hate the vice and savagery of the Ninevites, but they feared lest they too might eventually fall to the mighty army and suffer the same dehumanizing wickedness as other neighboring territories had done. Yes, "Nineveh" was equated with "enemy"; and since the iron dictator, Pul, the descendant of Tiglath-Pileser III, had seized the throne, the ruthless tyranny had only increased the depth of hatred and fear in the hearts of all the surrounding nations.

At this moment, God spoke to Jonah. "Go to . . . Nineveh and preach against it."

God was preparing a candlestick to carry His Candle into a very dark area at that precise moment in history, but the candlestick wasn't willing for the task. In fact, Jonah could not believe his ears. It was impossible—absolutely, totally impossible. God just could not mean it. Go to Nineveh? "Dear God, anywhere but not there!" No one would ever believe that God had sent him. He would be blacklisted, turned out by his own people. No one would support him. And deep down inside, though he did not say so, not even to himself, Jonah was scared stiff! No, God, no! Not that. "And anyway, if I did do anything so outlandishly foolish," Jonah may have reasoned with himself, "what on earth would I say to the Ninevites? They are good for nothing except extermination, to be wiped off the face of the earth. Oh, I know, You could tell me to warn them of judgment to come, and to talk to them about Your holy wrath against their abominable sins, but God, I also know that, in the end, Your mercy would prevail . . . and for me to be seen by my fellow Jews as a messenger of mercy and forgiveness and light to our arch enemy . . . No! Please God, no."

So Jonah fled.

Is not the situation today very similar? How many "candlesticks" argue with their Creator when He seeks to direct them to an apparently insalubrious spot or to a hard and unresponsive people? How many are even willing to be candlesticks, preferring rather to be saucepans?

A young Christian, who has been brought under conviction of sin by the Holy Spirit and to a state of true repentance and regeneration, is filled with a deep love for the Savior who died as his Substitute. He is determined to show that love in a life of service, but suddenly realizes that God is sending him out into the world of today to live a holy life. His heart shrinks within him as he contemplates the implications. Does God not understand just how sinful and wicked and immoral the world is today? It is surely impossible to stay clean in such a polluted atmosphere. And anyway, how could one holy life affect the vast torrent of unholiness all around? It would be like putting one tiny candle in a vast, unlit cathedral and expecting its light to expel the darkness!

So the Christian is tempted to turn tail and flee: maybe back into a local fellowship or small group of like-minded people: maybe, as Jonah, to go in the opposite direction anywhere except where God is pointing.

What has gone wrong with the love that wanted to serve? Is it perhaps that the motive that prompted the service was inadequate? If "I" want to show God how much I love Him, by giving all I've got to serve Him, whatsoever it may mean and wheresoever it may be, it is quite possible that this service may not be according to God's predetermined plan. "I" may find myself a potato trying to shine in a candlestick! The "I" is in the way. The motive is self-something: maybe self-gratification, self-satisfaction, or any of what A. W. Tozer calls "the hyphenated sins of the self-life." I am seeking to prove to myself that I am what I hope I am, or that I love whom I hope I love. This type of motivation is insufficient: it does not work.

Hatred of sin and love for the Savior must lead, first and foremost, to obedience. Obedience to the Word of God will show itself in service. Because I love Him, I delight to obey Him; because I obey Him, I delight to serve Him. This will be true godly service, a giving without any thought of gaining.

> I beseech you, therefore, brethren, by the mercies of God, that ye present your bodies a living sacrifice, holy, acceptable unto God, which is your reasonable service. And be not conformed to this world: but be ye transformed by the renewing of your mind, that ye may prove what is that good, and acceptable, and perfect, will of God" (Rom. 12:1-2).

"Reasonable service" is translated in newer versions as "spiritual worship." To be acceptable to God, both service and worship must be holy and in obedience to His command that we should offer ourselves as "living sacrifices." Christ died on the Cross as our vicarious sacrifice. Not only must there have been a decisive act in the past when I committed my life to Christ, being identified with Him in His death, but there must also be a continual daily identifying of myself with that death, in putting aside my own will and self-pleasing, in order to live according to His will and good pleasure. This is the deliberate daily choosing to "die" to self, in order to allow the Spirit of Christ to indwell me and to rule my choices, so that I can say with Paul: "I have been crucified with Christ and I no longer live, but Christ lives in me. The life I live in the body, I live by faith in the Son of God, who loved me and gave Himself for me" (Gal. 2:20).

The writer to the Hebrews says: "Let us have grace, whereby we may serve God acceptably with reverence and godly fear: for our God is a consuming fire" (Heb. 12:28-29). Expounding this verse, the *New Bible Commentary* puts it very clearly: "Let us appropriate the grace so abundantly available to serve God in ways well pleasing in His sight, i.e., to offer to God acceptable worship. In the presence of such a God and in the face of such a prospect this will be with a real sense of unworthiness and awe. Only those who thus follow after Holiness will survive His judgment, see the Lord, and reign eternally with Him"[1]

Let us look again at Jonah, and see what he did next. He had no idea that God could ever use the wicked and hated Assyrians as His rod of judgment against Israel. All Jonah could see was the impossibility of the situation in which he found himself.

"Surely God does not mean me to go and offer Salvation to that brutal city of Nineveh?" was his natural reasoning. Oh, yes, Jonah acknowledged God, acknowledged that He was the One unique Creator of earth and sea; and he wanted to serve God to show his allegiance, but . . . he was determined that he would choose how and where! Jonah was not yet so in love with God that obedience to His voice was an essential corollary, from which would flow God-directed service. He was not yet willing to be thought *peculiar*, nor to become the laughing stock of his own people: so he ran away from God's command and from the responsibility of obedience.

Is God really expecting us to reveal, by holy living, true godliness in the midst of the ungodliness that reigns in our world today? Would we not be like tiny candles in an ocean of darkness? Does He really expect every Christian "to say 'No' to ungodliness and worldly passions, and to live self-controlled, upright and godly lives in this present age" (Titus 2:12-13)? Jonah was scared stiff to face Nineveh; are we as scared to face our world?

Not only have we to be willing that God should mold us into His candlesticks for the individual jobs He has planned for us, but also we must be willing to do that prepared job in the way prescribed by God. Rightly to fulfil our designated task, we shall need instruction in the procedure to be adopted.

Some perhaps are tempted to ask if God's standards for service are really practicable in the twentieth century. Is it not necessary for us to rethink the procedure and re-word the instructions to suit today's culture in the light of today's corruption? Should we not contextualize the Scripture to fit in with modern thought? Such a verse as is found in Micah 6:8—

He has showed you, O man, what is good.
   And what does the Lord require of you?
To act justly and to love mercy
   and to walk humbly with your God.

—sounds so simple, but it just does not seem to fit in with the contemporary scene—or does it?

Firstly, "to act justly."

God is speaking. To understand what He means we must think as He thinks and judge whether our actions are just or not, by using the yardstick of His justice. We must acknowledge His right to determine the standards by which He will judge us and our actions. Of course, this is a tremendous challenge in an age that has slipped into an acceptance of "situational ethics" and a tacit agreement that there are no such things as "absolute standards." Today it is widely believed that standards must depend on culture, education, opportunities, economics, any or all of which can change from place to place, and from time to time.

We are being quietly yet steadily brain-washed into believing that Christianity is wrong, even that God's ways are actually unethical, and certainly that Holiness, as God describes it, is totally impracticable. For example, to maintain a standard of "giving service" in a climate of "getting advantage" may cause mockery and raised eyebrows. If we were to persist in such a stand, it could lead to a failure to receive deserved promotion.

A gentle hint that a little more pressure by a salesman, with a slightly decreased emphasis on truth, might well gain a needed promotion and increased salary. Given quietly at a moment of known need or family hardship, such a hint can be very difficult to resist; especially as "everyone else does it," and one's peers are leaving one behind in the proverbial rat-race. At that moment, to be able to detach oneself from the actual situation, to weigh up and consider impartially the underlying principles, and then to be true to one's convictions and stand for what one believes to be right, can be incredibly difficult.

To keep one's word even when this may be injurious to one's apparent interests; to be utterly loyal, when one might gain promotion by a little subtle gossip; to be honestly content, when a propitious hint could better one's lot; . . . these are standards of service that God laid before us when David wrote Psalm 15. . . .

This is God's prescribed standard of procedure. All my activities, public and private, must be "just" according to this standard, because "I am not my own." Christ has bought me with the price paid at Calvary. As His, I am to "mirror" Him, that others shall see Him in me. I am to act always and only as He would in each situation and under all circumstances.

The New Testament gives us very positive statements as to how to "act justly." Paul, in his letter to the Ephesian church, enjoined the young Christians to godly service in their community: "It was He who gave some to be apostles, some to be prophets, some to be evangelists, and some to be pastors and teachers, to prepare God's people for *works of service*, so that the body of Christ may be built up . . . " (Eph. 4:11-12, my italics).

He then went on to remind them that, to serve in a way pleasing to God, they must first put off their old, corrupt self, and then put on the new self "created to be like God in true righteousness and Holiness." He then detailed to them how this new nature would act, linking a negative demand to reject unjust behavior and to shun expediency with a positive command to practice goodness, both in obedience to God and in service to one another. As we read in Ephesians 4:25-32:

> Therefore each of you must put off falsehood and speak truthfully to his neighbor, for we are all members of one body. In your anger do not sin: Do not let the sun go down while you are still angry. . . . He who has been stealing must steal no longer, but must work, doing something useful with his own hands, that he may have something to share with those in need. Do not let any unwholesome talk come out of your mouths, but only what is helpful for building others up according to their needs, that it may benefit those who listen. And do not grieve the Holy Spirit of God, with whom you were sealed for the day of redemption. Get rid of all bitterness, rage and anger, brawling and slander, along with every form of malice. Be kind and compassionate to one another, forgiving each other, just as in Christ God forgave you.

Christian service is the overflow of superabounding devotion to God, as Oswald Chambers puts it: "God gets me into a relationship with Himself whereby I understand His call, then I do things out of sheer love for Him on my own account. To serve God is the deliberate love-gift of a nature that has heard the call of God"[2] But for that service of love to be acceptable to God it must be in accord with God's explicit commands. If, in serving, I lie to promote my own ends or increase my profitability, that service becomes unacceptable to God. If I blast off in anger at a colleague or at an employee, and fail to apologize for my loss of self-control, my service ceases to be acceptable.

If I allow myself to "fiddle" the books or make a knowingly false entry, for whatever purpose; if I join in conversation that is unseemly, laugh at jokes that are questionable, listen to language that dishonors the God I seek to serve; if I speak or act in any way to defraud another, out of malice or spite or revenge; if in any degree I cease to be kindly and considerate of others, I make my service unacceptable in the eyes of God.

To "act justly" in such a manner as Paul has detailed here is the only way for a Christian to know peace—peace with God, peace with himself, peace with his fellow men. It is the only way for a society to live together in harmony and prosperity. All the ills of society today are the result of a refusal to acknowledge God's right to declare what is just and to set absolute standards for our behavior. Is the selfishness that dominates our culture today not the result of each one wanting his own way, and setting up his own right to determine what is just? This reminds us of the state of affairs in the days of the Judges in the Old Testament: "In those days Israel had no king; everyone did as he saw fit" (Judg. 21:25).

To *act justly* is the way that God has planned for us to live, in order to achieve His purpose and to fulfil His will. It is the appointed way to "serve God acceptably," and to show forth the Holiness that the Spirit is creating in us.

This Holiness will reveal itself also in a God-given desire to "love mercy." We shall seek always to lift those who are down, to encourage those who are down, to encourage those who are discouraged, to help those in need. We shall be willing to think the best of another, rather than the worst; to be grieved when another fails, rather than to rejoice in his downfall; to pray rather than to gossip.

This Holiness will enable us to "walk humbly" with our God—as the New Bible Commentary says, "in utter dependence upon His enablement to lead a godly life, and in full recognition of the total lack of personal ability or merit which might furnish a base for pride or self-justification."[3]

To walk humbly with God we need to be transformed into His image by the Holy Spirit, and this is achieved by deliberate obedience to all He reveals to us. We must give Him all that we are and have. There has to be a total surrender and absolute submission of our will to His, a true echoing of the prayer of the Savior in the Garden of Gethsemane: "Not as I will, but as you will" (Matt. 26:39).

When, in prayer, we look at ourselves honestly and recognize our poverty of spiritual experience; our stunted growth and continuing immaturity; our lack of love and devotion to God and to our fellow men; our spirit of grumbling and discontent; our quickness to criticize others, we shall marvel that God has called us to be co-laborers with Him. Only then shall we walk humbly with our God, awed by His gracious patience and longsuffering forbearance.

"Acting justly" as Christ would, in each circumstance, and so revealing Christlikeness to others in all we do and how we do it: "loving mercy" and yearning over the welfare of suffering humanity around us, seeking by all means to bring them to Christ; "walking humbly" before God who has called us out of darkness into His marvelous light; this is Holiness, revealing itself in service.

When Paul wrote to Titus, that God's grace teaches us "that denying ungodliness and worldly lusts, we should live soberly, righteously and godly, in this present world;" he went on to say that it is for this that Christ has redeemed us: to "purify unto Himself a peculiar people, zealous of good works" (Titus 2:11-14). That is Christ's purpose for us: to be "a peculiar people" [meaning: God's special people] zealous in His service. . . .

The first of these three phrases: "denying ungodliness and worldly lusts," can be considered as the negative aspect of Holiness, the essential biblical "do nots." Ungodliness simply means leaving God out of our reckoning: acting as though there were no God. Men by their own reasoning have devised their own system of situational ethics, without regard to God's laws or standards. The result is not unlike what would happen if one filled a car with lemonade instead of petrol, or if a team played a football match to their own set of rules, without discussion with the opposing team. Chaos!

Though God created us, and therefore knows how we can function best, and has provided us with a book of instructions so that we can get the very best out of the life that He has entrusted to us, we can choose to ignore Him, go our own way and make up our own rules. That is ungodliness. Furthermore, questioning the very existence of God as Creator and Sustainer, as Savior and King, as well as questioning His relevance to our generation, and His right to set the rules, and His authority to demand our obedience, is ungodliness.

"Worldly lusts" are those forces that govern, direct and control much of today's world. As we look around the nations of the world, we see people governed by a vast, egocentric attitude. Greed, selfishness and pride often overshadow what is popularly called "our better nature." The desire to dominate, to be popular, or simply to make a success, drives many onward, no matter what means are employed.

To deny worldly lusts is to say "No to all that the world offers us that is not clearly in accord with God's character and standards, thereby showing the people among whom we live Whose we are, and Whom we serve.

The second of Paul's three phrases in his letter to Titus, to live "soberly, righteously and godly," can be considered as the positive aspect of Holiness; to say "Yes" to all that God shows us to be right and pleasing to Him. A public and visible declaration of intent to go God's way and to live self-controlled and upright lives is to say "Yes" to God's right to control my life according to His declared laws.

"Self-control" is one of the nine-fold fruit of the Holy Spirit. Those, who seek to live self-controlled and upright lives, will refuse to push themselves forward at another's expense. They will speak the truth with courtesy and restraint, and refrain from exaggeration that inflates the ego or avoids personal responsibility. They will refuse to deceive, or to use underhand means to gain more than is justly due, or to cheat in any form whatsoever to avoid just payment. They will behave with a quiet dignity that remains calm when falsely accused, and that refuses to get heated when slandered. They will maintain right standards even in the face of ridicule, and act justly even when by so doing an advantage is lost.

Instead of being dominated by the urgent question, "What can I get out of it?" a Christian should be steadily directed by the searching question, "What can I contribute to it?"

And so to the third phrase in Paul's letter to Titus: "to purify unto Himself a peculiar people, zealous of good works." Christ died to "redeem us from all wickedness" dealing with all the past by His death on Calvary; but also "to purify" us for service, enabling us by His risen life to live in the present in a manner pleasing to Him. We may be "zealous of good works," but for these good works to be acceptable to God, we must first know that we are being purified by His grace, in order that we may be His peculiar [special] people.

To return to the story of Jonah. He knew that God wanted His people to be "set apart" and distinct from those about them, in order that they might serve Him acceptably. Jonah could see quite clearly that God's ways and the ways of the world around him were diametrically opposed.

But he couldn't face the consequences of that fact.

He had to learn that a Christian cannot say "No, Lord." Either we say, "Yes, Lord," or we simply say "No," refusing to acknowledge our Savior as Lord. Once we say "Lord," we have to say "Yes," because His acknowledged lordship demands obedience.

Jonah knew that it was God's Voice that had said distinctly, "Arise, go to Nineveh," but he sought to argue. Yet even as he argued, the Holy Spirit showed him that he was wrong. He made him conscious of the fact that God did actually want him to go to Nineveh, to preach repentance, and probably to watch them turn to God and be forgiven!

Jonah loved God and wanted to serve Him, but he wanted to do it on his own terms. He lacked the basic essential of obedience—instant, unquestioning, unhesitating obedience—so God could not accept the proffered service. He must train Jonah first to obey Him.

Jonah did not submit easily to God's training!

"He rose up to flee from the face of the Lord," and probably "put out a fleece" to prove to himself that he was actually doing what the Lord really meant him to do.

"If I find a ship about to sail, with an empty berth, for which I have sufficient money, I'll know that is really where God meant to send me," may have been his thoughts—though he would not have needed a ship at all to go to Nineveh, just a camel! And sure enough, there was the ship, with the berth, and he had just the right money! All circumstances lined up to prove that this was right—to go west, when God's plan was to send him east.

How easily we can think like that, if our motive to serve, though possibly born of a real heart-love for the Savior and for mankind, is not actually governed by obedience. Are we willing to do the specific job that God wants us to do—that is, to carry the Candle to the place of His appointment?

"Yes, I'm willing to be God's candlestick, and that He should mold me to the shape and size He chooses.

"Yes, I'm willing to abide by the prescribed rules for carrying God's Candle, doing the job His way rather than my own.

"But I'm not sure if I am yet willing to let God choose the place of my service and that He alone should direct where I am to carry the Candle."

Is that our reaction?

When I came home from Africa in 1973, to share with my family in providing a home for our mother, she and I initially accepted an invitation to stay together at our Mission headquarters. We were both very happy and everyone was so good to us; yet after a few months I felt that it was wrong to remain there. It is not possible for the Mission to accept the care of the elderly parents of all our missionaries: headquarters simply is not big enough, has not sufficient staff, and lives at a pace impossible for the less able. We were, it seemed to me, presuming on their kindness.

So I looked round for employment. I felt that I needed a job that would both stretch me, and also give that elusive thing called "job satisfaction." Preferably, there should be a house provided with the job, with suitable living accommodation downstairs for my invalid mother. It would be good to have a sufficient salary to be able to pay someone to care for mother in the way she deserved, and to be a companion to her during the hours that I would be at work. I laid all that before the Lord, and mother and I prayed for His clear guidance.

Just the right job "came my way." The lady retiring from this job was seeking a Christian woman, with my qualifications, to take her place. It would be a five-year appointment initially, but with the expectancy of a fifteen-year tenure. There was a home, with absolutely the right ground-floor accommodation for mother. There would be a steady, secure and sufficient salary. This lady discussed it all with me, and urged me to apply for the appointment.

It was all so perfectly "right." Everything fitted exactly. It would be a great challenge, but I felt my previous experience would enable me to meet that challenge and to enjoy it. Even the timing was right; it would probably be fifteen years before the job became vacant again! "Yes, indeed," I reasoned, "God is good, and is obviously working on my behalf."

I resigned from our Mission and applied for the job.

God's ways are certainly mysterious at times, and this was one of those times. This turned out to be a case of what I call "negative guidance".

Every piece had fitted exactly into the jigsaw, or I would never have applied for the job, much in the same way as Jonah found a ship with an available berth. But God was at work behind the scenes for me, exactly as He had been for Jonah.

Once my resignation from the Mission and an application for this appointment were completed, my peace of heart left me. For a month, I was fretful and worried and anxious. I could settle on nothing. I could not sleep at nights. I dreaded going to the prayer meetings at headquarters, as I felt so ill at ease. Mother said I became irritable, almost unreasonable, even over small inconsequential matters. By the end of the first month, my mother urged me to withdraw my application for the job, and to ask the Mission to defer my resignation.

"You are like a bear with a sore head," she said, "and I just can't stand any more of it. It is so obviously not God's will for you!"

I was startled by her words. I honestly wanted God's will, yet uncertain as to the rightness of mother's reasoning, I hesitated. Was my nervousness possibly only fear of the unknown? Being a member of the Mission family had been my great security for twenty years. Was I simply afraid that I would not be able to manage the job, that it would prove too big for me? It would certainly demand even greater resourcefulness than all the tasks in Congo/Zaire, but the same God who undertook for me there could surely undertake for me now in this new venture. Yet I wondered, was mother right, that my loss of peace of mind signaled that I was venturing outside God's will for my life? So many voices clamored to be heard.

"Helen, give it up!" mother pleaded with me. "Get back into WEC! You'll see I'm right."

I did. She was. Peace returned at once.

God had reached through to show me what was His will, by showing clearly what was not His will. To do this, He had allowed me to think that the second alternative might be His will—and everything had looked so right. But God's peace was withdrawn. "Negative guidance" if you like, but still guidance, and that guidance confirmed when His peace was restored.

Jonah received the same type of "negative guidance!

Ship, berth, passage-money—all lined up—and he sailed away westwards, with his back to God's chosen destination, pleased that God had made everything fit so well. We have to learn that circumstantial guidance alone, even when everything seems to fit perfectly, is not a sufficiently sure proof that one is taking God's chosen pathway. This is particularly true when we know that there has been a moment of unwillingness on our part to do the particular job that God has appointed for us, and so an act of disobedience and a turning out of God's way have followed.

"Then the Lord sent a great wind on the sea," we read in Jonah 1:4, "and such a violent storm arose that the ship threatened to break up." You could say, there was no peace! But Jonah was not yet ready to listen.

Others could see the storm, and the sailors were all afraid. Doubtless all the other passengers, and the sailors and passengers of any other ships in their vicinity, were also filled with fear by the overwhelming tempest. "But Jonah had gone below deck," we read, "where he lay down and fell into a deep sleep" (Jonah 1:5). What an incredible picture! Everyone suffering except, apparently, the cause of it all. Ultimately the owners and commercial traders, as well as the sailors and the other passengers, were all to lose enormously because of the tempestuous storm: "they threw the cargo into the sea, to lighten the ship" (Jonah 1:5).

God allowed the situation to arise in order to teach Jonah a lesson, a deep lesson: namely, that our service for God must be the result of obedience to the Voice of God. Jonah may well have intended to preach God's message in Tarshish. The intention to serve was there, but he sought to decide what would be best for God's cause! That did not, and does not, work.

True Christian service, as the expression of God's Holiness in an individual, must be motivated by obedience to God's will. There can be no room whatsoever for any "self" in the motivation, or it ceases to be holy.

Jonah was afraid for his "self" and self's image, if he were to obey God and go to Nineveh. Yet God knew that at heart Jonah did want to act in accordance with His will. So God cornered him, in a situation from which he could not flee, and Jonah capitulated to God's right to determine the terms of his service. "Pick me up and throw me into the sea," said Jonah, "and it will become calm" (Jonah 1:12), for he knew that he was the cause of the ferocious wind and wild storm. He was no coward. He was willing to accept the responsibility for the mess they were in, and showed the sailors what to do to restore calm. Nevertheless, the sailors tried with all their might to spare Jonah: they struggled to reach land in a desperate bid to overcome the storms but to no avail.

So we are told in Jonah 1:15: "Then they took Jonah and threw him overboard, and the raging sea grew calm."

Instant calm! God's peace prevailed.

Jonah down in the fish's belly, realised that he had disobeyed God and, because of that, had lost God's peace in his heart. He acknowledged his fault and sought God's forgiveness, promising to obey His commands in the future; and God's Word tells us that "the Lord commanded the fish, and it vomited Jonah on to dry land" (Jonah 2:10).

It is very easy to offer God our service, as Jonah did, with certain reservations. I had told God that I was willing to be a candlestick and be molded to His design and that I was willing to carry His Candle in the prescribed way. I had gone where He had appointed me; but now I was unwilling for Him to change the place and the nature of my service. I wanted to attach conditions to my service.

Service, to be acceptable to God, must be given as an unreserved act of total obedience to His will, with no part of "self" involved. There can be no qualifying conditions.

During my first furlough, I had the joy of seeing more patients accepting the Lord Jesus Christ as their Savior during a six-month surgical residency in South Wales than I had seen during the four years of service at Nebobongo hospital. Ought I therefore to remain in medical service in the United Kingdom rather than return to the cross-cultural missionary situation at Nebobongo? The obvious flaws in such a simplistic evaluation of service hardly need attention drawn to them. If my ultimate objective was to see the largest possible number of people converted, then I would stay in the United Kingdom. If, however, my goal was to bring honor to God and glory to His name, I would obey Him and, answering His call, return to Nebobongo in Zaire.

The "flaws" in any system of evaluating the suitability of a candidate for a particular job are not always so obvious, and the enemy is intensely clever at muddling the issues.

It is, of course, right to seek to fit the right candle to the right candlestick, but this must not be in order to show off the workmanship of the candlestick! It must always be to seek what is best for the candle. Missionary service, as all other Christian service, if it is to be "holy and acceptable" to God, must flow from obedience, and not simply come from a desire to meet a need, however great that need may be. The fact that a missionary candidate appears to have the exact abilities needed to fulfil a particular task on the mission field, is, again, not sufficient evidence that that person is necessarily the one of God's choice.

It is obviously essential to try to know the state of the world we live in and to face the plight of millions of its inhabitants, in hunger and poverty; in ignorance or pain; under fanatical dictatorships or suffering from corrupt exploitation. World news on the media does move our hearts to realize the enormity of the task committed to us: "Go into all the world and preach the good news to all creation" (Mark 16:15).

This knowledge, however, does not in itself constitute a call to service. We can be stirred and challenged and made to face up to our responsibilities by these means, but the call to Christian service must be in obedience to His Word and personal call.

When God says: "Arise and go to Nineveh" it is not for us to consider whether Nineveh needs or deserves the message more than Tarshish, nor to reckon whether there is more probability of a response in Tarshish than in Nineveh. We are not asked whether Nineveh is in our program or not, nor are we to debate as to the greater likelihood of finding a language teacher in Tarshish!

Can the clay pot argue with the Potter: "Why have You not given me handles?"

Can a candlestick demand to be a saucepan, preferring to boil a potato to carrying the Candle into an unpropitious corner of the world?

Holiness will always show itself in obedient service. Andrew Murray has two most useful comments that we might look at here. He says:

> It has sometimes been said that people might be better employed in working for God than attending Holiness Conventions. This is surely a misunderstanding. It was before the throne of the Thrice Holy One, and as he heard the seraphim sing of God's Holiness, that the prophet said: "Here am I, send me." As the missions of Isaiah, and Moses, and the Son, whom the Father sanctified and sent, had their origin in the revelation of God's Holiness, our missions will receive

new power as they are more directly born out of the worship of God as the Holy One, and baptized into the Spirit of Holiness.

Secondly, he comments:

Note the connection between "sanctified," and "meet for the Master's use." True Holiness is being possessed of God; true service is being used of God. How much service there is in which we are the chief agents, and ask God to help and to bless us! True service is being yielded up for the Master to use. Then the Holy Ghost is the Agent, and we are the instruments of His will. Such service is Holiness.[4]

Inward Holiness is developed by the Holy Spirit in three "steps"—through hatred for sin, love for the Savior and obedience to God. This Holiness of character is foreordained by God for all His adopted children, as Paul tells us in Ephesians 1:4-6:

For he chose us in Him before the creation of the world to be holy and blameless in His sight. In love He predestined us to be adopted as His sons through Jesus Christ, in accordance with His pleasure and will—to the praise of His glorious grace, which He has freely given us in the One He loves.

Outward Holiness is revealed by the Holy Spirit in the life of the Christian, through the manifesting of the nine-fold fruit—love, joy, peace, patience, kindness, goodness, faithfulness, gentleness and self-control—in service to others. This Holiness of conduct is channeled into the good works that God has foreordained for each one of us: "For we are God's workmanship, created in Christ Jesus to do good works, which God prepared in advance for us to do" (Eph. 2:10). These good works are like the fragrance that filled the house when Mary broke the alabaster box, in order to pour out all the very costly ointment, to anoint the feet of our Lord Jesus Christ. He said that what she had done was "a good work, a beautiful thing".

Such service has to know the "must" of *obedience to love's compulsion.* All His life, Christ had this *must* upon Him.

As a twelve-year-old, in Jerusalem after the feast of the Passover, He said to His parents, "Didn't you know I had to be in My Father's house?" (Luke 2:49).

On His way from Jerusalem to Galilee, during His three years of ministry, it is said: "Now He [Jesus] had to go through Samaria" (John 4:4)—just to meet a needy woman, drawing water at the well.

As He went to the Garden of Gethsemane on that fateful last evening before Calvary, our Lord said to His disciples, "It is written: 'And He was numbered with the transgressors'; and I tell you that this must be fulfilled in Me" (Luke 22:37).

After the Resurrection, Jesus reminded His disciples of all He had taught them during His three years with them, and at the empty tomb, the angels said: "Remember how He told you, while He was still with you in Galilee: The Son of man *must* be delivered into the hands of sinful men, be crucified and on the third day be raised again" (Luke 24:6-7, my italics).

By His Holy Spirit, Christ challenges us with the same "must." "You will be told what you *must* do" (Acts 9:6, my italics), God said to Paul, and a little later, God sent Ananias to Paul saying: "I will show him how much he *must* suffer for My name" (Acts 9: 16, my italics). Paul and Barnabas taught the same message to the young converts in Galatia: "We *must* go through many hardships to enter the kingdom of God" (Acts 14:22, my italics).

All our conduct and the whole outward service of our lives must be an expression of Holiness, that results from the *must* of obedience.

One could quote endlessly to illustrate how Holiness always reveals itself in service that reaches out to help others, as light pours out into a dark place.

All the records of revivals, be it in 1859 in Ulster, in 1904 in Wales, in the 1940's in Ruanda, in the 1950's in Zaire and in the Hebrides, tell stories of changed lives and active witness, the longing to serve born of a new Holiness of character that just has to share the Good News of Salvation with those still in darkness.

The important point to realize, however, is that, underlying all such illustrations and stories of selfless service to others from church history and missionary chronicles, it is always *obedience* that motivates such service.

The person rendering that service may not necessarily look on it as an act of obedience, but rather as the overflow of love for God in gratitude for His overwhelming love for us. Nevertheless, it is the Holy Spirit in the believer's life who translates the need of one's heart to express this love into a life of obedience, poured out in service for others.

To clarify our understanding of the apparent overlapping of these four steps in the life of Holiness, may we look again at the illustration of the use of the four hoofs of a galloping horse? Each hoof is essential to the horse's progress. Each follows in steady rhythm, but the eye cannot observe the order which they move. So is the ministry of the Holy Spirit in the heart of each believer, as He seeks to transform us into the likeness of Christ, by developing Holiness in our lives. Each step is essential, but we are not always conscious of the order in which one step has led on to the other.

What we *are* determines what we *do*. Jesus Himself made this abundantly clear in His great Sermon on the Mount. The first section of the beatitudes show us what we are to be by the grace of God. We are to be poor in spirit rather than proud, mournful for sin rather than indifferent, meek in submission rather than obstinate, hungry and thirsty for God's righteousness rather than for worldly success, merciful and compassionate rather than vindictive and judgmental, pure in heart rather than conformed to a socially acceptable low ethic, peacemakers rather than troublemakers, willing to be persecuted rather than to compromise.

Then the Lord showed us how this inner character of Holiness would reveal itself in outward conduct and service: "You are the light of the world . . . let your light shine before men that they may see your good deeds and praise your Father in heaven" (Matt. 5:14-16).

Paul was inspired by the Holy Spirit to stress exactly the same order, when he wrote to the Philippians. He told them to be Christlike: "blameless and pure, children of God without fault in a crooked and depraved generation," before he enjoined them to "shine like stars in the universe" (Phil. 2:12-15).

Our urgent prayer must always be: "Let us be thankful and so worship God acceptably with reverence and awe. For our God is a consuming fire"' (Heb. 12:28-29).

Almighty God, in His terrible, awesome, holy Majesty, is a "jealous" God (where jealousy means intolerance of unfaithfulness). He is jealous for my undivided love and loyalty. He is jealous that I should be holy. He has commanded me to have no graven image, no second cause, no ulterior motive, no selfish factor—but that I should love, obey and serve Him only.

You shall have no other gods before Me. You shall not make for yourself an idol in the form of anything in heaven above or on the earth beneath or in the water below. You shall not bow down to them or worship them; for I, the Lord your God, am a jealous God . . . showing love to a thousand generations of those who love Me and keep My commandments (Exod. 20:3-6).

This jealousy of God is fire—fire that can burn out sin and dross, fire that can melt and warm our hard and cold hearts, fire that can purify and harden our will to obey, and fire that can heat and shine through our lives in daily service to others.

For we do not preach ourselves, but Jesus Christ as Lord, and ourselves as your servants for Jesus's sake. For God, who said, "Let light shine out of darkness," made His light shine in our hearts to give us the light of the knowledge of the glory of God in the face of Christ. But we have this treasure in jars of clay to show that this all-surpassing power is from God and not from us (2 Cor. 4:5-7).

May we be willing for all that God, our consuming fire, wants to do in our lives to make us acceptable candlesticks to carry Him, the Light of the world, wheresoever He wants to go: and may our prayer be:

Spirit of the living God, fall afresh on me.
Spirit of the living God, fall afresh on me.
Break me—dealing with all the sin—
Melt melt—filling me with Your Divine love—
Mould me—firing me to obedience to Your will—
Use me—sending me out to serve You acceptably—
Spirit of the living God, fall afresh on me.

17

The Arbiter of the Heart

Thomas Cook

Thomas Cook (1859-1913) was born in Middlesbrough, England. His father seems to have been indifferent to spiritual things for much of his life, but his mother was a godly, praying Methodist woman. Thomas made a commitment to follow Jesus in 1875 at age sixteen. His conversion was quiet and unremarkable from outward appearances; but the reality of Christ's saving work made such an impression on the teenager that he and a friend were soon of their own volition preaching on street corners to all who would hear about their life-giving Savior. In time, his ministry was much in demand, not only in his own denomination, but also among the Primitive Methodists, the Wesleyan Reformers, and the Salvation Army. In his twenty-second year alone, over 5,000 conversions were recorded!

Cook had no post-secondary education, so it was with some surprise in his denomination that he was called upon to become the first principal of Cliff College in 1903 for the training of lay ministers. He served the school faithfully and ably until his death in 1913.

The maintenance of a good conscience towards God from day to day is essential to the life of faith. True spirituality cannot exist unless accompanied by scrupulous conscientiousness, the purpose to do right at any cost. Archbishop Temple has truly said, "It is always a duty to obey conscience; it is never a duty to disobey." Conscience requires that we mean well, and do our best. It requires not only that we follow all the light we have, but all that we can obtain, and that we do this gladly. Conscience claims regency in everything that a man should aim to do or to be. "The word *ought* is the sovereign of all vocabularies."

But conscience guarantees only good intentions. Apart from knowledge and sound judgment, even those who are most conscientious may do immense mischief under the impression that they are doing the will of God. In some, conscience develops singular incongruities. Men are often very scrupulous in certain things, and very lax in other things. Frederick Robertson emphasizes the fact that scrupulosity about details often slides into laxity about the eternal laws of right and wrong. The brigands of Italy would go to the confessional most obediently before starting on an adventure of robbery and murder.

The Rev. John Newton, the author of some of the most valuable hymns in the English language, was once, as is well known, a slave-trader on the coast of Africa. After his conversion, his moral stupor was such that he saw no necessity for abandoning his diabolical trade. On his last voyage to the African coast for cargo, he said, he "experienced sweeter and more frequent hours of divine communion than he had ever known before." He wrote again of this infamous occupation: "No other employment affords greater advantages for promoting the life of God in the soul, especially to one who has command of a ship." This is the testimony of a slave-dealer. Yet the piety of John Newton at the time was scarcely less questionable than that of St. Paul. His moral sense had not been educated to see the exceptional depravity of the course he was pursuing.

The Bible itself speaks of conscience as seared, blunted, and blinded. We have scriptural warrant for saying that the conscience may be seared as with a hot iron. In Newton's case it was drugged, so as to give out delirious judgment. He had written several of the hymns for Christian worship, which the Church sings today, before he found out the depth of the moral abyss in which his moral nature was rotting. But when the awakening did come, he vaulted from the extreme of moral stupor to the extreme of moral hysteria. From the conviction that nothing was sin, his moral sense came to the conviction that everything was sin. For a time he could scarcely be persuaded to converse on other than religious topics, lest he should incur the guilt of "idle words."

Is there any tyranny worse than that of an unenlightened conscience? Of all our ignorances and infirmities, none is more disastrous to Christian character than to fall into bondage to the ascetic scruples and tyrannical prohibitions of a conscience not healthfully instructed and mollified by good sense. It is reported that Oberlin once fell on his knees in a remorseful prayer, because he had dispatched a letter in which he had neglected to cross the t's and dot the i's accurately. We may smile at his folly, but there are few Christians who cannot recall vagaries quite as foolish in their own lives, during temporary subjection to an austere conscience.

It is because of such possibilities of perversion and contortion that the human conscience is not always a safe and infallible guide. The moral sense in man is not designed to stand alone in the conduct of life and the building of character. God has provided the Christian with another arbiter to decide between good and evil, which is perfectly competent and reliable. "Let the peace of God," says the apostle, "rule in your hearts" (Col. 3:15). Much of the force of the expression is lost by the use of the colorless word "rule" which is translated "arbitrate" in the margin of the Revised Version.

"It is evident," says an eminent Bible exegete, "that St. Paul intended something peculiar by the use of the Greek word "arbitrate," found nowhere else in the Holy Scriptures, and styled "a remarkable word" by Bengal." "Wherever," says Bishop Lightfoot, "there is a conflict of motives, or impulses, or reasons, the peace of God must step in and decide which is to prevail." Dr. Maclaren explains that "the figure contained in the word translated *rule* is that of the umpire or arbitrator at the games, who, looking down on the arena, watches that the combatants strive lawfully, and adjudges the prize."

This arbiter is not peace with God, but the peace of God, the fathomless ocean of Christ's peace, which He has left as a legacy to His people. "My peace I give unto you." It is that deep repose of spirit which we receive when we enthrone the God of peace as the Lord of our hearts and lives. When this peace becomes the paramount consideration, everything that disturbs that profound rest of the soul will be instinctively avoided, and every act that would weave the thinnest veil between us and the face of our adorable Savior, we shall instantly shrink from. A man who is exploring an old well lowers a candle before him, knowing that where that can live, he can live. If the light goes out, he knows that it is not safe to go farther. The peace of God is the Christian's test-flame. Anything that in the slightest degree disturbs it should instantly be discarded, otherwise the storm has begun which will wreck the fair beauty and happiness of the soul.

The question of worldly amusements has been before the court of conscience for centuries, but no final decision has been reached. Before this arbiter, which the Gospel has called to the judgment-seat of the soul, the matter is quickly settled. What we cannot do quietly we cannot do safely. Whatever mars our tranquility or interferes with our inward repose, is detrimental to spiritual life. If we find that a given course of action tends to break our peace, we may be certain that there is poison in the draught, which, as in the old stories, has been detected by the shivered cup, and we should not drink any more. Conscience may discern no evil, but the peace of God is a more delicate instrument, dealing with questions too subtle for conscience to answer, and operating in a higher sphere.

The peace of God will approve of nothing into which Christ cannot be introduced and assigned the seat of honor. It should be to us what the barometer is to the sailor, and if it sinks, let us take warning. Whenever we find it in peril, we must retrace our steps. In all matters of doubt, when contending impulses and reasons distract, and seem to pull in opposite directions, our safety is to "let the peace of God" decide which is to prevail. Under His watchful rule the soul settles down into resolute and calm obedience to the law of Christ. The hearts and lives of men are made troubled, not by circumstances, but by themselves. We are restless because our wills are not in harmony with the will of God.

"A calm and heavenly frame" is only possible to those who let the peace of God have its way in their hearts. That stillness of the spirit is so sensitive, that it shrinks immediately in the presence of an evil thing. Our peace is gone immediately when we allow what it forbids. Happy are those who have enthroned the peace of God as the arbiter of their hearts! We share with Christ then, not only the peace that He gives, but "the peace which lay like a great calm on the sea, on His own deep heart."

The halcyon rest within,
Calming the storms of dread and sin.

18

Holiness and the Spirit-filled Life

Allan Brown

Allan Brown (b. 1944) has served as the chair of the division of Ministerial Education at God's Bible School and College, Cincinnati, Ohio, since 1996. Some of the courses he teaches are: Doctrine of Holiness; Holiness: Critical Issues; Hebrew Language; Wisdom Literature, Romans & Galatians; Christian Beliefs and the Epistle to the Hebrews; and Daniel & Revelation. He has his PhD from Bob Jones University, Greenville, South Carolina, in Old Testament Interpretation with an emphasis on the Hebrew and Greek languages.

Dr. Brown has served as a college professor for the past 40 years, during which time he also served as a senior pastor for 25 of those years, pastoring four different churches. He is married to Dr. Nadine Brown, who is involved in cancer research at the Children's Hospital Research Center in Cincinnati, Ohio; they have two married sons and 5 grandchildren.

<hr>

"As the deer pants for the water brooks, so my soul pants for Thee, O God" (Ps. 42:1).

"Blessed are they which do hunger and thirst after righteousness: for they shall be filled" (Matt. 5:6).

"And be not drunk with wine, wherein is excess; but be filled with the Spirit" (Eph. 5:18)

The ability to live a holy life comes from the power of the Holy Spirit.

In this chapter we will learn that one of the greatest blessings in the life of a Christian is the privilege of being filled with the Holy Spirit.

Christians Receive the Holy Spirit at the New Birth

The Holy Spirit is given to the redeemed person at his conversion. He creates within us the desire to live holy lives and empowers us to do God's will. It is the Holy Spirit who enables us to rejoice in and receive the love of God. He is also the One who enables us to love God and others. We see this in Romans 5:5: "The love of God is shed abroad in our hearts by the Holy Spirit which is given unto us."

There is a difference between being indwelt with the Holy Spirit and being filled with the Holy Spirit.

It is, however, biblically proper to distinguish the gift of the Holy Spirit received at conversion from what is often referred to as the "fullness of the Spirit." We are said to be "filled with the Spirit" only when as a Christian we invite Him to have full control of every aspect of our life.

If you wish to be filled with the Spirit, why not join me in the following prayer:

> *O God, I am hungry and thirsty for You. More of You is what I need. I ask You, through Your blessed Holy Spirit, to cleanse the intent of my heart and to enable me to turn over to the Holy Spirit full control of every aspect of my life. I pray this so that I may be empowered to love you completely and to serve You worthily. As I read this chapter, please help me to learn how to let the Holy Spirit have full control of my life. I pray this in Jesus' Name. Amen.*

Who is the Holy Spirit?

The Bible teaches that the Holy Spirit is the third Person of the Godhead. There is only one God, but the one God exists in three Persons: Father, Son, and Holy Spirit. We see this truth in verses such as, "The grace of the Lord Jesus Christ, and the love of God, and the fellowship of the Holy Spirit, be with you all" (2 Cor. 13:14). And after His bodily resurrection, Jesus commissioned his disciples, saying "Go therefore and make disciples of all the nations, baptizing them in the name of the Father and the Son and the Holy Spirit" (Matt. 28:19).

The Holy Spirit is a Person

The Holy Spirit is not simply a power or a symbol; he is a Person. Symbols and powers don't communicate; the Holy Spirit does. We read in Acts 13:2 of the Christians at Antioch, "While they were ministering to the Lord and fasting, the Holy Spirit said, "Set apart for Me Barnabas and Saul for the work to which I have called them." And Jesus said of the Holy Spirit, "When the Helper comes, whom I will send to you from the Father, that is the Spirit of truth who proceeds from the Father, He will testify about Me" (John 15:16).

The Holy Spirit has intellect, emotions, will, and can be grieved. This means that the Spirit has a personality. We are exhorted, "Do not grieve the Holy Spirit of God, by whom you were sealed for the day of redemption" (Eph. 4:30).

The Holy Spirit is the Spirit of Holiness

In addition to the name, "Holy Spirit," there are other titles that speak of the Spirit. He called "the Spirit of Jesus," "the Spirit of truth," the "Comforter" or "Helper," the "Spirit of God," the "Spirit of wisdom and understanding, counsel and might, knowledge and judgment," the "Spirit of grace," and the "Spirit of life," to mention just a few of his many titles.

One title of the Holy Spirit especially important for this chapter is "the Spirit of holiness" (Rom. 1:4). The "Spirit of holiness" speaks of the sanctifying Spirit who would have all Christians live in purity before the Lord. It is the Holy Spirit who actively works in a believer's life to enable holy living. Peter writes to believers as those "chosen according to the foreknowledge of God the Father, through the sanctifying work of the Spirit, for obedience to Jesus Christ" (1 Peter 1:2). Through His work of sanctification, the Holy Spirit enables believers to be obedient to the Lord Jesus Christ.

Paul wrote, "We should always give thanks to God for you, brethren beloved by the Lord, because God has chosen you from the beginning for salvation through sanctification by the Spirit and faith in the truth" (2 Thess. 2:13). The Holy Spirit is the One who graciously works in the life of a Christian to transform him or her into the likeness of Jesus Christ (2 Cor. 3:18).

Other Important Activities of the Holy Spirit

Because the work of the Holy Spirit is so important, let's quickly summarize some of the major activities the Spirit accomplishes in God's plan to make Christians holy.

First, the Holy Spirit is the One who convicts sinners of their sins. The Apostle John recorded Christ's words when he said, "But I tell you the truth, it is to your advantage that I go away; for if I [Jesus] do not go away, the Helper will not come to you; but if I go, I will send Him to you. And He, when He comes, will convict the world concerning sin and righteousness and judgment; concerning sin, because they do not believe in Me; and concerning righteousness, because I go to the Father and you no longer see Me; and concerning judgment, because the ruler of this world has been judged" (John 16:7-11).

Because God is merciful and loving, He sends the Holy Spirit to unsaved individuals to convict them of their sin and draw them to Jesus (Titus 2:11-12). The Holy Spirit graciously works in the mind and life of a sinner to help him realize his need for Christ. The Spirit's work of convicting a sinner through his conscience plays a vital part in his salvation.

Second, the Holy Spirit is also the Agent of the New Birth. Jesus wrote of the regenerating work of the Holy Spirit when he said to Nicodemus, "'Truly, truly, I say to you, unless one is born again he cannot see the kingdom of God.' Nicodemus said to Him, 'How can a man be born when he is old? He cannot enter a second time into his mother's womb and be born, can he?' Jesus answered, 'Truly, truly, I say to you, unless one is born of water and the Spirit he cannot enter into the kingdom of God. That which is born of the flesh is flesh, and that which is born of the Spirit is spirit. Do not be amazed that I said to you, You must be born again. The wind blows where it wishes and you hear the sound of it, but do not know where it comes from and where it is going; so is everyone who is born of the Spirit'" (John 3:3-8).

When you became a Christian, you were born of the Spirit. The Holy Spirit regenerated and renewed you, thereby making you holy. Paul writes that God "saved us, not on the basis of deeds which we have done in righteousness, but according to His mercy, by the washing of regeneration and renewing by the Holy Spirit, whom He poured out upon us richly through Jesus Christ our Savior" (Titus 3:5-6).

Third, at the moment of the new birth the Holy Spirit entered your life to live within you. On the day of Pentecost, Peter told the unsaved people who wished to become Christians, "Repent, and each of you be baptized in the name of Jesus Christ for the forgiveness of your sins; and you will receive the gift of the Holy Spirit" (Acts 2:38).

As the Agent of the new birth, the Holy Spirit dwells within you, creating and sustaining your spiritual life. The biblical expressions indicating the Holy Spirit's presence in a Christian's life are terms like, "have," "dwell (s)" or "receive." For example, Paul said of Christians, "You are not in the flesh but in the Spirit, if indeed the Spirit of God dwells in you. But if anyone does not have the Spirit of Christ, he does not belong to Him" (Rom. 8:9). Paul asked the Galatian Christians, "Did you receive the Spirit by the works of the Law, or by hearing with faith?"

Because the Holy Spirit comes to dwell in your life, your physical body becomes a temple for the Holy Spirit. The Holy Spirit requires that His dwelling place be holy. For this reason Paul wrote, "Flee immorality. Every other sin that a man commits is outside the body, but the immoral man sins against his own body. Or do you not know that your body is a temple of the Holy Spirit who is in you, whom you have from God, and that you are not your own? For you have been bought with a price: therefore glorify God in your body" (1 Cor. 6:18-20).

Fourth, in addition to becoming a holy temple for the Spirit to reside, the Holy Spirit makes you a part of the body of Christ—the Church. Induction into the body of Christ is termed, "the baptism by the Holy Spirit." It is a spiritual baptism performed by the Holy Spirit at the moment of the new birth. Paul tells us, "For by one Spirit we were all baptized into one body, whether Jews or Greeks, whether slaves or free, and we were all made to drink of one Spirit. For the body is not one member, but many" (1 Cor. 12:13-14).

The Witness of the Holy Spirit

One of the ways that you know you are a Christian is through the witness of the Holy Spirit. "The Spirit Himself witnesses with our spirit that we are children of God" (Rom. 8:16).

The Holy Spirit is the One who gives assurance to us that God is our heavenly Father, and that we have been adopted by God and are now his children. Paul wrote in Romans 8:15 that the Holy Spirit is the One who causes Christians to be adopted into the family of God and by Him we have the great privilege of saying to God, "Abba, Father."

The Fruit of the Holy Spirit

The Holy Spirit is the source of the "fruit of the Spirit" in a Christian's life. "The fruit of the Spirit is love, joy, peace, patience, kindness, goodness, faithfulness, gentleness, self-control" (Gal. 5:22-23), qualities of holiness that are essential to holy living. In order for these fruit to mature in a Christian's life, the Christian must put away all known sin and learn to follow the prompting and checks of the Holy Spirit. This is called being "led by the Spirit." Paul explains, "We are under obligation, not to the flesh, to live according to the flesh. For if you are living according to the flesh, you must die; but if by the Spirit you are putting to death the deeds of the body, you will live. For all who are being led by the Spirit of God, these are sons of God" (Rom. 8:12-14).

The Filling with the Holy Spirit

We come now to the important truth of being filled with the Spirit. In Ephesians 5:18, Paul writes to Christians who already have the Holy Spirit dwelling in them, and commands: "Do not get drunk with wine, for that is dissipation, but be filled with the Spirit." In the original language, this command to be filled with the Spirit actually translates, "be being filled with the Spirit." In other words, "become filled and keep on being filled with the Spirit."

From statements in the chapters in the Book of Ephesians that precede the command to be filled with the Spirit (Eph. 5:18), we can establish that Paul is writing to believers. He characterizes them as both "holy ones" and "faithful" to the Lord (Eph. 1:1). They have been "quickened together" with Christ, "raised up together" and "seated together" with Christ in heavenly places (Eph. 2:5-6). Further, they have been "sealed" with the Holy Spirit and have been warned about grieving Him (Eph. 1:13; 4:30). There is no question that Paul believed his readers to be true Christians in whom the Holy Spirit lived. What then does it mean to be "filled" with the Spirit?

What do you think of when you hear the command, "Be filled with the Spirit?" Do you think in terms of quantity, volume or measurement? This is not the point Paul is making. Although becoming drunk requires the intake of alcohol, Paul is speaking of the effects of being drunk and the effects of being Spirit-filled. Just as being "drunk" is to be under the influence or control of alcohol, so being "filled with the Spirit" is to be under the control of the Holy Spirit. Please note: when you are filled with the Spirit, you do not get more of the Spirit. To be filled with the Holy Spirit means He gets all of you: by faith you surrender to the Holy Spirit full access and absolute control of every aspect of yourself.

The passive voice of the Greek verb, "be being filled with the Spirit," indicates the method of the filling. We must submit to the Holy Spirit. We must consciously allow the Holy Spirit to have control of every aspect of our lives. Submission is the crucial element. The Holy Spirit takes full control only of those who willingly and totally submit to him. He never takes control by force.

Perhaps I can illustrate what it means to be fully surrendered to the Holy Spirit by an analogy of driving a car. To some people, the idea of a fully surrendered life would be the equivalent of removing ourselves from the driver's seat and letting the Holy Spirit drive. That would eliminate the stress of decision making. It would let us take a passive role. Instead, the Holy Spirit insists that we stay in the driver's seat. He is going to ride with us, but instead of driving, He is going to tell us what to do. So He issues instructions (through the Word and through our conscience in the form of prompts and checks), and we, as the driver, decide moment-by-moment whether or not we will continue to be submitted to His control and obedient to His directions.

This analogy highlights the fact that the fullness of the Spirit is not a simplistic "let go and let God have His way," a one-time decision that becomes automatic from that point forward. It is not simply a state of being, nor is there anything passive or automatic about it. A person who has fully surrendered to the control of the Holy Spirit must live out his surrender in obedience. As he moment-by-moment submits to the Spirit's control he moment-by-moment maintains the fullness of the Spirit.

A Contrast and a Comparison

Have you ever wondered why Paul chose to place a command not to be drunk next to the command to be filled with the Spirit? There must be some basis of contrast as well as comparison between drunkenness and Spirit-fullness. The contrast between being drunk with wine and being filled with the Spirit lies in the contrast between self-indulgence and Spirit-enabled self-control. A person becomes drunk with wine only through self-indulgence. On the other hand, a Spirit-filled person is enabled to bring all the desires of the flesh and mind under the control of the Holy Spirit and this produces self-control.

The comparison between being drunk with wine and being filled with the Spirit is that of being under the influence of a controlling substance. To be drunk is to be under the influence of alcohol. To be filled with the Spirit is to be under the control of the Holy Spirit.

Characteristics of a Spirit-filled life

There are definite changes that the Holy Spirit wishes to produce in the life of a Christian who becomes filled with the Spirit. The command to be filled with the Spirit is followed by five present participles, speaking, singing, making melody, giving thanks, and submitting, which express both inward and outward changes he wishes to produce in the life of a Spirit-filled Christian. Paul wrote: "And do not get drunk with wine, for that is dissipation, but be filled with the Spirit, speaking to one another in psalms and hymns and spiritual songs, singing and making melody with your heart to the Lord; always giving thanks for all things in the name of our Lord Jesus Christ to God, even the Father; and be subject to one another in the fear of Christ" (Eph. 5:18-21).

The Spirit-filled Christian, living daily under the controlling power of the Holy Spirit, will find his or her talk and taste in music changing ("speaking to one another in psalms and hymns and spiritual songs, singing and making melody with your heart to the Lord" - v.19). The Holy Spirit wishes to enable Christians to become a people who will spiritually strengthen others by guiding our talk and our outlook on life as we overflow in praise and thanksgiving to the Lord through singing and making melody with our hearts to the Lord.

Further, the Spirit-filled Christian will find his attitude toward life and others will be changing ("always giving thanks for all things in the name of our Lord Jesus Christ to God, even the Father"- v. 20). He or she will be led by the Spirit to make it a practice ("always") to give thanks to God for all things, for the Holy Spirit is the Spirit of praise and thanksgiving. When tempted to complain about circumstances, the Spirit will check the Christian and will lead him to thank God for His control over circumstances and His promise to work in every situation to make him more like Jesus (Rom. 8:28-29). The Spirit-filled Christian will find himself drawn to verses such as Ps. 34:1, "I will bless the Lord at all times, His praise shall continually be in my mouth," and Hebrews 13:15, "By Him therefore let us offer the sacrifices of praise to God continually, that is the fruit of our lips giving thanks to His name." The Spirit will enable him to take every thought captive and make it obedient to Christ (2 Cor. 10:5).

The Spirit-filled Christian will also find his relationships with other people changing ("submitting yourselves one to another in the fear of God" v. 21). The Spirit-filled person will be prompted by the Spirit to be kind to other people, not only in words, but also in one's thoughts (1 Cor. 13:5). The Holy Spirit desires to help us to have holy and pure intentions toward other people. Further, the Holy Spirit will enable a Spirit-filled Christian to gain a new sensitivity to, and respect for, the opinions and rights of others. The Spirit will prompt him to treat others as he would wish to be treated in reverse circumstances (see Phil. 2:3; Rom. 12:3).

In sum, the Spirit-filled Christian is totally given over to pleasing God in everything (Col. 1:9-10). Obeying God is the driving force of his life, the consuming passion of his heart. The Spirit-filled Christian will sacrifice anything for His Lord.

How to be Filled with the Spirit

Have you been filled with the Holy Spirit? If not, there are several steps to take in order to be Spirit-filled.

First, be sure you are born again. Do you know for sure that you are a child of God? You can be sure of your relationship with God if you are walking in all the light you have (1 John 1:7).

Second, you must be biblically convinced that you need to be filled with the Spirit. Hopefully, our study of Scripture has convinced you that all Christians are commanded to be filled with the Spirit subsequent to the new birth (Eph. 5:18).

Third, you must desire with all your heart to be filled with the Spirit. God pronounces a blessing upon those who seek Him with the whole heart (Ps. 119:2). If your desire is not whole-hearted, ask God to increase your desire to be filled with the Spirit. Ask yourself, "What keeps me from desiring to be under the full control of the Holy Spirit?" Ask God to show you your heart as He sees it.

If you meet these three requirements, you are ready to be filled with the Spirit. This necessitates a deliberate surrender of the control of your life to the Holy Spirit, and the faith to believe that the Holy Spirit will fill you right now as you surrender to His full control. Believe the promise of 1 John 5:14-15, "This is the confidence which we have before Him, that, if we ask anything according to His will, He hears us. And if we know that He hears us in whatever we ask, we know that we have the requests which we have asked from Him." According to Ephesians 5:18, it is God's will for all Christians to be filled with the Spirit!

Lastly, Scripture urges us to confess with our mouth that which we have believed in our heart (Rom. 10:9). Let others know of God's wondrous work in your heart.

Closing Prayer

Dear Heavenly Father, Thank you for the gift of Your Son, Jesus Christ. I desire with all my heart to be filled with the Holy Spirit. Please cleanse my heart of anything that would hinder me from giving the Holy Spirit full control of my life. I now open my heart to the fullness of the Spirit, and consciously, deliberately, yield my past, my present, and my future to your sovereign control. Whatever you wish to change, I give you full permission to change. I only ask that you grant me the grace to obey you in everything and to become the person you wish me to become. I claim the promise, "Blessed are they which do hunger and thirst after righteousness: for they shall be filled" (Matthew 5:6).

Holy Spirit, I thank you for taking full control of my life. In Jesus' Name I pray, Amen.

A Hymn to Memorize: "Fill Me Now"

Hover o'er me, Holy Spirit,
Bathe my trembling heart and brow;
Fill me with Thy hallowed presence,
Come, oh, come and fill me now.

Refrain:
Fill me now, fill me now,
Holy Spirit, fill me now;
Fill me with Thy hallowed presence,
Come, oh, come, and fill me now.

Thou canst fill me, gracious Spirit,
Though I cannot tell Thee how;
But I need Thee, greatly need Thee,
Come, oh, come and fill me now.

I am weakness, full of weakness,
At Thy sacred feet I bow;
Blest, divine, eternal Spirit,
Fill with pow'r, and fill me now.

Cleanse and comfort, wholly save me,
Bathe, oh, bathe my heart and brow;
Thou dost sanctify and cleanse me,
Thou art sweetly filling now.
(Elwood H. Stokes, 1879)

19

Toward Christian Maturity

W. T. Purkiser, Richard S. Taylor, Willard H. Taylor

W. T. Purkiser, Richard S. Taylor, and Willard H. Taylor were all scholars within the Church of the Nazarene tradition. W. T. Purkiser (1910-92) was a prolific writer, respected scholar, and well-loved preacher, who also had a significant voice in the larger evangelical Christian community. He authored and contributed to some of the most widely disseminated and enduring works in the Wesleyan-Holiness tradition. Richard S. Taylor (1912-2006) was a professor of theology and missions at Nazarene Theological Seminary. His significant contributions as an author include *The Disciplined Life* and *Life in the Spirit*. Willard H. Taylor (? -1993) served as dean and professor of biblical theology at the Nazarene Theological Seminary. He also served in the pastorate for ten years. He wrote for numerous periodicals, theological dictionaries, and scholarly journals.

It was in Antioch that "the disciples were for the first time called Christians" (Acts 11:26). Here Barnabas exhibited the instinctive sense of responsibility toward new converts that gripped the Early Church, exhorting "them all to remain faithful to the Lord with steadfast purpose" (v. 23). Babes were not abandoned; they were nurtured. Their growth and final salvation was never taken for granted (Acts 8:14f; 13:43; 15:36).

But what is evident in Acts becomes dominant in the Epistles. All of the letters are directed to Christians and clearly have as their aim precisely what Paul specifies as the function of "all scripture." The Epistles were designed to be not only "profitable for teaching" but also for "reproof, for correction, and for training in righteousness, that the man of God may be complete, equipped for every good work" (2 Tim; 3:16-17).

What happens after the crisis experiences of salvation is clearly therefore of major importance in the New Testament perspective. Two burdens run parallel. One is that a vital and growing relationship with the Lord be maintained; the other, that the Christian's relationship with his fellows be exemplary. The first we may call Christian devotion; and the second, Christian ethics.

The mature Christian is one who has attained to a high degree of stability and credibility in both areas. This chapter will be devoted primarily to the progress of the soul—without implying that this can be a real experience apart from simultaneous and corresponding attention to ethics. Using Micah's trilogy (6:8) we will consider the last first: "to walk humbly with your God." Only by so walking can the "salt of the earth" retain its "saltiness" (Matt. 5:13).

The Responsibility of the Believer

While the Early Church leaders carried a heavy sense of responsibility toward converts, it was no stronger than the sense of responsibility urged upon the believer himself. "But grow in the grace and knowledge of our Lord and Savior Jesus Christ" was Peter's final command (2 Pet. 3:18), an injunction epitomizing the viewpoint of the New Testament. Apparently growth is not inevitable or automatic. Growing is what the believer does by choice (cf. 2 Pet. 1:5-10). While the grace available is so adequate that dismay is never justified, it is not so overwhelming as to justify trifling or presumption. For "how shall we escape if we neglect such a great salvation?" is the unanswerable challenge to those among the Hebrews who already had tasted salvation's power (2:1-4; cf. 3:12-14; 5:12—6:12; 10:26-29, 35-39; 12:1-17).

While we must guard against a humanistic self-reliance by remembering that we "by God's power are guarded" (1 Pet. 1:5), we must not fail to add what the Bible adds: "through faith." Jude strikes the balance by saying, "Now to him who is able to keep you from falling" *after first* commanding, ". . . keep yourselves in the love of God" (24, 21). John says, "Look to yourselves, that you may not lose what you have worked for, but may win a full reward" (2 John 8). Paul insists that while "God is at work" in us "both to will and to work for his good pleasure," our task is to "work out" our own "salvation with fear and trembling" (Phil. 2:12-13). "This exhortation," says A. T. Robertson, "assumes human free agency in carrying on the work of one's salvation."[1] And the same apostle who is sure that Christ "is able to guard until that Day what" He has "entrusted to me," admonishes Timothy, almost in the next sentence, "Guard the truth that has been entrusted to you by the Holy Spirit" (2 Tim. 1:12, 14; cf. Heb. 2:1; James 1:25).

Perhaps the most frequent and urgent admonitions are given by Jesus himself. The imperative "Take heed" is found no less than 12 times in His sayings, exclusive of parallels. And when "many believed in him" following one of His controversial discourses, He said to them simply: "If you continue in my word, you are truly my disciples" (John 8:30-31). There is no way to minimize or escape the total and consistent New Testament teaching on the importance of going forward in the Christian life; nor that this essential progress is squarely up to the believer (cf. Eph. 2:10).[2]

The Province of Growth

It has been apparent that some deficiencies in the Christian are unacceptable and are therefore to be corrected immediately, by confession, self-cleansing, consecration, prayer, and faith. No allowance is made or license given to love God with less than our whole being at any moment, or to love our brother less than ourselves, or to be walking behind light, or to fail to be spiritually minded. Nor are worldly-mindedness and lukewarmness treated as innocent weaknesses which the Christian is exhorted to overcome gradually.[3]

Yet the New Testament has much to say about progress in the Christian life. What are the areas which are legitimately matters of growth and development but that require time and process? It is important that we "rightly divide" here, lest we confuse the two categories and suppose that some facets of Christian deficiency that God designs to correct crucially are proper subjects of growth, or that areas properly in the sphere of growth are to be struggled over under the illusion that they are subject to instant correction.

The matter is clearly expressed by Donald S. Metz:

The Corinthians had accepted the gospel as a new and revolutionary way of life. Yet many problems persisted in the church. In the Christian life some problems, such as actual sins and transgressions, are solved in the new birth (1 John 3:8-9). Other problems, such as carnal affections and attitudes, are solved by the cleansing power of the Holy Spirit in the crisis of entire sanctification (1 Cor. 3:3; 2 Cor. 7:1; Eph. 5:25-26). Other problems not related to sin or to the carnal mind are solved by spiritual maturity, growth in grace, and enlarged understanding. The problems of the church at Corinth were due primarily to the carnal mind, although some, such as the problem of marriage and celibacy, may have been due to lack of understanding.[4]

It is important therefore that we give careful attention to passages that plainly mark out the areas which belong to the sphere of progress and growth.

Christlikeness of Personality. While a holy man is Christ-centered, and while his Christian witness is not tarnished by [deliberate] sinning, he is only relatively Christlike in total personality. There may be many crudities and blunderings, even ill-advised reactions, which on the surface do not remind others of Jesus.

The veil of spiritual blindness that lies over the heart of unbelievers has been removed. Paul writes: "We all, with unveiled face, beholding the glory of the Lord, are being changed into his likeness from one degree of glory to another; for this comes from the Lord who is the Spirit" (2 Cor. 3:18). The image of Christ is the important lodestar. The general meaning of "image" (*eikon*) is visible, recognizable likeness to or of an original, perhaps now invisible (cf. Matt. 22:20; Rom. 1:23; 1 Cor. 11:7; 15:49, et al). The inner likeness or conformity (*summorphous*) to this image is the predetermined goal of the divine calling (Rom. 8:29).

The inner conformation is essentially ours through regeneration and sanctification, fitting us for eternal exhibition of triumph when Christ stands as "the first-born among many brethren" (Rom. 8:29; cf. Heb. 2:11). But the *metamorphosis*, the complete transformation of character, includes the translation of the inner conformity into outward personality, and in this respect is a gradual process.[5] We are to take on Christlikeness "from glory to glory," or from one degree of visible resemblance to another. A high degree must have been recognizable in the personality and face of Commissioner Samuel Brengle when after a visit to the home a little girl said to her mother, "Would Jesus have looked like Brother Brengle if he had lived to be 75?"

The import of the present tense in Romans 12:2 might be debatable. There we are dealing not with a simple statement of fact, as in Corinthians, but a command, which seems to be the counterpart of "Do not be conformed to this world." This too is present tense, but the sense of crisis immediacy is obvious.[6] If, however, the transformation of Romans is to be given a progressive sense (as is clearly the import of the Corinthian reference), then we may understand the "renewing of your mind" to constitute the inner change immediately possible and obligatory. The transformation would be the external change in lifestyle, taking shape increasingly, as new light comes; yet the *pattern* of conformity with the world is to stop at once. The renewing of the mind is brought about by the sanctifying of the Holy Spirit (Titus 3:5; cf. Eph. 4:23); but a truly renewed mind will gladly stop any remaining worldly conformity and will progressively translate its own thorough renewal into whatever outward changes are consonant with it (cf. Phil. 2:12). The result of such progress will be a growing recognizability of Christlikeness.

Acquiring Maturity. The function of the special ministries within the Church, Paul says, is "for the equipment of the saints,[7] for the work of ministry, for building up the body of Christ" (Eph. 4:12). The goal of this edifying is mature manhood in spiritual things, a maturity which is defined as a "measure of the stature of the fullness of Christ" (Eph. 4:13). The "equipment" (*katartismos*) includes as a presupposition whatever *mending* is necessary, the possible nature of which is suggested elsewhere in the Epistle (1:18f; 3:13f; 4:1-3, 20-32; 5:15-21, 25-27). This mending may be either internal (sanctification) or external (manner of walk, ethics). But the "perfecting" (KJV) does not stop with complete and satisfactory spiritual adjustment. It includes that nurturing and training which leads to two indispensable marks of maturity: *doctrinal stability* and *smooth functioning* in the Body. Both ideas are interwoven here and are interdependent. This kind of progress occurs only as the Christian learns to combine verbal fidelity to the truth with love (v. 15).[8]

Marks of Maturity

From one standpoint maturity is open-ended, therefore difficult to define. Even relatively mature Christians are still growing. Self-satisfaction with one's attainments is fatal. Yet when John addressed all as "little children," then subdivided into "young men" and "fathers" (1 John 2:12-14), he must have had in mind categories that were recognizable.[9]

Christian perfection as holiness, or a sanctified frame of mind, is the disposition to count all things but loss for Christ, and to "press on in order" to lay hold of the ultimate goal (Phil. 3:7-16, NASB). This is the foundation. But what are the marks of Christian perfection conceived as *maturity*? Doctrinal stability and adjustment within the body of Christ have already been noted. But there are other marks.

Contentment. Paul's own testimony furnishes the main clues. In spite of imprisonment and impoverishment he says: "I have learned, in whatever state I am, to be content" (Phil. 4:11). This is not the contentment of indifference or of vegetation, which neither desires nor prays for change. It is rather a sanctified self-sufficiency, which has inner resources in Christ for the hour of adversity.[10] Yet this level of unflappable composure is in part the acquirement of years of "learning experience." While such learning is a process, often painfully slow, the constative aorist tense here would suggest that Paul has learned his lesson well. It does not have to be relearned every time something goes wrong. Emotional stability is a mark of Christian maturity.

Discernment. There are several facets of Christian discernment.

1. One is mature perception of doctrinal truth in distinction from error (Eph. 4:14; Heb. 5:11-14). The mature Christian is not easily fooled. This insight into truth also extends to ethical issues (Eph. 5:11-17).

2. Another important facet is a discernment of true spirituality. To inculcate a proper concept of spirituality could almost be said to be the whole of Paul's burden in both Corinthian letters. The Corinthians measured spirituality in terms of gifts, the showier and more spectacular the better. This, Paul chided, was thinking like children, not like spiritual adults (1 Cor. 14:20). Paul measured spirituality (negatively) in terms of freedom from carnal traits (1 Cor. 3:1 ff.), and (positively) in terms of perfect love (1 Corinthians 13), which fosters stability, faithfulness, and patience.[11]

Paul reminds the shallow Corinthians that he had "visions and revelations" which put all their gifts in the shade. But he refuses to glory in these lofty experiences; instead he says, "I will all the more gladly boast of my weaknesses, that the power of Christ may rest upon me" (2 Cor. 12:9). What power? To perform miracles? No, the power to be victorious over thorns. Superficial Christians would have measured Paul's spirituality by whether or not he received healing. True spirituality perceives that the greater miracle is not deliverance from the thorn but deliverance from preoccupation with it. True spirituality is exhibited in that pure devotion to Jesus which gladly accepts the grace rather than the miracle, the moment one perceives that in this path lies greater glory to the Lord.

3. A yet further aspect of discernment is acquaintance with the Spirit" is the movings and leadings of the Holy Spirit (1 Cor. 2:9-16). Walking "in the Spirit" is the essence of the normal Christian life (Gal. 5:25); but it takes time to learn the art of such walking as will teach a Philip how to recognize the voice of the Spirit when He prompts action (Acts 8:29), and will teach a Paul and Silas the meaning of the Spirit's restraint (Acts 16:6-7). The anointing "by the Holy One" (1 John 2:20, 27; 4:1-3) is through the Spirit, who touches our eyes and gives spiritual insight, generally into truth, sometimes into people (Acts 5:1-5). As we grow, our sensitivity to the reproof or promptings of the Spirit grows apace (Eph. 4:30; 1 Thess. 5:17).

Balance. Peter provides one of the most comprehensive expositions of personal progress in spiritual matters to be found in the New Testament (2 Pet. 1:5-7). His emphasis is on the development of all the essential graces, that the character may become full-orbed.[12] Regenerating and purifying *faith* is the foundation. By faith we escape the "corruption that is in the world because of passion," and by it we are made "partakers of the divine nature" (2 Pet. 1:4). Faith, however, must be supplemented with *areten*, which is not "virtue" in the modern sense of the term, but "resolution" (Moffatt). For a believer to become complacent is to prevent all spiritual progress, if indeed any holiness at all can be maintained (cf. Phil. 1:10; 2:12f.; 3:13-15).

To our resolution we are to add *knowledge*. We must be intelligent in our zeal, remembering always the peril of "zeal without knowledge." Good religion is made better by the addition of common sense.[13]

Similarly, our knowledge must be supplied with *self-control*, for the man who knows much without applying that knowledge to his own life is self-condemned. Our self-control, if it is to be complete, must be supplemented with *steadfastness*, because the need for discipline is not temporary. We shall not reach a place where we can afford to become flabby or to let down our spiritual and moral guard.

Our *perseverance*, however, must be supplied with *godliness*, i.e., habitual prayerfulness and piety, lest it degenerate into a mere human tenacity and unbending stubbornness. Dogged persistence without warmth or flexibility ceases to be a Christian virtue. On the other hand, our prayerfulness and piety must be supplemented by *brotherly kindness*, which in this case is a true liking for people, a fraternal sociability essential to happy human relations. This sociability must at the same time avoid unseemly levity or frivolity which would breed compromise and grieve the Spirit (cf. Eph. 4:29; 5:4).

But "brotherly kindness" (*philadelphia*) will fall short if it is permitted to stand alone. Sooner or later, natural liking for people will break down, especially when we discover things about them that we do not like, or when we become victims of some rascality. Therefore brotherly love can be perfected and preserved only by a massive infusion of *agape*—Christian love—available through the constant supply of the indwelling Holy Spirit. Such love transcends the natural dimensions. Going far beyond the joys of congeniality, it actively seeks the welfare of others, even when at times congeniality must give way to pain (cf. Col. 3:12-14).

"For if these qualities are yours and are increasing, they render you neither useless nor unfruitful in the true knowledge of our Lord Jesus Christ" (2 Pet. 1:8, NASB). In the light of the extreme gravity of the issues at stake, according to verses 1-11, the word increasing should be underscored. It is in these specific qualities of Christian character, and particularly in the symmetry of their development in relation to each other, that we find the marks of growth and maturity (cf. Gal. 5:22-23; Phil. 4:8; Col. 3:12-16).

20

The Ongoing Warfare—The Flesh Against the Spirit

Gordon D. Fee

Gordon Fee (b. 1934) is Professor Emeritus of New Testament at Regent College, where he taught for sixteen years. His teaching experience also includes serving schools in Washington, California, Kentucky, as well as Wheaton College (five years) and Gordon-Conwell Theological Seminary.

Dr. Fee is a noted New Testament scholar, having published several books and articles in his field of specialization, New Testament textual criticism. He also published a textbook on New Testament interpretation, co-authored two books for lay people on biblical interpretation, as well as scholarly-popular commentaries on 1 and 2 Timothy and Titus and on Galatians, and major commentaries on 1 Corinthians and Philippians. He is also the author of a major work on the Holy Spirit and the Person of Christ in the letters of Paul.

The Spirit-flesh conflict in Paul has to do not with an internal conflict in one's soul, but with the people of God living the life of the future in a world where the flesh is still very active.

A good friend wrote recently, "Christians seem to me to divide into two groups these days: the first lot don't think that sin matters very much anyway, and the second know perfectly well that it does, but still can't kick the habit."[1] This chapter picks up the concern of the second lot. Indeed, we now come to the real world! Painfully, for many of God's people the subject of this chapter tells the story of their Christian life, a story of ongoing inner conflict of soul. They take some comfort in believing that Paul was their companion in this struggle. If Paul, the great apostle of the faith, could write, "what I want to do I do not do, but what I hate I do" (Rom 7:15), then what hope is there for us? So they simply resign themselves to the struggle.

People come by this comfort by reading Galatians 5:17, the single Pauline text that speaks about a *conflict* between the Spirit and the flesh, in light of Romans 7:14-25—although the Spirit is not so much as mentioned in the Romans passage, where Paul describes the conflict that goes on in the soul of a person living under law and without the Spirit's help. People accept this unfortunate reading of Paul at face value, because the text in Romans vividly describes something they know only too well. Sadly, for the vast majority of those who adopt such a view, the flesh usually wins. Thus Paul's passion, namely, the sufficiency of the Spirit for all of life in the present age, is brushed aside as unrealistic in favor of one's own personal reality.

To be sure, such war does rage in the hearts of many. Often the warfare—and the sense of helplessness to live above it—is the direct result of the intense individualism of Western culture. Both secular psychology and much Christian teaching focus on the inner self: How am I doing, according to some set of criteria for wholeness? Focused on the inner struggle, we can scarcely see Christ or walk confidently in the way of the Spirit. Instead of living out the fruit of the Spirit, in constant thankfulness for what the Spirit is doing in our lives and in the lives of others, our individualistic faith turns sourly narcissistic—aware of our personal failures before God, frustrated at our imperfections, feigning the love, joy, peace, and gentleness we wish were real. Our turmoil crowds out openness to the Spirit himself. In such spiritual malaise God almost always gets the blame.

But as real as this is for some, Paul is not addressing this issue when in Galatians 5:17 he speaks of the Spirit and "flesh" as in utter opposition to each other. Indeed, he would not even understand it. His world is that of Psalm 19, not that of "the introspective conscience of the West."[2] In consecutive verses (12-13), the psalmist acknowledges first his "errors" and "hidden faults" and then the possibility of "willful sins." The former is an acknowledgment of the depth of our fallenness; for these "hidden faults" he asks forgiveness. His concern—and it does not take the form of a struggle—

is with the "willful sins." About these he prays that they will "not rule over me."[3] Paul's view is similar. In Galatians 5:17 he is not addressing a struggle over "hidden faults" but open disobedience to God in the form of "willful sins."

At issue for us in this chapter, therefore, is Paul's own view of the conflict between the Spirit and the flesh, between living *kata sarka* ("according to the flesh") and *kata pneuma* ("according to the Spirit"). Every occurrence of these terms in Paul has to do with our present eschatological existence—what it means for believers to live together as a people, defined by the already/not yet fulfillment of God's promises, in contrast to a former life defined and determined by the world. My point: Nowhere does Paul describe Christian life in the Spirit, as one of constant struggle with the flesh.[4] He simply does not speak to that question. His point rather is the sufficiency of the Spirit for God's new end-time people.

Basic to Paul's view is that, as with Torah observance, the time of the flesh is over for followers of Christ. According to Romans 7:4-6, Christ and the Spirit have, with the new covenant, brought an end to the time of the law and the flesh, which belong to our existence *before* and *outside* Christ. Continuing to live this way is incompatible with life "according to the Spirit" (Rom 8:5-8). But Paul's view does not represent triumphalism, as though people who lived by the Spirit were never tempted by the old life in the flesh or that they never succumbed to such. They have, and they do; and there is forgiveness for such, and gracious restoration.

A careful analysis of the key texts Galatians 5:17 and Romans 7:14-25 demonstrates that this is Paul's perspective. But we will be helped in that analysis by looking first at Paul's use of the term "flesh."[5]

The Meaning of "Flesh" in Paul

The place to begin such a study is with the Old Testament, since Paul's usage originates there. The Hebrew word *bāśār* refers primarily to the flesh of bodies, and by derivation sometimes to the bodies themselves. On a few occasions the term is extended to describe human frailty and creatureliness, usually in contrast to God as creator. Thus a common expression for all living beings, especially humans, is "all flesh," meaning "every creature." When the psalmist asks in light of his trust in God, "What can flesh do to me?" (Ps. 56:4), he means that with God as his protector what can a mere human do to him (cf. Jer. 17:5). In his anguish Job asks God, "Do you have eyes of flesh? Do you see as humans see?" While "flesh" is not a neutral term when used in this way, neither does it express a negative moral judgment; rather, it expresses the frailty of human creatureliness. It would be unthinkable to the Hebrew that sin lay in the flesh, since sin's origins lie in the human heart.

Although Paul rarely uses the Greek term *sarx* in its basic sense, as referring to the physical body, he regularly uses it in the extended sense as referring to our humanity in some way or another. Thus he can speak of "Israel according to the flesh" (1 Cor. 10:18), or Abraham as our forefather "according to the flesh" (Rom 4:1), or of Jesus as descended from David "according to the flesh" (Rom. 1:3), meaning in each case "according to ordinary human descent." In the same mode Paul recognizes present human life as still "in the flesh" (e.g., Gal. 2:20; 2 Cor. 10:3), that is, lived out in the present human body, characterized by frailty as it is.

Paul also uses *sarx*, however, in a more unusual sense, derived in part from intertestamental Judaism, but marked by his own basically eschatological view of life in the world. "Flesh" for him denotes humanity not simply in its creatureliness vis-a-vis God, but in its *fallen* creatureliness as utterly hostile to God in every imaginable way. It is in this sense that he contrasts life "according to the flesh" over against life "according to the Spirit." The one describes the present evil age in terms of human fallenness, where by nature each has turned to his or her own way; the other describes the eschatological age that has dawned with the coming of Christ and the Spirit, ...

This does not make *sarx* an easy term to translate. The NIV often uses "sinful nature."[6] That translation works well in Romans 7, where Paul is describing the failure of his former life under the law. The "flesh" represents "another law in his members" that rises up to defeat the law of God and thus to render the law helpless. That "other law" is his own "sinful nature." But this rendering does not work well in other places, where he is describing what characterizes the whole world in its present fallenness.

The clearest instance in which Paul plays on the two basic senses of this word ("human frailty" and "human fallenness") is in 2 Corinthians 10:2-4. Accused by them of acting "according to the flesh" in the morally negative sense, Paul allows, for the sake of his argument, that he does indeed live "in the flesh," by which he means "in the weaknesses and limitations of present mortality." But, he goes on, I do not engage in warfare *"according* to the flesh," in keeping with the fallenness which characterizes the present age that, because of the cross and resurrection, is on its way out. This argument does not work at all if "flesh" is morally negative in both instances.

Our interest lies strictly with this latter sense, human fallenness, which has completely lost its relationship to the physical and has become strictly eschatological—and morally negative—describing existence from the perspective of those who do not know Christ, who thus live as God's enemies. It describes believers only *before* they came to be in Christ and live by the Spirit. Any conflict in this matter has to do with believers in Christ, people of the Spirit, continuing to behave according to their pre-Christ perspective and values. Paul's point always is, "Stop it." "Put off your old self," he says, and "put on the new self" (Eph. 4:22, 24). My point, then, is that whenever "flesh" occurs in contrast to the Spirit, it always bears this eschatological sense.

The Spirit-Flesh Contrast in Paul[7]

That Paul viewed the flesh as belonging to the past for believers, in the same way as he viewed Torah observance, is specifically stated in Romans 7:4-6: "When we *were* living in the flesh, the passions of sin, aroused by the law, *were* [also] at work in us; . . . but now, by dying to what once bound us, we have been set free . . . to walk in the new way of the Spirit." How Paul understands this is set forth vividly in 2 Corinthians 5:14-17:

> For Christ's love compels us, because we are convinced that one died for all, and therefore all died. And he died for all, that those who live should no longer live for themselves but for him who died for them and was raised again. So then, from now on we regard no one from the perspective of the flesh. If indeed we once considered even Christ from this perspective, now we know him in this way no longer. So then, if anyone is in Christ, a new creation; the old things have passed away; behold, the new have come.

The death and resurrection of Christ and the gift of the Spirit have changed everything. The former order of things is described in terms of flesh, that basically self-centered, creature-oriented point of view, which has caused the Corinthians to regard Paul as he had formerly regarded Christ, as weak and therefore not of God. The flesh perceives things from the old age point of view, where value and significance lie in power, influence, wealth, and wisdom (cf. 1 Cor. 1:26-31).

To be sure, such a worldview is still about. But for those in Christ, all of that has passed away; behold, the new has come, the time of the Spirit, in which there has been a total change in the definition of what has value or significance. The new model is the cross: the power lies not in externals but in the Spirit, who indwells believers and by grace is renewing the "inner person" (2 Cor. 4:16), transforming us into God's own likeness (ultimately portrayed in Christ through the cross).

This eschatological view of the Spirit/flesh contrast is found in other passages as well:

1. "I could not speak to you as Spiritual, but as fleshly," Paul tells the Corinthians (1 Cor. 3:1). The irony of this sentence lies in the fact that the Corinthians, who think of themselves as Spirit people, are thinking just as they did before they met Christ, just like those leaders of this passing age, who crucified Christ (2:6-8). Their attitude toward Paul's suffering and his message of the cross in effect makes them bedfellows with those who killed Christ, viewing things from the perspective of the flesh.

This is obviously eschatological terminology. Moreover, it does not reflect some internal struggle in the believer between these two kinds of existence. On the contrary, it describes the essential characteristics of the two ages, which exist side by side in unrelieved opposition in our present already but not yet existence. The one, flesh, has been condemned and is on its way out; they are to be done with that. Paul is cajoling them to live the real life of the Spirit.

2. Similarly, in Philippians 3:3, Paul warns against those who would insist on circumcision. He describes believers as those who serve "by the Spirit of God" and who put no confidence in "the flesh." Here "flesh" refers to self-confidence based on a presumed advantaged relationship with God evidenced by circumcision. But as noted in chapter 9 above, the Spirit also stands opposed to, by fulfillment, any form of Torah observance. Thus these too are basically eschatological realities. To revert to circumcision, that is, to

put "confidence in the flesh," is to go back to the way that has come to an end with the death and resurrection of Christ and the gift of the Spirit.

3. The strong contrasts in Romans 8:5-8 likewise do not deal with internal conflict. Paul is again describing the two kinds of existence, and indicating their utter incompatibility. Those who walk according to the flesh—and it is clear in context that this does not mean believers, but those still outside Christ—"have their minds set on what the flesh desires" (v. 5). Such a mind -set is hostile to God, does not—indeed, cannot—submit to God's law, cannot please God (how in the world could it?), and ends up in death. That simply does not describe the Christian life, not in Paul and not anywhere else.

The people of God, who walk according to the Spirit, live in bold contrast to flesh-walkers. Their minds are set on the things of the Spirit (their minds have been renewed by the Spirit, after all); in place of hostility to God, they live in peace; and instead of death, they know life.

That this is the conflict Paul describes is made certain in Romans 8:9, where he addresses his Christian readers: "but you" he says, "are *not in the flesh* [in the sense that the flesh-walkers in vv. 7-8 are], but in the Spirit (a whole new way of existence], since indeed the Spirit of God dwells in you ."

But Paul also recognizes that life in the Spirit is not just a stroll in the park. So in Romans 8:12-13 he applies all of vv. 1-11 to their lives, by reminding them that by the Spirit they must continue to kill that to which they have already died (the already/not yet again). They were formerly controlled by, and thus under obligation to, the flesh. Their new obligation is to the Spirit, to walk in his ways, led by him (v. 14).

Life in the Spirit is not passive; nor is obedience automatic. We continue to live in the real world; we are, after all, both already and not yet. Therefore, the imperative for the already is walk in/by the Spirit. That assumes that we live in a world very much controlled by the flesh; but it also assumes that we now live in that world as different people, led by the Spirit and empowered by the Spirit to produce the fruit of righteousness, rather than to continue in the works of the flesh.

That leads us finally to Galatians 5:17 and Romans 7:13-25. We begin with the latter, since it does not have to do with this contrast at all; and conclude by another look at the Galatians passage. . . .

The Struggle in Romans 7:13-25

What about the intense, deeply emotional narration of Paul's own internal conflict in Romans 7:13-25? Doesn't this passage suggest that Paul himself, even though a man of the Spirit, continually struggled in his inner person with the pull of the flesh? At first glance, and taking the passage out of context, one might think so. But three things reveal otherwise: the surrounding context, what Paul actually says, and what he does not say.

The context throughout has to do with the place of Torah in the Christian life. In vv. 1-6 Paul has made it clear, by repeating himself yet one more time, that the believer has no relationship to it at all. In the death of Christ we have died with respect to the law (v. 4). Not only so, he adds, but we have also died with respect to the flesh (vv. 5-6; note the past tense, "when we were in the flesh"). But Paul is also aware that he has been extremely hard on the law in his argument to this point, which will hardly sit well with his readers who are Jewish Christians. Besides, he does not really consider the law a bad thing—quite the contrary. His problem with the law was with its inadequacy, its helplessness to empower what it required.

So in vv. 7-25, he sets out to exonerate the law from any suggestion that, because it was implicated in our death, the law itself was a bad thing. To make this point, he argues in two ways. First, he says in vv. 7-12, what killed "me" (and "me" in this paragraph stands for all other Jews as well as for himself) was not the law but the innate sinfulness that the law aroused. The law is implicated in his "death," to be sure, but as an abettor, not as a direct cause.

This, too, could put the law in a bad light, so he starts all over again (v. 13), this time insisting that the law is not really to blame at all. Its fault lay in its helplessness to do anything about the sin it has aroused in us by making us vividly aware of sin's utter "sinfulness." This is said with great intensity, and in a way in which all who try to please God on the basis of law can empathize. In the final analysis it is a totally useless struggle. For the person under law, who has not experienced the gift of the Spirit, sin and the flesh are simply the stronger powers.

Enter Christ and the Spirit (Rom 8), as God's response to the anguished cry of 7:24. Not only is there no condemnation in Christ (that is, the judgment we all so richly deserve has been put into our past through the death of Christ), but we now live by a new "law," that of the Spirit of life (8:2).

What the law was unable to do, Christ has now done for us (positionally) and the Spirit "fulfills" in us (experientially) as we "walk in the Spirit" (vv. 3-4).

Three simple points, then, in conclusion:

1. What Paul describes throughout is what it was like to live under the law; and whatever else is true of the Christian Paul, he did not consider himself to be under the law. What he describes, from his now Christian perspective, is what it was like to live under law before Christ and the Spirit. The use of "I" and the present tense of the verbs only heighten the intensity of his feelings toward the utter helplessness of the law to do anything about the real problem of sin.

2. The person here described never wins. Being under the helpless law, in the face of the more powerful flesh and sin, means to be sold as a slave under sin, and thus incapable of doing the good thing the law demands. Such a description is absolutely incompatible with Paul's view of life in Christ, empowered by the Spirit.

3. There is not a single mention of the Spirit in the entire passage (vv. 7-25). The Spirit was last mentioned in v. 6, as the key to our new life in Christ, who has brought our relationship with the law and the flesh to an end. Christ and the Spirit are then picked up again in 8:1-2 as the divine response to the anguished cry of the person struggling with sin, but with the helpless law standing by, pointing out the sinfulness of our sin, unable to do anything about it.

Thus the only questions Paul himself raises in this entire passage have to do with Torah, whether it is good or evil, and, once this is affirmed as good, how this good thing is still implicated in our death. Life under Torah alone is under scrutiny.

Galatians 5:17 in Context

But what of Galatians 5:17, where Paul says (literally), "for the flesh has desires over against the Spirit, and the Spirit over against the flesh; for these two [realities] are in opposition to each other, so that whatever things you may wish [= feel like doing], these things you may not do"? Does this not indicate that there is an internal struggle of the Spirit against the flesh? In context, not so. In fact, this text is precisely in keeping with the texts previously looked at, where this contrast appears.

Verse 17 comes at the heart of an argument dealing with one urgent question: Since Torah observance is now a thing of the past because of the coming of Christ and the Spirit, what is to ensure righteousness? That is, Paul is arguing against (perhaps anticipating) Jewish Christian opposition that would see his bypassing Torah observance as a sure invitation to license and ungodliness. Indeed, as Romans 3:7-8 makes clear and Romans 6:1 implies, Paul has been charged with this very thing.

Paul takes up this question, typically, not in terms of the individual believer in a one-on-one relationship with God, but at the very point where the Galatians are living as they used to, when the flesh held sway. Paul therefore warns the Galatians not to let their new freedom in Christ serve as a base of operations for the flesh (5:13), meaning in this case to continue to engage in strife within the community of faith (v. 15). Rather, in love they are to "perform the duties of a slave to one another" (v. 13). For love like this "fulfills the law" (v. 14).

Paul's response to vv. 13 and 15 is vv. 16-26. He begins in v. 16 with the basic imperative—and promise. "Walk in the Spirit," he urges them, "and you will not carry out the desire of the flesh." Since this responds to v. 15, he is not talking about the inner life of the believers, but of giving in to ungodly behavior within the community. After all, the works of the flesh that follow, have to do with behavior, and eight of the fifteen items mentioned are sins of discord within the believing community.

Verse 17 functions to elaborate to elaborate v. 16, and does so by way of what has been said in vv. 13-15. The elaboration simply says what we have seen him say elsewhere: walking in the Spirit is incompatible with life according to the flesh, because these two are in utter opposition to one another. And because they are utterly incompatible, those who live in the Spirit may not do whatever they please, that is, their new freedom in Christ does not permit them to continue living as they used to, by eating and devouring one another.

Thus the flesh-Spirit contrast has to do with those who have entered the new way of life brought about by Christ and the Spirit; Paul is urging them to live this way by the power of the Spirit. His point is that the Spirit stands in opposition to the other way of living, and is fully capable of empowering one to live so. It is not that Paul does not care about the inner life; he does indeed. But here he cares especially that the way God's people live provide a radical alternative to the world around them. Those who so walk by the Spirit will not keep on destroying the Christian community through strife and conflict.

In all the passages where Paul sets the Spirit against the flesh he insists that through the death of Christ and the gift of the Spirit, the flesh has been mortally wounded—killed, in his language. It is not possible, therefore, that from Paul's perspective a Spirit person would be living in such a way that she or he is sold as a slave to sin, who is unable to do the good she or he wants to do because of being held prisoner to the law of sin.

Believers live between the times. The already mortally wounded flesh will be finally brought to its end at the coming of Christ. The Spirit, already a present possession, will be fully realized at the same coming. To the degree that the old age has not yet passed away, we still must learn to walk by the Spirit, to behave in keeping with the Spirit, and to sow to the Spirit. We can do so precisely because the Spirit is sufficient. In Paul's view, we live in the flesh, only in the sense of living in the present body of humiliation, subject to the realities of the present age; but we do not walk according to the flesh. Such a way of life belongs to the past, and those who live that way are outside Christ and "shall not inherit the [final eschatological] kingdom of God" (Gal 5:21).

Paul is always a realist. The "new righteousness" that fulfills Torah, effected by the Spirit, is itself both already and not yet. To return to the preceding chapter, the coming of the Spirit means that "divine infection," not divine perfection, has set in. Our lives are now led by the one responsible for inspiring the law in the first place. But that does not mean that God's people cannot still be "overtaken in a fault" (Gal. 6:1). The resolution of such between-the-times trespassing of God's righteous requirement is for the rest of God's Spirit people to restore such a one through the Spirit's gentleness. It means regularly to experience God's forgiveness and grace. It does not mean to accept constantly living in willful sin as inevitable, like a slow leak deflating our lives, as though the Spirit were not sufficient for life in the present.

If this explanation does not satisfy those of you who live in a constant struggle with some besetting sin, my word to you is to take heart from the gospel. I do not minimize the struggle. But you are loved by God, and that love has been "shed abroad in your heart by the Spirit." The key to life in the Spirit for some is to spend much more quiet time in thanksgiving and praise for what God has done—and is doing, and promises to do—and less time on introspection, focused on your failure to match up to the law.

Whenever you do feel like getting even for what someone has done to you rather than forgiving them as Christ has forgiven you, you are made to realize once more that you do still live between the times, between the time the infection set in and the perfection will be realized. But by the Spirit's leading, neither do you do whatever you wish—tear into somebody for what they have done to you—as you used to do without thinking. The Spirit, God's own presence—his *empowering* presence—is within, and will lead you into appropriate responses.

Finally, to bring this discussion full circle, here is where your being a member of the body comes in. Since the ultimate goal of salvation is for us individually to belong as a growing, contributing, edifying member of the people of God, others in the body exist for the same purpose, and thus should serve you in the same way. Don't try to be a lone ranger Christian, slugging it out on your own. Seek out those in the community to whom you can be accountable and let them join you in your desire to grow into Christ's likeness.

21

Some Rules for Living a Holy Life

Johann Arndt

Johann Arndt (1555-1621) was born at Ballenstedt, in Anhalt, Germany. While he was in school, studying medicine and the sciences, he became quite sick with a painful disease. His physicians gave him no hope for recovery. At that juncture he vowed that if God would heal him, he would devote his life to the Lord's service. He recovered and kept his word. At that time, not only were reformers at odds with the Roman Church, they were quarreling with one another. Some of the changes in Arndt's life were the direct result of these theological differences.

Arndt was concerned that theologians taught Christians to put too much emphasis on the legal achievement of Christ on the cross while neglecting the necessary heart change which alone could make a true Christian. Consequently, he encouraged his contemporaries to worship from the heart. They must have a "practical Christianity." His large book of meditations and prayers, *Sechs Böcher vom Wahren Christentum*, ("Four Books Concerning True Christianity") was widely read. His writings influenced John Wesley, who published an edited volume of Arndt's *True Christianity*.

"Exercise thyself unto godliness. For godliness is profitable unto all things, having promise of the life that now is, and of that which is to come" (1 Tim. 4:7-8).

In this apostolical sentence is contained a brief description of a Christian's life, and of the main study about which he is employed, namely, the study of godliness, or of Christian piety, which comprehends in it the whole train of Christian virtues. The apostle makes use of two motives to recommend this heavenly study and the constant practice of it. First, says he, "Godliness is profitable unto all things." Godliness is of most admirable service, as soon as our words and actions are influenced by it. It renders the whole life acceptable to God, and useful to our neighbor. The second motive is, because godliness is accompanied with a gracious reward both in this life, as appears from the examples of Joseph, of Daniel, and of others, as well as in the life to come; where we shall reap without ceasing, provided we do not faint while we dwell here (Gal. 6:9). For our better encouragement in the practice of piety, let us endeavor to keep in remembrance the following rules and considerations.

1. If you cannot live up to that degree of holiness which the Word of God requires, and which you yourself desire, yet you must never cease ardently to wish for it; for such holy breathings are always acceptable to God. God does not so much regard the outward action of a man, as the heart whence the action proceeds. But after all, never neglect to crucify the flesh, and never permit it to rule over you.

2. In all that you think and do, be careful to preserve the purity of your heart. Set a watch over it, lest you be defiled with proud thoughts, words, or actions, with wrath, or other such works of the flesh, and of the devil. Sin opens the door to the devil, and shuts the heart against God.

3. Study continually to maintain the Christian liberty of your soul. Do not allow yourself to be enslaved, or brought into bondage, by any inordinate love of the creature, or of the things of this world. Consider the value of your soul, which certainly is of a more noble nature than this present perishing world. Why should you degrade it so far as to subject it to the frail, base, and frivolous things of this life?

5. Beware of the care and sorrow of this world, because it produces death (2 Cor. 7:10). As worldly sorrow begets death, so godly sorrow begets life, and lays up an eternal treasure! Worldly sorrow springs from avarice and envy, from excessive care, from unbelief and impatience, and other temporal sources. Godly sorrow proceeds from a knowledge of your sins,

and those eternal punishments which follow them. This sorrow produces many salutary effects in a penitent soul, and "works repentance to salvation, not to be repented of" being attended with spiritual joy, and solid peace or tranquility of mind. No loss of a temporal kind ought to afflict you so much as the remembrance of your sins, by which you have offended the infinite goodness of God.

5. If you cannot bear your cross with joy and cheerfulness, yet take it at least with patience and humility, and acquiesce calmly in the divine will and providence. For, truly, the will of God is always good; nor does it intend anything but your benefit and salvation. Whatever, therefore, God shall be pleased to appoint you in his wisdom, gratefully accept it, and be either joyful or sorrowful, poor or rich, high or low, vile or excellent, as he orders your lot. Let this saying always be in your mind: "Thus it seems good unto God, and so it must need be expedient and useful for me also. His will, not mine, be done." Let not that, therefore, which pleases God, displease you; but rather rejoice that all things are ordered according to His pleasure and your salvation. Remember that "the Lord is righteous in all his ways, and holy in all his works" (Ps. 145:17). Hence it is but just that the will of God should be done, because it is always good and profitable, and that your own will should be subdued and unaccomplished, because it is always evil and hurtful.

6. Whenever the Lord visits your soul with heavenly joy, accept the same with gratitude and humility. But when he is pleased to withdraw the comfortable light of his presence, then consider that the mortification of the flesh must be of greater profit to you than exalted joy in the spirit. Through overmuch spiritual joy, many fall into spiritual pride. But whatever causes mortification and sorrow, is far more useful in subduing the flesh, than that which is delightful and pleasing to nature. The Lord best knows whom to lead in a pleasant and agreeable path, and who are to be brought through an unpleasant, stony, and difficult way. Always esteem it best to arrive at thy journey's end by that way which divine Wisdom has chosen for you, however different it may be from your own choice, or from the devices of your own heart. Remember, that "sorrow is better than laughter;" and that "by the sadness of the countenance the heart is made better." And if

you will be wise, trust to the experience of the wise man, who tells you furthermore, that "the heart of the wise is in the house of mourning; but the heart of fools is in the house of mirth" (Ecc. 7:3-4).

7. Make an offering to God of all that you have and undertake. If you cannot bring offerings of a high and exalted devotion, of prayer, of thanksgiving, and of other similar acts of religion, offer at least what you have, with a good will, and a fervent desire. Wish, at least, that it may prove acceptable unto the Lord; for to have such a desire, or to be willing to have it, is no contemptible offering, but is very agreeable to the kindness of God. In what measure you desire to offer up your devotion, your prayer and praise, in that measure God accepts the same. He requires no more at your hands than he himself works in you by his grace; nor can you return him more than he has first conferred on you.

In the meantime, entreat the Lord Jesus that he would graciously please to supply what is defective in you, by his own more perfect oblation and sacrifice. Because he, and he only, is the perfection of our imperfect worship and service. Say, therefore, in faith: "O my God, and my Father, I beseech you, let my devotion, my prayer, and thanksgiving, together with all the acts of my faith and worship, be graciously accepted by you in your beloved Son, Jesus Christ. Esteem them, not according to what they are in themselves, but according to what they are made by the merit of the all-sufficient sacrifice offered up by your Son. O look upon that, and upon all that he has wrought for me in the flesh; and as his most perfect works must be pleasing to you, so let mine also be acceptable to you for his sake. He, O my God, shall abundantly make up whatever is defective in me."

By this means, our devotion, our prayer, and thanksgiving, how imperfect, weak, and obscure they may be in themselves, acquire a certain luster, worth, and dignity derived from the merit of Christ, whereby our works are rendered acceptable to the Lord. As a naked and unclean infant is offensive to everyone that sees it, but becomes sweet and lovely when it is thoroughly cleansed, and covered with fine linen, in like manner, all the works which you do in your *natural* state, are polluted with sin, and of no account before God; but no sooner are you covered with the perfection of Christ (Isa. 61:10), than your works are acceptable to God. As fruit, which is not valuable in itself, surprises the spectator into a love of it, when served up in vessels of precious gold, so our prayers and acts of devotion, though of no account in themselves, are exalted in Jesus Christ, in whom, as in the beloved, we are made accepted with God (Eph. 1:6).

8. If your sins and manifold frailties (as they should do), make you sad, yet let them not lead you to despair. If they be many in number, remember that there is yet more mercy with Christ, and "plenteous redemption with him" (Ps. 130:7). If your imperfections be ever so great, remember that Christ's merits are yet greater, and say with the royal penitent: "Have mercy upon me, O Lord, according to the multitude of thy tender mercies!" (Ps. 51:1). And when, by the grace of God, you truly repent, and behold Christ Jesus, that great sacrifice for sin, then God himself relents of the evil which was to be inflicted upon you; and absolution and remission of sin instantly follow so good and salutary a sorrow (Ezek. 18:23; 33:11).

As the leper, upon his application to Christ was immediately delivered from his evil, so is also the penitent sinner. No sooner did he say, "Lord, if you will, you can make me clean," than Christ freely replied: "I will; be clean" (Matt. 8:2-3). So also the merciful God, inwardly and in the spirit, makes you clean, comforts you, and says: "Be of good cheer; your sins are forgiven you" (Matt. 9:2). This wonderful mercy of the Lord in cleansing and absolving you of your sins, as it is forcibly represented by the example of that leper, so it ought by no means to give you an occasion to sin the more, but to love God the more, and to say, "Bless the Lord, O my soul; and all that is within me bless his holy name" (Ps. 103:1).

9. Let not injuries, reproaches, and revilings provoke you at any time to wrath, indignation, or revenge; but rather take them as so many trials of your heart, and of the inward state of your soul. Hereby God designs to prove you, that it may appear what is hidden within, and whether meekness and humility, or wrath and pride, sway your mind. For that which lies concealed in a man, is stirred up and made manifest by reproaches and provocations. If, therefore, your heart be endued with meekness and lowliness, you will easily bear contempt and injuries; nay, you will accept them as so many paternal chastisements designed for the good of your soul.

Moreover, you must consider that contempt and reproaches are part of the chastisements which the Almighty sends, and you should patiently bear whatever the Lord shall be pleased to allot to you. "Let us go forth," says the apostle, "unto him, bearing his reproach" (Heb. 13:13). Behold with what lowliness of heart did he undergo the affronts of a profane world! And should not we submit to the same with meekness, and with an unshaken evenness of mind? Say not then, "Should I suffer these things from so contemptible a fellow as this?" But rather submit, in consideration of that patient and meek spirit which was in Christ, and displayed itself in his whole life and conduct.

Lastly, consider the kindness of God toward those that suffer for his sake. So faithful is he, and so kind to those that bear any disgrace on his account, that he confers the greater marks of honor and favor upon them. Thus David, when Shimei vented his malice upon him, took it for a pledge that God would bestow a token of great honor upon him; and this accordingly came to pass. "It may be," says he, "that the Lord will look on my affliction, and that the Lord will requite me good for his cursing this day," and turn his curse into a blessing (2 Sam. 16:12). Be not, therefore, at all disturbed at the evil report that wicked men may raise against you; but rejoice rather, since the Spirit of glory rests on those that are reproached for the name of Christ (1 Peter 4:14).

10. Study to overcome and to pacify your enemies, by bestowing upon them tokens of love and kindness. No man will ever be reconciled by wrath, or revenge, or returning evil for evil, for victory consists in virtue, not in vice. And as one devil does not drive out another, so it cannot be expected that one evil should be subdued by another, or that enmity against you should be extinguished by affronts and provocations offered by you. A man that is full of sores and bruises is not likely to be healed by the addition of more blows; and if he be so mad as to beat and to cut himself, he is to be pitied, and to be treated with the greater kindness and leniency. In like manner, if a man be full of spiritual distemper, and of hatred, he is to be handled with the more love and gentleness, if, perhaps, by such lenient means as these, he may be softened into a better temper. Consider the method which God himself uses for overcoming our natural obstinacy. Does he not conquer our malice with his goodness, and our wrath with his love? And does he not invite us to repentance by many endearing marks of love and benignity? (Rom. 2:4). This method is prescribed by St. Paul: "Be

not," says he, "overcome of evil, but overcome evil with good" (Rom. 12:21). This is victory indeed.

11. When you observe that God has adorned your neighbor with gifts above you, take heed not to envy him on that account, but rather rejoice and give thanks to God for the same. Consider, that since all true believers make up together but one body, it must needs follow, that the beauty of every member is communicated to the whole body, and to every member thereof. On the other hand, when you perceive the misery of your neighbor, lament over it as if it were your own, considering that the condition of all men is equally subject to evil, and that misery and affliction are the lot of mankind. Christ has also set you here an example. And, truly, whoever does not commiserate and sympathize with the misery of his neighbor, let him pretend to be what he may, he is no living member of the body of Christ. For did not Christ look upon our misery as his own, and by be compassionate toward our deplorable state, deliver us from all our miseries? This mutual love and sympathy are inculcated by St. Paul: "Bear ye one another's burdens," says he, "and so fulfil the law of Christ" (Gal. 6:2).

12. As for love and hatred in relation to your neighbor, make the following distinction. It is but fit that you should hate his vices and crimes as the very works of the devil; but then, beware of hating the person while you abhor his sin. On the contrary, it is your duty to bewail the case of your neighbor, who, being carried away by so many irregular passions, enjoys no solid rest in his soul. Offer up his cause to God, and pray for him, as Christ did for his enemies when he was nailed to the cross (Luke 23:34). Do not, therefore, hate any man, but hate his vices only; for whosoever hates a man, and seeks his ruin, can in no wise be pleasing to God, since it is the very nature of God to be kind, and to desire that "all men should be saved, and come unto the knowledge of the truth" (1 Tim. 2:4). This was also the end for which Christ took our flesh upon him. He came into the world, "not to destroy men's lives, but to save them" (Luke 9:56).

13. Consider all men as being frail and imperfect, but none as more frail and imperfect than yourself; for before God, all men stand equally guilty, and there is no difference. We have all sinned, and have thereby been de-

prived of the image of God, and of all the glory which attended it (Rom. 3:23). How great a sinner, therefore, your neighbor may be, never fondly persuade yourself, that you are better before God. Remember this warning of the apostle: "Let him that thinks he stands, take heed lest he fall" (1 Cor. 10:12). He that makes himself the lowest of all men, is in the fairest way of being preserved, by the grace of God, unto salvation. And certain it is, that thou stand no less in need of the grace and mercy of God, than the greatest of sinners. Where there is a great measure of humility, there is also a great measure of grace. Wherefore St. Paul accounted himself the "chief of sinners" (1 Tim. 1:15); and it was in this order he obtained mercy, and had so much longsuffering bestowed upon him. And in another place he declares that he will glory in nothing but in "his infirmities, that the power of Christ might rest upon him" (2 Cor. 12:9).

14. True illumination is always accompanied with a contempt of the things of the world. As the children of the world have their inheritance here upon earth, so the children of God have theirs laid up above in heaven. The treasures which the children of this world have chiefly at heart are temporal honors, perishing riches, earthly splendor and glory. But the treasures of the children of God are poverty and contempt, persecution and reproach, the cross and death, trouble and sorrow. Thus did Moses prefer "the reproach of Christ before the treasures in Egypt" and the affliction of the people of God, before the pleasures of sin (Heb. 11:25-26).

15. Remember, that by the name of a Christian written in heaven is intimated that solid, practical knowledge of Christ which is grounded in faith, and by which we are transplanted into Christ. From this knowledge flow all the living virtues which the Lord will praise in the great day of retribution (Matt. 25:34f). He will then also bring to light all those treasures which we have laid up in heaven (1 Tim. 6:19), together with all such works as have been wrought in God (John 3:21). Never has a saint lived upon earth, but he has been particularly eminent in one virtue or other, and this virtue shall never be forgotten (Ps. 112:6). Whether it is faith, love, mercy, patience, or any other virtue in the practice of which he has been so conspicuous, it shall make up that eternal name which is written in heaven (Rev. 2:17; 3:12). This will be the note and character of the saints, and their eternal memorial be-

22

Pressing On to the Mark!

Erich Sauer

Erich Sauer (1898-1959) was a masterful German evangelical theologian and teacher. His scholarly writings, written with a devotional touch, have warmed the hearts of thousands of God's people. Four of his books, *The Dawn of World Redemption, The Triumph of the Crucified,* and *From Eternity to Eternity,* and *In the Arena of Faith,* have had a wide circulation.

Sauer was born in Berlin, Germany, and died in Wiedenest, at age 60. He was raised in the Open Brethren Church, to which both his parents belonged. He taught in a Bible school in Wiedenest from sometime in the 1930s until his death.

⁓⊸⊸⊸

"Wherefore lift up the hands that hang down, and the palsied knees; and make straight paths for your feet, that that which is lame be not turned out of the way; but rather be healed. Follow after peace with all men, and the sanctification without which no man shall see the Lord: Looking carefully lest there be any man that falleth short of the grace of God; lest any root of bitterness springing up trouble you, and thereby the many be defiled (or poisoned)" (Heb. 12:12-15).

Christianity is eternity in time. With the appearance of Christ a new sprig was planted into the withered ground of the world of man. And all who have been grafted into it have become partakers of eternal life. Thus Christians have found the fountain of eternal youth. The genuine life of faith never grows old. "Though our outward man is decaying, yet our inward man

231

is renewed day by day" (2 Cor. 4:16). "They that wait upon the Lord shall renew their strength; they shall mount up with wings as eagles; they shall run, and not be weary; they shall walk, and not faint" (Isa. 40:31). A really healthy life of faith is like one running in an arena whose freshness of the starting-post is maintained to the finish.

And yet! The Christians of the *Letter to the Hebrews* had grown tired. After a richly blessed start (Heb. 10:32) their inward life had begun to droop. Their hands were hanging down and their knees had become feeble (Heb. 12:12). The attendance at their gatherings had decreased (Heb. 10:25). Their life of faith was no longer to be compared to running in an arena but rather to the slow and painful walk of a sick or paralyzed person. Instead of looking towards the goal, they began to turn their eyes to times gone by. Instead of looking forward to the consummation at the coming of Christ, they looked backward to the Old Testament ages of preparation. Instead of considering the glories of the Spirit and the fulfilment of all prophecy in Christ's person and work, they began to yearn for the types and symbols of the divine service of the Old Covenant which they had known as so beautiful and impressive. So the glory of grace had become darkened for them. It appeared desirable to them to return to the law. The danger of "being hardened" had arisen (Heb. 3:13). Indeed, they had even to be told: "Take heed, brethren, lest there be in any one of you an evil heart of unbelief, in falling away from the living God" (Heb. 3:12).

How can they be helped?

Only by renewed contact with the Fountain of power. The exceeding glory and reality of the New Testament salvation must come before their minds and hearts as a fresh vision. They must be brought to acknowledge that leaving the ground of grace means robbing oneself; returning to the old is sinking into the depth, turning back to the past is losing the future. Only grace can lead to the goal. Only the New Testament type of salvation can guarantee the promised eternal glory.

For this reason the main purpose of Hebrews is, as to its essence, a message of "re-formation." No doubt the Letter to the Hebrews contains a good deal of doctrine. In fact, it is the document of the New Testament which gives us the deepest insight into the inward relationships of preparation and fulfilment, of shadow and reality, of Old Testament sacrifices and the New Testament priesthood of Christ. But the chief object is not that of instruction but of renewal, not that of doctrinal presentation but of practical restoration, not that of leading the readers for the first time into the knowledge of full salvation, but rather that of leading them back to that which they had already acknowledged and experienced from the very start of their Christian life. Here the reader is not encouraged to lay hold on salvation but rather to hold it fast. It is not so much the matter of being "formed" as of being "re-formed."

For this reason Hebrews is, within the New Testament, the sister letter to the Epistle to the Galatians. In both letters the purpose is the same. They are the main "re-formatory" epistles of the New Testament.

In the Galatian letter, as also in the Hebrews, people are dealt with who were in danger of falling back from the New Testament heights of salvation to the Old Testament introductory stages of Divinely revealed history. The main difference is that the Galatian Christians were originally heathen who had since come under wrong Hebrew-Christian influences, while the leaders of the Letter to the Hebrews were Israelites who had accepted the Messiah, perhaps even priests or Levites (Acts 6:7).

This made a different type of presentation of thought necessary.

"Law and grace" is the theme of both letters. But the Galatian letter treats it with special reference to the moral laws of the Mosaic dispensation, while the Hebrews speaks especially of its ceremonial laws. The Galatian letter refers chiefly to jurisdiction, Hebrews to worship and cult (Divine Service).

In Galatians, Paul points out that it is not allowable in law to alter testamentary documents which have already been officially recognized (Gal. 3:15-20), and he speaks of legal forms of the educational system of antiquity (Gal. 3:23-29), and of the respective legal position of slaves and of sons before they become of age (Gal. 4:1-7). So the Galatian letter uses pictures and comparisons taken more from the legal practice, but Hebrews (especially chs. 5-10) refers more to the symbolical language of the Old Testament forms of Divine Service, to priesthood, sacrifice, tabernacle. Galatians places us more in a law court, Hebrews in a temple.

But the theme is the same: the relationship of law to grace, the greater glory of grace, freely bestowed, and, as the result of this, the holy demand and serious warning: Never go back! "Hold that fast which thou hast, that no one take thy crown" (Rev.3:11).

Paralyzing Powers

How did it come about that the Hebrew Christians lost their original freshness of faith? How happy they had been at the beginning! What would they not have done for Christ in those early days? They received into their houses the persecuted witnesses of Christ (Heb. 10:34). They endured personally all sorts of indignities and trials (Heb. 10:33). Even the loss of their possessions on account of their Christian confession they had endured, and had done it not only without complaining, but, indeed, with rejoicing. "Ye took joyfully the spoiling of your goods" (Heb. 10:34).

And now everything had become different. Instead of the former freshness and vigor, their hands hung down; instead of marching manfully onwards, a paralysis had set in. They no longer pressed on, running on the racecourse, but had halted, and indeed were in danger of stagnation. In fact many had definitely become backsliders (Heb. 12:12-13). The enemy had begun his work of inducing paralysis.

1. *The external difficulties* had been used by him in order to weaken and to eliminate these joyful witnesses of God. Again and again they had to meet with bitter hatred against Christ. Continually the world mocked at and despised them. Ever and again outward loss, social ostracism, and injury in their business or professional standing made them feel the lack of legal rights. By all this the enemy had been able to wear them down. It was not the first shock of suffering that brought him this success but the continuing pressure of persecution.

However, the extremity of persecution had not yet been reached. Martyrs' blood had not yet flowed. And this fact is used by the writer of the Hebrews letter to encourage them: "ye have not yet resisted unto blood, striving against sin" (Heb. 12:4). This is not intended to mean that "You have not yet taken seriously enough the struggle against your own sin which is within yourselves. You have not yet shown sufficient energy of faith, readiness for service, devotion, initiative, and resolution in your personal sanctification." But the sin which is spoken of here is the persecuting might of the enemy and the world which approaches from outside. It is meant not as the subjective, but as the objective power of evil, of the enmity of the world; so that the meaning is that "the battle has not yet become so fierce that some of you have had to die for the sake of the testimony of

Christ." So far there has not been shedding of blood. Though the situation was hard enough, they had thus far been spared the hardest of all.

But they must remember that others had made this supreme sacrifice! The immediately preceding chapter, Hebrews 11, had spoken of those who had been "stoned" or "sawn asunder," who had been tortured, or put to death by the sword, and who had accepted no deliverance, though they could have obtained it easily, if only by one word or one action they had denied their faith (Heb. 11:35-37). But they refused to do this in order "that they might obtain a better resurrection" than such an earthly deliverance, which last might have been comparable to a "resurrection" by being immediately freed from prison and martyrdom. And now, though certainly recognizing the seriousness of your present situation, how much less are your difficulties! Therefore do not overestimate your hardships!

And have we today not much more reason to keep in mind this same exhortation? What are our sufferings for the testimony compared with those of many men and women in the glorious history of the heroes of the church of former times?

In the course of my travels I have often visited places where Christians in times gone by suffered death for their faith. Think of the dreadful subterranean prison cells hewn into the frightful fortress of the Spilberg in Brünn (Moravia). Or think of Prague, where 27 crosses, composed of small stones in the pavement in front of the old Town Hall, remind us today of the "Bloody Judgment" of Prague (1620, two years after the beginning of the Thirty Years' War). Small paving-stones mark also the exact spot of the scaffold on which the 27 leaders of the Protestants were beheaded. They are in the form of a large crown of thorns, with two long, crossed judgment swords. Think of the cells of the Bloody Tower on the Thames in London, where one can still see under glass plates verses of the Bible and comforting words which were carved into the walls by those men in the times of their greatest distress. Or I think of the marketplace in Florence where the gallows and stake of the great Italian forerunner of the Reformation, Savonarola, stood. I remember walking through the catacombs of ancient Rome, with the secret meeting places of the early Christians during the times of the persecutions, and in the arena of the Coliseum in Rome where hundreds of witnesses to the faith in the second and third centuries allowed themselves to be torn in pieces by wild animals. Only a few years ago I stood in the evening twilight in the graveyard of the Scottish town of Kilmarnock at the side of the graves of seven whose blood was shed about 300 years ago for their unflinching stand for their biblical evangelical faith. Just before this we had held an open-air meeting in the marketplace of the town at which I had opportunity to give my testimony. The place where we stood with our gospel caravan and loudspeaker was very significant to me. It was just over against the spot where the Covenanter, John Lisbet, was executed in 1688 (14th of April), a man who had pledged himself not to deny the biblical covenant of faith and who had been willing to suffer the sentence of death. Here again the exact spot where the gallows stood is marked by special small paving stones. Many of these heroic Scottish Covenanters signed with their own blood their "covenant" never to deny Christ or His word. And now we stood on exactly the same spot and proclaimed exactly the same message for the sake of which this man had laid down his life. Afterwards I went with a Scottish friend to an old, historic cemetery. The stars had already come out and quietly we stood at the gravesides of seven others of these witnesses of Christ. Special framed inscriptions show the site.

How small and feeble one feels, standing on such spots! A feeling of veneration and reverence comes over one for these heroes of God in whom the might of Christ was so powerful! Those were men and women for whom Christ meant more than their own life. And we ourselves are often so timid and do not give a clear testimony. How often we tend to make compromises! How easily we are afraid of being put at a disadvantage, or of not being promoted in life and profession, or of having to hear a sarcastic remark or getting a superior look, a shrug of the shoulders, or even only to be smiled or laughed at. But the Lord wants fighters, men who really sacrifice themselves for His interests, men who have counted the cost of true Christianity and who are prepared to pay it. In truth we are in the same position as the Hebrew Christians: we have not yet resisted unto blood. Blood has not yet been demanded from us. Therefore we must not overestimate the difficulties which we take upon ourselves for Christ's sake. On the other hand, come what may, we want to be ready for anything.

The real reason, however, for the signs of fatigue, noticeable amongst the Hebrew Christians, was not so much their externally difficult situation, but their internal reaction to it. Inwardly they had become weak. And therein lay the real root of the danger of their failure.

2. *Inward weakness and signs of fatigue.* Their prayer life had slackened, the numbers at their gatherings had decreased, and their spiritual energy had fallen off. They were to be compared to a pilgrim who had roused himself to leave the "City of Destruction" in order to go to the heavenly Jerusalem but who had become tired and weary on the way and could now only force himself forward with "feeble knees" (Heb. 12:12).

Their actions and ambitions were no more those of the athlete in a race. They were in danger of giving up the battle altogether. No longer were they runners who were "pressing on." Old attractions of their former worship which had long since been eclipsed, and had lost their glory by Christ having risen as the Sun in their hearts, began to shine again. Their whole life of sanctification had become problematic, and with this also their attaining the radiant goal and their abundant entry into the high glories of their heavenly calling. So that it was necessary to exhort them: "Follow (lit., pursue) . . . the sanctification without which no man shall see the Lord" (Heb.12:14). Run in the race (v. 1).

And what shall we do? It is not our task to rebuke these Hebrew Christians. Is it not a fact that the picture of their situation is far too often an exact description of our own inward state? What about our own zeal? How often do we go to hear God's Word and to pray? Do we regularly take part in the prayer meetings of our churches and assemblies, striving together by prayer in the battle of the Lord? If we do not, our knees are "paralyzed." Does peace rule among us? Do we watch over our fellow-pilgrims to help them in love? Is it our earnest desire to be a blessing to others? If this is not the case we have ourselves grown weary. All quarrelling among believers is a sign of spiritual slackness. Instead of our making use of all our energies in the front line of battle, the enemy has succeeded in getting *agents* of his demoniac power behind our lines and these inspire divisions amongst us, so that valuable energy is spent in this battle dealing with the *partisans* behind the front lines.

How can all this be overcome? This faint condition without victory can never be the normal state of a sound Christian!

Here only continual reformation can help—only an ever renewed and fresh vision of Christ, only keener devotion and increased practical surrender of our life to our Lord. "Let us look unto Jesus!"

Quickening Powers

"Therefore lift up the hands which hang down, and the feeble (lit., paralyzed) knees."

The picture at the beginning of our chapter is perhaps still valid. One cannot "run" in the arena of faith, "pursue" and press on to the goal of sanctification—as in the very next verses we are called to do—if our knees are feeble and our hands hang down. For "wrestling matches" require strong hands, and "athletic races" demand knees which do not grow tired.

Thus a real and manly renewal of strength in the power of God is required. With verve, indeed even with rhythm, is this brought out in the poetical language of the verse in which this renewal is demanded. The author of this passage becomes quite poetical in his exhortation, clothing it in the original language in the form of a Greek hexameter. As with a clarion trumpet call he wakes up the sleepers and the lingerers:

And make straight paths for your feet,
Lest that which is lame be turned out of the way,
But let it rather be healed.

Looking unto Jesus gives us renewed freshness. The fatigue disappears. The paralysis is overcome. Those who have strayed from the way or who are wounded are "healed" (Heb. 12:12-13). New courage and confidence fills our souls. We get the right standard to estimate our troubles. We do take them seriously; but we no longer overestimate them. Overestimation of difficulties is always a sign of fatigue. But looking unto Jesus brings strength. Only from His hand can we receive the true yardstick. After all, the extent of our sufferings is not appointed and destined by the enemy but by the Lord. Golgotha proves that God loves us, and should not God, who did not spare His only begotten Son, give us with Him all things? (Rom. 8:32). Thus we gain new courage, and looking away to the great Immanuel, the eternal "God with us," who suffered for us on the cross and won the victory, we receive new joy, and we experience the truth of the prophet's word: "The Lord thy God in the midst of thee is mighty" or, literally translated: "Yahweh, thy God, is in thy midst, a saving hero-warrior." "Light is sown for the righteous, and gladness for the upright in heart" (Ps. 97:11).

Looking unto Jesus gives us peacefulness and fellowship. All strife wears us out. Conflicts between the redeemed rob us of our verve. All self-seeking controversy about things of but illusory value consumes spiritual energy. This is the connection between the necessity to overcome all signs of fatigue and the exhortation: "Follow (pursue) peace with all men" (Heb. 12:14).

By the word "follow on, pursue eagerly" (Gk. *diokete*), the writer of Hebrews resumes the picture of the race from the beginning of the chapter. Paul uses this same word twice in Philippians 3, where he describes the Christian life as a holy race in such detail as he does in no other portion of his epistles: "I press on! . . . I press on! (Gk. *dioko . . . dioko*) toward the goal unto the prize" (vv. 12-14). Just as Paul in Philippians 3, had in view the final end, the heavenly prize, so the writer of Hebrews regards here the leading of a life of peace with all men as an immediate object necessary to reaching that final object. "The believer is to be as zealous in walking in peace as the racer is to secure the crown. In a world marked by greed and contention this is indeed a strenuous affair. It will not be obtained haphazard, but only by such as pursue it as an all-worthy, all-desirable object, and who make every sacrifice to secure it" (G. H. Lang).

Difficulties amongst believers can always be overcome. Looking unto the Reconciler makes us conciliatory. There is no time to quarrel but rather to love. "Let us look unto Jesus."

"Peace" is here classed together with sanctification. "Pursue peace with all men, and the sanctification without which no man shall see the Lord." Striving after peace brings with it a right attitude towards our fellow-men, striving after holiness a right attitude towards God. Peace gives unity and fellowship here below; holiness arises out of fellowship with the Lord who is above. Both are indispensable. But neither peace nor sanctification are to be won without effort and diligence. Both are attained only by steadfast "running." Therefore: "Press on!"

"Peace," in the full meaning of the biblical word, is more than mere absence of strife. Peace is harmony, inward working together, being tuned in to one another, heart fellowship, love.

The church was born out of eternal love. She owes her life to the act of love on Golgotha. She lives by love and is therefore also ordained to live in love. Love is one-mindedness, a desire for fellowship, the highest form of inward unity and heart-felt oneness. Where this love does not exist, all outward formal unity is mere self-deception and lifeless pretense.

We believe in the one holy, universal church. There is one foundation—the sacrifice of Golgotha; there is one power of God in her—the indwelling of the Holy Spirit. There is one object and goal—the rapture and the perfecting. There is one Lord and Master—Jesus Christ, our common Redeemer. Therefore we must also be of one mind in our attitude of love, and, regardless of all the differences amongst us, we must find the way of peace with each other. We must cultivate practical unity, offer one another the right hand of fellowship and receive one another as Christ received us.

Loving is, however, not simply "loving at a distance" by means of which one imagines oneself to be in fellowship with all the world, but at the same time forgetting to seek the brother who is one's neighbor. This notion of love is very nebulous. We must guard against thinking more of the absent ones than those who are present with us.

Love is not simply a "denominational affair." It is not enough to be enthusiastic for showing unity and fellowship between the various circles of believers, but at the same time not being able to have real fellowship with the individual child of God. Love is nothing sentimental or merely a matter of feeling. It is not something vague and indefinite, but something very real. Love is will, is practical action, is the purposeful energy of God, is the manifestation of God's world in the midst of the world here below.

Love seeks the brother. Love believes in the work of Christ in his soul, and we must humble ourselves deeply and, in repentance before God and men, confess that we have often been too slow in this seeking of our brother, and that, with all our faith in God, in this sense we have often been too unbelieving in our belief.

Love is able to bury old strife between brethren. Love can forget the dark past and make a new start. Love kills, in the power of the life of God, all fatal division. Love is the soul of all peace and fellowship amongst believers. Love brings together. Love unites the hearts and leads to fellowship in work at home and abroad, in our own assemblies and churches as well as on the mission field. Love leads to combined effort in order to reach the great aims of God.

Every one of your fellow-men is to be compared to a mirror. He reflects what is confronting or shining upon him. Every unkindness on your part causes a shadow on his face, even if only for a second; but every act of love brings out brightness in the expression of his countenance, and this brightness will shine back into your own heart. "Through service to joy!"—this word of old Father Bodelschwingh may well be engraved in our own hearts, wills, and souls.

Love and service are forces which draw hearts nearer together. People who are cold always feel cold; people who are warmhearted create a warm atmosphere around them. In what sort of a relationship do you stand to your surroundings? Do you feel yourself being treated coldly or warmly by the others? Seek to a great extent in your own heart the reason for the answer to this question.

Our pursuit of peace and holiness enables us at the same time to serve others. Here again the relationships in the biblical text are very dear and deep: "Pursue peace with all men, and the sanctification . . . looking diligently lest any man fall short of the grace of God " (Heb. 12:14-15). Only he who strives after holiness, and tries to live in harmony with his neighbors, has the authority and capacity to serve others. Only service which is done in this attitude of mind has any chance of being fruitful. And this leads to a further consideration.

Looking unto Jesus brings new commissions. Our eyes begin to see the needs and distresses round about us. We recognize our responsibility that we should be active in helping those around us insofar as they have become feeble, tired, and paralyzed. We begin to see the necessity and possibility of mutual brotherly care and discipline. Looking to the greatest proof of love which ever has been given by love in the history of the whole universe, opens our eyes to the necessity, the privilege, and the many opportunities of ourselves giving practical proofs of watchful love and selfless service in mutual spiritual and bodily care for one another. Looking unto Jesus gives us a new outlook upon the world. It opens our eyes. "Look diligently!" "Lift up the hands which hang down and the feeble knees!"

In the context it is obvious that not so much the hands and knees of the readers themselves are meant, as if they are exhorted to make a fresh decision in order to get new freshness and life, but it speaks of the hands and knees of others. The readers are expected to be a help for the reviving of these others, "that that which is lame be not turned out of the way; but rather be healed. . . . Strengthen ye the weak hands and confirm the feeble knees. Say to them that are of a fearful heart, Be strong! Fear not! " This passage, taken from the prophets and here quoted in Hebrews, is the background of our exhortation (Isa. 35:3-4).

There may be many in your neighborhood who are spiritually lame and weary. Keep in mind that you ought to be the means in God's hands of their restoration and revival. Do not pass by their external and internal need. Your eyes ought to see their dangers. Looking unto Jesus sharpens our eyesight concerning the distresses of our brethren. "Look carefully lest there be any man that falls short of the grace of God; lest any root of bitterness springing up trouble you, and thereby the many be defiled; lest there be any fornicator or profane person, as Esau" (Heb. 12:15-16). "Let us consider one another to provoke unto love and good works" (Heb. 10:24).

In this spirit of love let us become active Christians. We must awake from our sleep of pious self-centered idleness. It is not enough to affirm the commandment of God with mere feelings. Our Christian life must have muscles. Our strength must become evident in everyday life. God and the world want to see actions.

But work costs effort. He who shuns the heat of the day is no workman. The man who only sits on the spectator's seat will never become victor. During the race in the arena all our energy must be mobilized. Even in ordinary human life it is a true saying, "What is worth doing at all is worth doing well." Work that we do for others but that does not cost us anything, is scarcely worth doing. Thus Scripture says that we should give "all diligence" (2 Peter 1:10), that we should fight, do battle, pursue after, and press forward (cf. Phil 3:12), that we should put forth the "labor of love," that we should be "zealous of good works" (Titus 2:14). Idlers are a ubiquitous people. There are many lazy spectators and passive critics, but "the laborers are few," says the Lord (Matt. 9:37). And what sort of a person are you, my reader? Are you a laborer or a spectator? Are you an active fighter or a mere onlooker?

Work requires self-denial. Many are quite willing to be active for Christ and His interests as long as it involves no self-sacrifice. This kind of service has in reality no true value: "For whosoever will save his life shall lose it" (Matt. 16:25). Only those who sow with tears will reap with joy (Ps. 126:5). We can easily do light work, work which does not cost us any effort, or pain, or sacrifice; but if this is our only work for Christ we need not be surprised if at the great harvest-home we shall appear with empty hands.

The aim, however, of this mutual spiritual love and care is not merely the recovery of the individual but the preservation and protection of the whole. This is the meaning of the words: "Lest any root of bitterness springing up trouble you, and thereby the many (= the majority) be defiled." This does not mean that this mutual shepherding will hinder bitter feelings arising in the heart of the individual—although this, of course, can and should be attained where such spiritual mutual care is present—but the author means here apparently persons whom he calls "roots." He is referring in a free type of translation to a word of the Old Testament law, well-known to his Jewish readers (Deut.29:18).

In this passage Moses warns of the danger of there being "among you man, or woman, or family, or tribe, whose heart turneth away from the Lord . . . lest there should be among you a root that beareth gall and wormwood." And it might even happen that a man who is such a "root" would feel very self-confident and say in his heart, "I shall have peace" (Deut. 29:19), but God will not forgive and will not spare him: "The anger of Yahweh and His jealousy shall smoke against that man" (vs. 19, 20). The relationship between the text in Hebrews, speaking of the "root of bitterness," and that in Deuteronomy, speaking of the "root that beareth gall and wormwood" is obvious. Both passages speak of persons who, although living within the people of God, turn away from God and become a spiritual hindrance and a stumbling block to their fellow-Christians. Thus it is a matter not so much of certain feelings in the soul-life of the individual but rather of the individual himself as a person and a member of a fellowship.

It is easily possible that a member of the people of God fails and "comes short of the grace of God" and exercises a harmful influence upon the others, so that he infects his surroundings like a "plant with bitter sap and bitter fruits." Thus a Christian who lives in an unspiritual state of heart, poisons God's vineyard, the church, like a root that bears gall and wormwood. Apparently the author has in mind the picture of a poisonous plant, or rather of a plant infected with a ruinous disease, which, when it is mature, harms everything around it. Every failure of an individual is a twofold danger, not only to himself but also to others, because his sin might cause these others also to fall. A single member of the church can, if he is given over to sin and allowed to go on with it, exercise such a dreadful influence on the whole circle that the many individuals which make up this fellowship become defiled by sin. This should be prevented by mutual spiritual care. Thus shepherding the individual soul is at the same time a preservation and help for the whole community.

And in this you must see quite clearly that it is therefore possible for yourself to become such a "root of bitterness." Growing weary in spiritual life is an infectious illness. Through the bitter fruit which arises in your life, poison and weeds can be sown in the lives of others. Either you are a help to your environment or a hindrance. Either you lift up the others or you weigh them down, either you further sanctification or you are a seed of defilement. Some kind of influence always radiates from us, even if unconsciously. Either you are "salt of the earth" or you may become "pepper for the world," either useful or annoying, either a fruit tree or a poisonous plant, either a channel of blessing or a means of harm.

On the other hand if you devote yourself to holy service for others, you may be sure that being a blessing to others brings blessing to yourself. If we work for the revival of others we are ourselves revived. You will overcome the signs of fatigue in yourself if you give yourself up wholly to the Lord to be commissioned by Him to overcome paralysis and feebleness in others. He who loves and nurses his ego makes himself spiritually old. Selfishness makes weary. The service of love keeps us young.

Further, looking unto Jesus brings with it new spiritual initiative and power of resolution. Let us note the clear commands: "Lift up! . . . Make straight paths! . . . Pursue peace!" (Heb. 12:12-14). To own a Bible involves effort. Hearing God's Word imposes obligations. Perhaps many of us need new devotion. One does not overcome weariness by remaining weary. We must "awake" from our sleep (Eph. 5:14). We must respond to God's call. There must be a new turn towards a more definite attitude of faith and increased active faithfulness. In this deep spiritual sense of the word, we must personally return to "that which was from the beginning," that is Christ Himself (1 John 1:1).

It is true that mere good intentions will not help us very far. How often we have become bankrupt! But the Scripture says clearly that "with purpose of heart" we should cleave to the Lord (Acts 11:23). Such Spirit-wrought purposes of heart are required. For devotion is not something which God does in our stead, but it has to be done on our part. Christ devoted Himself in order that we should follow His steps and in like manner devote ourselves to God. "I sanctify Myself that they themselves also may be sanctified in truth" (John 17:19). It may be necessary that we get alone with God and ourselves, bow our knees in prayer, and rededicate in a practical sense our life and will to the Lord. . . .

And is it not a fact that even after our new birth we have often become lukewarm, superficial, and weary to such an extent that the great things of our great God, as the all-overpowering and all-overshadowing realities, no longer overwhelm us? Have we not also often experienced the fact that the mere acknowledgment of weaknesses and shortcomings did not themselves produce progress? Perhaps we have been too afraid of making "good resolutions" and have therefore not had the spiritual energy to come to a holy "purpose of heart" (Acts 11:23) and thus to make a new start by a definite act of personal devotion. Spiritual awakening and remaining fresh do not come automatically or by magic. No, you must yourself act—not of course in a dead, legal manner, but definitely, in faith. Start again to serve your Redeemer and Lord anew and faithfully. Deny yourself and bear witness to Him. Then continue! You will yourself advance experientially: one learns prayer by praying, witnessing by witnessing, serving by serving, helping by helping. And your life will become fresher. Your days will become useful, and your heart happy.

You yourself must, however, really desire this and give to it your whole will without any reservation (Rev. 22:17). The Bible says nowhere that the will of man must be "broken." Such expressions sound very devoted and humble and are, no doubt, meant sincerely by those who use them, but in reality no one is helped by such unscriptural terms—neither believers nor those who are willing to believe, and certainly not the opposers or despisers of the Christian faith. What Scripture shows is that it is not the "will" which has to be broken but rather the egocentric "self-will," not our personal energy, but rather man's rebellion against God. As to the will itself, the regulation principle is that it has to be brought into line with the will of God. Our will should certainly remain "will," but has only by the power of the Holy Spirit to will what God wills. And just in this "willing of the will of God" it will become a real and strong will, that is, a powerful energy of a true personality. As long as it remained "self-will" it was not really a will at all, but merely a plaything in the hands of the mighty power of sin which oppressed and forced it to do its will (Rom. 7: 19-20). At the

highest estimate, it was only a striving, a searching, a wishing, and a yearning—for sin degrades and enervates us. But in Christ we awaken to ourselves. In Him alone do we become "personalities" in the real God-planned
sense of the word. Only by subjecting ourselves to the Lord of lords, do we
creatures receive a real "will."

Also in the life of the church as a whole all signs of fatigue must be
overcome. It is a fact which almost regularly repeats itself in the history of
the people of God that every new generation of the church is accompanied
by a crisis. Very often the third generation, especially of a spiritual movement has failed. It has so often given up spiritual energies and biblical
truths and convictions which by the pioneers of their movement, the fathers
of earlier revivals, had been held to be precious and holy. One can recognize this in Old Testament history. "And the people served Yahweh all the
days of Joshua [first generation], and all the days of the elders that outlived
Joshua [second generation] who had seen all the great work of Jehovah that
He had wrought for Israel. . . . And also all that generation were gathered
unto their fathers: and there arose another [the third] generation after them
which knew not Yahweh, nor yet the works which He had done for Israel . . .
and they forsook the Lord the God of their fathers . . . and followed other
gods" (Judges 2:7, 10, 22). How very grave! Let us not lull ourselves to sleep
in false security. No group of Christians, whether arising out of State
church or Free church, whether organized or unorganized, has any guarantee of retaining the freshness and vigor which it had at its beginning. Every
new generation in the local churches as well as in spiritual movements in
general must "lay hold" (1 Tim. 6:12) afresh for themselves, quite directly,
personally and individually, of the blessings which had been received and
held fast by their spiritual fathers. Spiritual possessions cannot be merely
"inherited."

The Letter to the Hebrews itself grew out of the crisis connected with
the arising of a new generation. The letter is a warning and an appeal by the
Spirit of God to that second generation to hold fast the confession in witness and life of the first generation.

A "crisis" need not of necessity be a "catastrophe." Trials are opportunities for victories. The ever-available power of the omnipresent Christ,
which never grows old, is at hand for new times and new people.

This is at the same time the meaning of the well-known verse, " Jesus

Christ is the same yesterday and today, yea and for ever" (Heb. 13:8). This word should be read in connection with Hebrews 11 and 12, and in relationship to its own context. It had just been said: "Remember them that had the rule over you, who spake unto you the word of God, and considering the issue of their life, imitate their faith" (v. 7). Immediately after this text follows that radiant word dealing with the ever-living, mighty, divine Lord of all times and all history.

This means: Men and women are called away. Generations sink into the grave. The leaders of past generations are no longer here. But Christ remains. In the midst of the coming and going of the generations, He is the rock of His church. He is far above all changes in situations and persons. He is the One who binds the generations together. He is the living link between "yesterday" and "today" in the history of His people, the connection between each generation at any given time and all generations before and after. He is the Head who unites all the redeemed through the generations past, present, and future. So He is the living, personal uniting principle of the church. This is true from the viewpoint of the contemporary "horizontal" cross-sections of the church, that is, of each generation living simultaneously in all parts of the earth. It is also true from the viewpoint of the "vertical" longitudinal sections of the church's history, that is, throughout the successive centuries and generations, forming the entire development of the church from the day of its founding to its completion, rapture, and perfecting at His coming. This means that in spite of all individual changes in detail, the spiritual essence of the life of the church remains in Christ unchanged throughout all generations. The death of the heroes of faith, those forerunners, leaders, and examples (Heb. 13:7, 17, 24), does not cause the slightest loss in the essence of the life and faith of the people of God. Even though the teachers go, the teaching remains the same. It is true, as I read on John Wesley's tomb in Westminster Abbey, that "God buries His labourers but His labour and work goes on." Therefore, do not grow weary! The Lord is ever-present.

Years ago I visited in Stuttgart the widow of the well-known German Christian writer, Professor Bettex. In the study of this brave confessor of Christ I saw a picture which Professor Bettex had painted himself. It represented a rock in the midst of the wildest waves. The waves are represented as surging mightily against this rock. But they flow back broken and smashed.

Friedrich Bettex was an author who helped thousands of his readers by his numerous apologetic works, which were most reliable in their many scientific statements, biblically sound, and deeply impressive and persuasive in their witness to Christ. By this picture he wished to show the main object of his own life: In the midst of time stands Christ, the Rock of Ages. The billows of doubt and the waves of hatred of God and Christ surge against Him, but it is the waves that are broken. He, the Rock, is unmoved.

Thus Christ gives His own the victory. One can throw His servants in this world into prison; one can banish them to scorching deserts or freezing steppes. They are "stoned, sawn asunder, tempted" (Heb. 11:37). But their experience will always be the same as that of the men in the fiery furnace: One is with them who comes down from heaven and who is able to keep them from hurt and harm, in any case inwardly, though He does not always do so outwardly (Dan. 3:20-27). "They looked unto Him and were lightened" (Ps. 34:5). "In all these things we are more than conquerors through Him that loved us" (Rom. 8:37).

This encourages us greatly. It should be also a holy stimulus and incentive. For if Christ our Savior is such a firm rock, our hearts also should be strong and firm (Heb. 13:9). Christ will never forsake His people. Therefore His people must never forsake Him. The younger generation especially must take this to heart. Faithfulness for faithfulness! The "today" of the church is under obligation on account of its "yesterday," and both are under obligation because of the faithfulness of Christ, who was and is "the same yesterday, and today, yea and forever."

This is the reason why the words about the bygone human leaders and the eternally living Savior (Heb. 13:7-8) are immediately followed by the exhortation and encouragement: "For it is good that the heart be established by grace" (v. 9).

The home-call of faithful servants of God brings with it a holy obligation for all those who remain behind.

Our life is short. Our days fly by. Earthly things are not the real things. That which really matters lies somewhere else, not in time, but in eternity, not in that which passes by, but in that which remains, not in the past or the present, but in the future. Thus we must press forward with a serious turn of mind and yet inwardly comforted, not trusting in ourselves and yet full of courage, not looking at our own powerlessness but looking to Christ's victorious power. "Therefore seeing we have this ministry, even as we have obtained mercy, we faint not" (2 Cor. 4:1).

When Abraham at the end of his life wanted to win a bride for his son Isaac, he sent the eldest of his servants to his relatives in Mesopotamia. Then, before leaving, this servant asked him: "Peradventure the woman will not be willing to follow me unto this land [Canaan]: must I needs bring thy son again unto the land whence thou camest?" (Gen. 24:5). Abraham answered—and in the Bible report one can feel and sense the energy of his will and the strength of his emotions and sentiments—"Beware thou that thou bring not my son thither again! and if the woman be not willing to follow thee, then thou shalt be clear from this my oath: only thou shalt not bring my son thither again!" (Gen. 24:6, 8).

"Not thither again!" "Beware thou!" "Not thither again!" These three expressions show the intensity of the decision and the feelings of the Patriarch. The father of faith demands of the coming generations the practical recognition of the irrevocability of the patriarchal call. What the first generation has attained in faith must never be given up by the second or third generations. The children must show themselves worthy of the attitude and devotion of their spiritual fathers. The following generation should faithfully administer the inheritance of their forefathers in the faith.

We often deplore—and unfortunately often rightly so—that the people of God in our time show so little of being really alive and keen for Christ. We recognize that we are lacking the Spirit of revival and that the last twenty years of the last century and the first ten years of the present century, generally speaking, saw more of the powerful working of the Holy Spirit. In those times many more people awoke out of their sleep of sin than today. There were leaders and shepherds in private and public Christian life in a measure unknown today. We think of the times of Finney, Moody, Torrey, Baedeker, George Muller, Spurgeon, and many others. But with all this recognition and regret perhaps we remain ourselves unchanged. Our yearning and desire may be honest, but is apparently not Spirit-filled enough. We wait, and probably also pray, for the Lord to send a revival. And in the last analysis it begins to appear as though God were the real cause of there being no widespread revival, simply because He does not answer our prayers.

And yet the situation is really quite different!

Nowhere is it taught in the Bible that we should wait for a revival. Revivals must be! But the children of God have not to take up a waiting attitude towards them. Never does Holy Scripture place the emphasis on practical holiness and on witnessing in the future, either near or distant. It brings us a present Christ, a Savior who desires to make our life fruitful and to fill us with power today and now. For if the revival were to come only after some years' time (God grant that it may come sooner) what should we be doing in the meantime? No, we dare not forget the "today." The past exists in our memory, the future in our expectancy; what we possess is the present. Mastering the ever-present moment means mastering life. And if you do not serve the Lord today there is no guarantee that you will serve Him tomorrow.

The King's business is urgent. What we can do today, let us not put off till tomorrow. If the Spirit incites us today to witness for the Lord in order to win a soul for Him, let us obey today. When tomorrow comes the enemy will certainly have found a thousand new reasons why we should not follow the voice of God. It belongs to true service to God that we should have a heart and mind clearly determined to do God's will today. "Whatsoever thy hand findeth to do, do it with thy might" (Eccles. 9:10). "Go, work today in the vineyard" (Matt. 21:28).

Then new blessings will come. When you yourself have been awakened, you will be able to wake up others, and so small circles of spiritually awakened Christians will arise, little cells from which the light can be spread further. You should belong to such. The Lord wants to use you, even though perhaps, in the sight of man, you may not have a conspicuous position, simply because God wishes you to do in obscurity a hidden and quiet service. In eternity you will be surprised that God could effect so much through your life only because it was really devoted to Christ, revived and remaining full of life till the goal was reached. That is God's will. Therefore it must be your will and decision also, and this just now and today.

We read in the life-story of Isaac: "And Isaac digged again the wells of water, which they had digged in the days of Abraham his father; for the Philistines had stopped them after the death of Abraham: And he called their names after the names by which his father had called them" (Gen. 26:18).

This is spiritually our situation. Our fathers in the faith digged "wells" and named them with names. The well of the Word of God, the well of prayer, the well of fellowship of the saints, the well of happy witnessing, the well of missionary service—all these were heavenly springs from which they drew water and which kept their personal life of faith fresh, as well as the life of their churches.

But the first generation has been called away and the "Philistines" have come—sin, worldliness, strife among brethren, lukewarmness, lack of interest in God's word and work, cowardice in witness, lack of sacrifice and missionary spirit—and the "wells" of the fathers have been stopped. Withering of the life of faith, lack of prayer and unfruitfulness in witness, spiritual stagnation in church life, subjection under the bondage of human tradition, narrowness of horizon, are the consequences.

What shall we do?

We must dig again the wells of the fathers. We must learn to pray again as our fathers prayed. We must bear witness as they did. We must sacrifice for the spread of the Word of God and for missionary service as they used to do. We must love the brethren as they loved and practiced the fellowship of the saints. We must listen afresh to God's Word and open our hearts to the working of the Holy Spirit. Our place in church or chapel must not be empty. Our contribution towards church and mission work must always be given with readiness of heart. Our prayers must be regular and sincere. Our mouth must not be silent. We must witness for Christ and be soul-winners just as the former generations of believers, who, in spite of failures and shortcomings which, of course, had been in their lives as in ours, had yet seen the mighty deeds of God.

"Isaac" must dig again "Abraham's" wells. Then new water of life will flow in our churches, and this promise of Scripture will be fulfilled in an ever deeper, richer degree:

And the Lord shall guide thee continually, and satisfy thy soul in dry places and make strong thy bones; and thou shalt be like a watered garden, and like a spring of water, whose waters fail not. And they that shall be of thee shall build the old waste places: thou shalt raise up the foundations of many generations; and thou shalt be called, The repairer of the breach, The restorer of paths to dwell in

(Isa. 58:11-12).

Therefore once again: "Lift up the hands which hang down! Make straight paths! Press on!"

In the arena of faith: "Let us look unto Jesus."

23

Thirsting for the Holy God

Ralph I. Tilley

Ralph I. Tilley (b. 1944) was converted to the Lord Jesus Christ at the age of 16. He is a graduate of God's Bible School & College (Th.B.; Bible, theology, New Testament Greek); Andrews University (M.A.; New Testament Studies); and Trinity Theological Seminary (D.R.S.; Religious Studies).

Ralph pastored for 38 years and has taught at the Bible college, university and seminary levels. He was the editor and publisher *Life in the Spirit Journal* for 20 years, and presently serves as the journal's online editor. He has served as the executive director of Life in the Spirit Ministries since 1993. *Called to Be Saints* is the eleventh book he has either authored or edited. He and his wife Emily reside in Sellersburg, Indiana; they have two married daughters and three grandchildren.

Thirst and hunger are two natural appetites that are innate to the human condition. Man was created by God with the need to drink and eat in order to sustain his earthly, biological life and existence. Without either food or water over a protracted period of time, death is certain.

In satisfying our appetite for food and water under normal circumstances, rarely do we consciously process what we are doing when we take a bite of food or lift a cup to our lips. The acts of eating and drinking are so instinctive in our daily rituals, that they are practically involuntary. For example, just before I sat down to the computer to begin this article, I helped myself to a few nuts and drank a glass of water—I barely gave it a conscious thought. Eating and drinking—we do it regularly.

Can you imagine what it would be like *not* to have a healthy appetite for food and water? How would we know when to eat or drink? Since we know our biological clocks as well as we do, most of us in the Western world eat three main meals each day. And as they say, we eat—whether we're hungry or not!

Just as the Creator made man with an appetite for food and water in order to sustain his biological needs, so this same Creator-God made man with spiritual appetites in order to sustain his inner spirit. When God created Adam, he endowed him with a spiritual capacity and need for fellowship with his Creator. In order for Adam to satisfy this innate need, God gave him an appetite—a strong desire—to know God intimately, to worship God habitually, to glorify God in all that he did, and to commune with his God and Father in every breathe he breathed. To Adam and all his offspring—from Eden's Garden to the present day—spiritual sensations of hunger and thirst were given to each person by their Creator.

But while we have all been given an inborn appetite for God, not everyone slakes his appetite by drinking from the water of life and the wells of salvation. Not everyone goes to Christ to drink-in his holiness, to experience his spiritual refreshment.

The sacred Scriptures record a wide range of God-thirsty men and women—in divergent circumstances and cultures—giving expression to an intense desire for the living God. These men and women were hungry for God's holiness; they were thirsty for God's righteousness. In a passage that has become the classic cry of every God-thirsty soul down through the centuries, the psalmist yearningly cries in Psalm 42:1-2,

As a deer pants for flowing streams,
  so pants my soul for you, O God.
My soul thirsts for God,
  for the living God.[1]

A Common Denominator

I often asked the Lord in years gone by, in one form of question or another, *Was there a common denominator—a special quality—that characterized those believers who had developed a close walk with you? If there was, what was it?*

I believe every disciple of the Lord Jesus Christ would agree that this is a legitimate question, and if there is indeed an answer to this fundamental inquiry, such an answer should be invaluable to Christ's Church and every earnest believer.

Although I asked that question many times, I don't need to ask it any longer. Why? Because the Lord has given me—and his Church—the answer in his inspired Word. The answer does not lie on the surface, but is carefully and clearly woven by the Spirit throughout its sacred pages. Whether one is reading Genesis or Joshua, Habbakuk or Hebrews, John or James, he will in time perceive that those men and women who became most intimately acquainted and walked in close communion with God, did so because they enjoyed a hearty and healthy appetite for their Father-God. They rose head and shoulders above all others. Why? Because they had an insatiable thirst for God. They panted for God. They longed for God. They were God-thirsty men and women—men and women who embraced God's holiness; men and women who possessed great appetites for God.

These giants in the faith never contemplated merely surviving on a spiritual diet of just having "a little talk with Jesus." Their appetite for God would not allow them to settle for a measly appetizer or pacifier. They were men and women who ate heartily and drank deeply from the wells of salvation, from the depths of God's holiness. Their soul capacities were forever expanding. They were God-thirsty saints. They burst forth again and again with God-thirsty longings and cravings—as did Israel's sweetest singer and song writer when he wrote (Ps. 63:1),

> O God, you are my God;
>   earnestly I seek you;
>   my soul thirsts for you;
> my flesh faints for you,
>   as in a dry and weary land where there is no water.

We read these repeated exclamations and heart-cries of soul-thirst bursting forth from thirsty saints throughout the centuries. Listen, for example, to Fredrick Faber (1814-1863) as he explodes in love for the Lord Jesus:

O Jesus, Jesus, dearest Lord!

Forgive me if I say,
For very love, Thy sacred name
  A thousand times a day.

I love Thee so I know not how
  My transports to control;
Thy love is like a burning fire
  Within my very soul.

Then listen again as he expresses his desire for a deep inner cleansing and holiness:

Burn, burn, O love, within my heart,
  Burn fiercely night and day,
Till all the dross of earthly loves
  Is burned, and burned away.[2]

A Paradox

Both the psalmist and Faber were experienced God-walkers, but nonetheless, they regularly gave vent to outbursts of soul-thirst. They were hungry for intimacy—intimacy with God. They were hungry for holiness—the holiness of God.

There is an apparent contradiction in the spiritual realm regarding this matter of thirsting for God. For example, Jesus said to the sin-weary seeker at Jacob's well,

"Everyone who drinks of this water will be thirsty again, but whoever drinks of the water that I will give him will never be thirsty again. The water that I will give him will become in him a spring of water welling up to eternal life" (John 4:13-14).

On the other hand, Jesus announced later to his disciples one day,

"If anyone thirsts, let him come to me and drink. Whoever believes in me, as the Scripture has said, 'Out of his heart will flow rivers of living water'" (John 7:37-38).

It is worthwhile to note that the grammatical tense (imperfect) used for "let him come to me and drink" suggests a continuous coming and drinking: "let him keep coming and let him keep drinking." To one person Jesus said that if she drank, she would never thirst again; to others, he said that they should drink and keep on drinking.

The explanation for this paradox is clear. For the woman who was thirsting for salvation, Jesus said that once she tasted the eternal life that he gives to all repentant, believing sinners, she would never experience the desire for salvation again because her need would have been satisfied through experiencing God's merciful, saving grace.

This truth is beautifully illustrated in the words of twentieth century poet Clara Tear Williams (1858-1937):

All my life-long I had panted
From a draught from some cool spring
That I hoped would quench the burning
Of the thirst I felt within.

Hallelujah! I have found Him—
Whom my soul so long has craved!
Jesus satisfies my longings;
Thro' His blood I now am saved.[3]

The audience Jesus was addressing in John 7, to whom the invitation was given: "If anyone thirsts, let him come to me and drink"—to this audience Jesus was speaking of the promised Spirit: "Now this he said about the Spirit, whom those who believed in him were to receive, for as yet the Spirit had not been given, because Jesus was not yet glorified (v. 39).

On the Day of Pentecost, the Holy Spirit was poured out on the disciples, and they were all "filled with the Holy Spirit." Yet, we discover throughout the Book of Acts that these same disciples were repeatedly filled with the Spirit. Moreover, Paul exhorts the Ephesian believers to be "continually filled with the Spirit" (Eph. 5:18). Now what do John 7, Acts 2 (as well as additional Acts' texts), and Ephesians 5 suggest about this matter of soul-thirst? Simply this: If the earnest disciple of Jesus Christ accepts his Lord's invitation to pursue a vital connection with him by being continuously filled with the Holy Spirit, he must have a healthy appetite that draws him habitually to Christ, that he might be regularly replenished in his own inner spirit: "If any man thirsts . . ."

Only the thirsty can be filled continually with the Holy Spirit. Only the thirsty will abide in the Vine. Only the thirsty will have a desire to intimately know, worship, glorify, and commune with their Father-God. Only the thirsty experience an increasing realization of God's holiness.

A. W. Tozer underscored the reality of this truth when he wrote, "To have found God and still pursue Him is the soul's paradox of love, scorned indeed by the too-easily-satisfied religionist, but justified in happy experience by the children of the burning heart."[4] Bernard of Clairvaux (1090-1153) expressed many years ago the same idea in poetic verse:

We taste Thee, O Thou Living Bread,
And long to feast upon Thee still;
We drink of Thee, the Fountainhead
And thirst our souls from Thee to fill.[5]

To feel an intense thirst for God, often means we have experienced a depletion, a draining in our spirit that needs replenished, refreshed. Paul said our inner man should be renewed day by day. And that is so true. But one often is drawn out by the Spirit with an intense, prolonged desire for a fresh infilling of the Spirit, a fresh encounter with God's holiness. It may be that you will be preaching/teaching the Word of God. It may be that God is preparing you for a new mission, a new step of faith. You may not even know at the time why you are experiencing such soul-thirst, such longing after God. But you feel inexorably drawn to God, to the place of prayer.

I went through (again) one of these experiences just yesterday [written in 2012]. It was Sunday evening. I had been relaxing in the afternoon, but when evening came, I felt the need to be alone, to be with God. I went to the back of our property, where we have a swing, and sat down. I bent over, with my face toward the ground, and was struck by the cracks in the soil (we had an unusually dry summer). I then cried out from the depths of my heart, "O God, that's a picture of my heart; I feel so dry. I need you to re-plenish my spirit with water from heaven."

I had no sooner expressed my need to my merciful, heavenly Father, when his words came strong and clear—words penned by the prophet centuries ago: "I will pour water on the thirsty land, and streams on the dry ground" (Isa. 44:3). I knew the "land" of my spirit was dry; however, before I left the swing that Sunday evening, my spirit was refreshed with fresh water—the very freshness of the Spirit of God, the living God, was renewing my inner spirit; I experienced a renewed cleansing—encountering God's holiness once again.

Models and Mentors

Living in an age when Christianity is reputed more for its *glitter* than for its *gold*, we twenty-first century followers of the Lord Jesus Christ would do well to seek out those saints in biblical and church history literature—as well as looking for those among our contemporaries—who evidenced an insatiable appetite for God and his holiness: Men and women who instinctively rejected shallow discipleship and *cheap grace* in all its hues. We should select as our spiritual models and mentors those godly, God-glorifiers who have developed through grace a worshiping heart and a holy lifestyle.

These men and women won't be found on every page of the Bible or in every book of church history. They may not be found in every pew or in every local church, but you will find them in God's Word, and you will find them both in classic literature as well as in today's Church. They may not be in every local church, but God still has his "seven thousand who have not bowed their knees to Baal."

You can find God's holy, thirsty-hearted remnant among the Catholics (no, that's not a typographical error) and Protestants, among the Pentecostals and Reformed, among the Calvinists and Arminians. The only biblical qualification for getting to know God and experiencing his holiness, and getting to know him more intimately, is to continually come with a thirsty appetite to the Lord Jesus Christ: "If any man thirsts, let him come to me and drink."

Spiritual Exercises

There are no easy steps or formulae for developing a greater thirst for God and his holiness, but there are some practices and habits of the soul that are common to all the God-thirsty of all the ages. There is a personal price one must pay; there are Spirit-exercises which must be pursued. Here are a few of those exercises and practices.

The Practice of Solitude. Aloneness and solitude are not the same. A Christian may be the only person in a building and yet may never truly be alone, as it were, with God. Nevertheless, it is important for one who is vitally interested in developing a healthy appetite for God to regularly separate him and herself from the company of all others. Jesus observed such a practice, for example, by spending time alone with his Father on the mountain and in the Garden.

The Practice of Meditating on Scripture. Note, I did not say *reading* the Scripture. A person may be a regular, systematic Bible reader and be woefully ignorant of spiritual truth. In order for the truth of God to take root in our lives, and the holiness of Christ to permeate our lives we must slowly and prayerfully contemplate what we are reading, asking the Spirit for understanding. This takes time. It is far better to read one verse of Scripture with understanding, than to read ten chapters and remain unchanged.

The Practice of a Worshiping Heart. Whether on our knees, driving down a highway, studying for exams, preparing a meal, mowing the lawn, or cleaning the house; whether we are in the home, at the office, in the classroom, or on a vacation, the God-thirsty—God's holy people—carry with them everywhere they go a worshiping heart, a praying heart, a grateful heart, a thirsty heart. Brother Lawrence (1614-1691) called it "practicing the presence of God."

Such individuals have learned that any attitude or action that disrupts communion with their Companion and Friend, must be corrected immediately. They jealously protect their intimacy with Christ. They jealously guard against grieving the Holy Spirit. When their "garment" becomes defiled in the least—they flea to the Refiner and Purifier of spirits. That leads us to our next point.

The Practice of Confession. While we should not buy into the "miserable sinner" theology on the one hand, or "sinless perfectionism" on the other hand, every authentic, God-thirsty soul—who knows himself better than any other person, and knows that God knows him even better than he knows himself—understands when he kneels before his holy and righteous Father, that he has nothing to boast of, but can only acknowledge his shortcomings, omissions, trespasses, debts, sins, and failures to love perfectly at all times all people, under every circumstance.

The biggest souls and the humblest saints through the ages, have practiced confession before God—men such as Augustine of Hippo, Martin Luther, John and Charles Wesley, Isaac Watts, George Whitefield, Andrew Murray, Dietrich Bonhoeffer, F. B. Meyer, A. W. Tozer—and so will we if we are cultivating a healthy appetite for God and his holiness.

The Practice of Authentic Fellowship. One of the most powerful means of grace God has give to his Church for developing a healthy appetite for himself and his holiness is fellowship—authentic Christian fellowship.

When the New Testament speaks of fellowship, it makes reference to believers coming together in Christ's name for mutual edification. And this is most effectively achieved in small groups. While not every believer, for one reason or another, has the opportunity to involve himself in a small group, where true fellowship is properly practiced great blessings follow and one's thirst for God and his holiness is thereby enhanced. Believers must zealously avoid isolating themselves from the Body of Christ. Fellowship is to be sought and cherished.

An Example of a God-Thirsty Person

On this theme of thirsting for God and his holiness, I recall the adventure of an African young man by the name of Samuel Morris (1873-1893). Following his remarkable conversion to Christ, this new convert wanted to know more about God and his holiness, and particularly more about the Holy Spirit than the missionaries could tell him. But the missionaries told him if he could get to New York City, there was a man who lived there by the name of Stephen Merritt, who could tell Sammy more about the Holy Spirit.

When Sammy arrived in New York City, he was graciously welcomed by Stephen and Mrs. Merritt. He was taken on a tour of the city and shown many of the attractions. Merritt was a busy man. He invited Sammy to go with him to a funeral where he was to speak. On their way, Sammy asked his new friend, "Did you ever pray while riding in a coach?" Merritt said he had not "formally" prayed in a coach. Sammy told him that they should pray, then Sammy prayed: "Father, I have been months coming to see Stephen Merritt so that I could talk to him about the Holy Ghost. Now that I am here, he shows me the harbor, the churches, the banks and other buildings, but does not say a word about this Spirit I am so anxious to know more about. Fill him with Thyself so that he will not think, or talk, or write, or preach about anything but Thee and the Holy Ghost."

Merritt later said that he had been in many religious meetings during the course of his ministry in the church, but that he had "never experienced the burning presence of the Holy Spirit as he did while he was kneeling in that coach, beside Sammy Morris who was penniless and clad in tattered garments."[6]

One's thirst for God and his holiness may be felt in multiple ways, depending on the particular need at the time. But however it may be experienced at a particular moment—and acted upon—it always leads to a greater knowledge and intimacy with God; it always leads us to exalt the Lord Jesus Christ; it always expresses itself by honoring the blessed Holy Spirit; and it always ends by reaching out to others—to saints and to sinners.

Now, what about you, dear reader? Has this vain world spoiled your appetite for God? Is what you're feeding on robbing you of your thirst after righteousness and true holiness—after the Lord Jesus Christ? Or will you identify with the psalmist (Ps. 42:1) and the prophet (Isa. 6:1-8)?

As a deer pants for flowing streams,
  so pants my soul for you, O God.
My soul thirsts for God, for the living God.

In the year that King Uzziah died I saw the Lord sitting upon a throne, high and lifted up; and the train of his robe filled the temple. [2]Above him stood the seraphim. Each had six wings: with two he covered his face, and with two he covered his feet, and with two he flew. [3]And one called to another and said:

"Holy, holy, holy is the Lord of hosts;
  the whole earth is full of his glory!"
[4]And the foundations of the thresholds shook at the voice of him

who called, and the house was filled with smoke. 5And I said: "Woe is me! For I am lost; for I am a man of unclean lips, and I dwell in the midst of a people of unclean lips; for my eyes have seen the King, the Lord of hosts!"

6Then one of the seraphim flew to me, having in his hand a burning coal that he had taken with tongs from the altar. 7And he touched my mouth and said: "Behold, this has touched your lips; your guilt is taken away, and your sin atoned for."

8And I heard the voice of the Lord saying, "Whom shall I send, and who will go for us?" Then I said, "Here I am! Send me."

Are you thirsty for God and his holiness? Come to the God of David! Come to the God of Isaiah! Come to the Lord Jesus Christ! Come often!

Appendix

Daily Aspirations

Ralph I. Tilley

Dear Fellow Christian:

The following "Aspirations" were originally written by me to serve as reminders in my own walk with Christ. Though Scripture references are not included (except in the last section), the serious Bible student will readily discern that each aspiration is biblically based. Of course, these aspirations are not an exhaustive list of biblical imperatives and exhortations to holy living; you will think of others to add to use in your own walk with Christ.

Life in the Spirit is no more and no less than the indwelling Christ living his life in and through the believer by the presence and power of the Holy Spirit. I pray the Spirit will use these "Daily Aspirations" to cause you to search the Scriptures diligently, and to seek the face of God daily, in order that you may aspire to live a life pleasing to God—all to His glory.

O God, my Father, graciously incline my heart *today* to . . .

worship You—Father, Son, and Holy Spirit—exclusively

exalt Your Son highly

honor the Holy Spirit attentively

obey You completely

keep Your commandments loyally

delight in Your Word incessantly

glorify You supremely

look to Jesus steadily

love You passionately

serve You wholeheartedly

praise and thank You repeatedly

rejoice continually

commune with You warmly

know You intimately

follow You closely

abide in Christ constantly

walk with You humbly

seek to live righteously

listen to Your voice eagerly

pursue holiness thirstily

keep in step with the Spirit unwaveringly

rest in You trustingly

understand Your will clearly

believe Your promises unswervingly

share the gospel unashamedly

declare Your Word boldly

speak the truth lovingly

pray ceaselessly

offer requests confidently

intercede in prayer fervently

act and react gently

speak prudently

guard my heart meticulously

engage in good works routinely

edify the saints insightfully

accept Your providences uncomplainingly

Daily Aspirations

walk before You purely

nonconform to the world discerningly

run the marked-out course perseveringly

relate to others sensitively

use my Spirit-gifts freely

eat and exercise moderately

contribute my resources generously

resist the Adversary immediately

accept Your discipline profitably

maintain a good conscience carefully

deny myself consistently

carry my cross gladly

imitate the faith of noble saints relentlessly

forbear the weaknesses of others silently

clothe myself with humility unpretentiously

conserve the unity of the Spirit vigilantly

receive all true believers non-judgmentally

manage time wisely

relax discreetly

fulfill my calling faithfully

perform duties assiduously

serve others selflessly

treat Your creation responsibly

respond to trespasses forgivingly

love the sinner mercifully

submit to authority meekly

acknowledge my faults unguardedly

confess my sins honestly

end the day reflectively

remember I will be judged by You rightly

**I believe, holy Father, in the name of Your Son,
the Lord Jesus Christ, and through the power of Your indwelling Spirit,
to answer these Spirit-formed petitions, as You are . . .**

cleansing me from all sin and unrighteousness unfailingly (1 John 1:9)

making me holy through and through thoroughly (1 Thess. 5:23)

enabling me to live in Your light transparently (1 John 1:7)

renewing me in the spirit of my mind deeply (Eph. 4:23)

strengthening me with all might powerfully (Eph. 3:16)

transforming me to the likeness of Jesus Christ increasingly (2 Cor. 3:18)

controlling and filling me with the Holy Spirit vitally (Eph. 5:18)

growing the fruit of the Spirit in me progressively (Gal. 5:22-23)

generating rivers of living water through me continuously (John 7:38)

protecting me from the Adversary knowingly (Jude 1:24)

perfecting what is lacking in me perceptively (Phil. 4:12-16)

using me to bless others meaningfully (Rom. 15:2)

---

*"Now to him who is able to do far more abundantly than all
that we ask or think, according to the power at work within us,
to him be glory in the church and in Christ Jesus throughout
all generations, forever and ever. Amen."*
Ephesians 3:20-21 ESV

*"Yet, my brothers, I do not consider myself to have 'arrived,' spiritually, nor do I
consider myself already perfect. But I keep going on, grasping ever more firmly that
purpose for which Christ grasped me.
My brothers, I do not consider myself to have fully grasped it even now. But I do
concentrate on this: I leave the past behind and with hands outstretched to
whatever lies ahead I go straight for the goal —
my reward the honor of being called by God in Christ."*
Philippians 3:12-14 Phillips

Endnotes

Introduction

1. Unless otherwise indicated, all Scripture quotations in the Introduction are from *The Holy Bible, English Standard Version*® (ESV®), copyright © 2001 by Crossway, a publishing ministry of Good News Publishers. Used by permission. All rights reserved.
2. J. C. Ryle, *A Call to Holiness* (Grand Rapids: Baker Book House, 1976, reprint), 47-48.
3. Timothy George in *For All the Saints,* edited by Timothy George and Alister McGrath (Louisville: John Knox Press, 2003), 7.

Chapter 1: Called to be Saints

1. Genesis 2:23. Unless otherwise indicated, all Scripture quotations in this chapter are from The Holy Bible, English Standard Version® (ESV®), copyright © 2001 by Crossway, a publishing ministry of Good News Publishers. Used by permission. All rights reserved.
2. John Bunyan, *The Pilgrim's Progress* (Westwood, NJ: Barbour and Company, reprint; originally published 1678), 1-4.
3. Taken from "At Calvary" by William R. Newell.
4. Taken from "And Can it Be?" by Charles Wesley.
5. J. Sidlow Baxter, *The Master Theme of the Bible* (Wheaton, IL: Tyndale House Publishers, 1973), 53-54.
6. Taken from "O Love Divine, What Hast Thou Done!" by Charles Wesley.
7. Dallas Willard, *The Divine Conspiracy* (New York: HarperCollins, 1998), 36.
8. This chapter addresses almost exclusively the NT usage of the term "saint." The are 21 occurrences of the word in the OT (ESV), with 20 of these appearing in either Psalms or Daniel; the other occurrence is in 2 Chronicles 6:41.
9. H. C. G. Moule, *The Epistle to the Romans*, edited by Philip Hillyer (Fort Washington, PA: CLC Publications, reprint, 1958), 26.
10. 1 Peter 1:14-16.
11. Oswald Chambers, *My Utmost for His Highest*, September 1. utmost.org.
12. 2 Corinthians 7:1 NASB.

Chapter 5: What Holiness is, and Why it Matters

1. See also J. I. Packer, *God's Words: Studies of Key Bible Themes* (Grand Rap-

269

ids: Baker Book House, 1988), ch. 14. "Holiness and Sanctification," 169-79; *Keep in Step with the Spirit* (Old Tappan: Fleming H. Revell, 1984), chs. 3-4, 94-169.

2. I have included J. I. Packer's quote of J. C. Ryle in Chapter 3.
3. Richard Baxter, *Poetical Fragments* (1681).
4. G. W. Allport, *Pattern and Growth in Personality* (New York: Holt, Rinehart and Winston, 1961), 34.
5. Chris Brain and Robert Warren, "Why Revival *Really* Tarries—Holiness," Renewal, 181 (June 1991), 35; quoting James Philip, *Christian Maturity* (London: Inter-Varsity Press, 1964), 70. I have attempted to make the same point briefly in *Knowing Man* (Westchester: Cornerstone, 1979) and more fully with Thomas Howard in *Christianity: the True Humanism* (Dallas: Word Books, 1985).
6. Philip, *Christian Maturity*, 65.
7. Philip, *Christian Maturity*, 67-69.

Chapter 6: Attention and Obedience

1. Ghéon, *The Secret of St. John Bosco*, 197.
2. C . C. Martindale, *The Vocation of Aloysius Gonzaga*, 62.
3. Tyerman, *Wesley's Designated Successor*, 18.
4. J. Jorgensen, *St. Francis of Assisi*, 28.
5. Cassels, *Men of the Knotted Heart*, 140.
6. Coley, *Life of Thomas Collins*, 68, 121.
7. Carr, *To Heaven Through a Window*, 111.
8. Streeter and Appasamy, *Sadhu Sundar Singh*, 93.
9. *Autobiography of St. Thérèse of Lisieux*, 146.
10. Booth-Tucker, *Catherine Booth*, Vol. I, 79.
11. Padwick, *Henry Martyn*, 152.
12. Rattenbury, *David Hill*, 69.
13. Gummeie, *John Woolman*, 158.
14. Cropper, *Flame Touches Flame*, 121.
15. Whyte, *James Fraser*, 84.
16. John Ward, M. P. for Hackney 1710-?. J . G . O'Leary, *The Book of Dagenham*, 65 f.
17. 2 Corinthians 3:18.
18. *Histoire Littéraire dii Sentiment Religieux en France*, VII.15.
19. Box, *The Ethics of Socialism*, 17.
20. Thorold (English Translation edn. 1935), 6f.
21. Ibid., 9, 53.

22. Ibid., 74.
23. Ibid., 45, 98.
24. Ibid., 15.
25. Thorold (*English Translation* edn. 1935), 29.
26. Ibid., 51.
27. Ibid., 64.
28. Ibid., 78.
29. Ibid., 130.
30. Ibid., 84.
31. Thorold (*English Translation* edn. 1935), 101.
32. Ibid., 94.
33. Thorold (*English Translation* edn. 1935), 83f.

Chapter 14: "Look Not to Your Own Interests"

1. Some may interpret Jesus' practice of withdrawing from the crowds to pray as an act of self-interest, but I doubt that. He seemed to be seeking additional spiritual resources so that he could give of himself to the people.

Chapter 15: How to Be a Living Sacrifice

1. Robert S. Candlish, *Studies in Romans 12: The Christian's Sacrifice and Service of Praise* (Grand Rapids: Kregel Publications, 1989), 33-34.
2. John Calvin, *The Epistles of Paul the Apostle to the Romans and to the Thessalonians,* trans. Ross MacKenzie (Grand Rapids: Wm. B. Eerdmans, and Leicester, England: Inter-Varsity Press, 1973), 264.
3. Leon Morris, *The Epistle* to *the Romans* (Grand Rapids: Wm. B. Eerdmans, 1988), 433-434.
4. Robert Haldane, *An Exposition of the Epistle to the Romans* (MacDill AFB: MacDonald Publishing, 1958), 554. See also John Murray, *The Epistle to the Romans,* 2 vols. in 1 (Grand Rapids: (Grand Rapids: Wm. B. Eerdmans, 1968), vol. 2, p. 111. Murray notes the depreciation of the body in favor of the spirit in Greek thought and argues that against that background an emphasis upon the body by Paul was a Christian necessity.
5. See Mike Bellah, *Baby Boom Believers: Why We Think We Need It All and How* to *Survive When We Don't Get It* (Wheaton, Ill.: Tyndale House, 1988), 27.
6. Handley C. G. Moule, *The Epistle of St. Paul* to *the Romans* (London: Hodder and Stroughton, 1896), 324-325.
7. J. I. Packer, *Rediscovering Holiness* (Ann Arbor, MI: Servant Publications,

1992), 12-13.

8. J. C. Ryle, *Holiness: Its Nature, Hindrances, Difficulties and Roots* (Cambridge: James Clark, 1959), and Jerry Bridges, *The Pursuit of Holiness* (Colorado Springs: NavPress, 1978).

Chapter 16: Acceptable Candlesticks: Service

1. *New Bible Commentary*; IVP production.
2. Oswald Chambers, *My Utmost for His Highest* (reading for January 17th), published by Oswald Chambers Publications Association and Marshal, Morgan and Scott.
3. *New Bible Commentary*; IVP production.
4. Andrew Murray, *Holy in Christ* (reading for the twenty-seventh day).

Chapter 19: Toward Christian Maturity

1. A. T. Robertson, *Word Pictures in the New Testament* (New York: Harper and Brothers Publishers, 1933), 4:446.
2. When a Christian worker builds with "wood, hay, and stubble," yet *on Christ* as the Foundation, his salvation is not forfeited, only his work (1 Cor. 3:10-15). But when a believer has reverted to overt sinning, the final salvation of his spirit is in jeopardy (1 Cor. 5:1-5). The Epistle to the Galatians groans with an agonizing distress in Paul which reflects a real fear for their ultimate salvation (2:15-21; 3:1-4; 4:8-9, 19-20; 5:1-4, 7, 15, 16-26; 6:1-8). Timothy is urged: "Take heed to your teaching; hold to that, for by so doing you will save both yourself and your hearers" (1 Tim. 4:16; cf. 2 Cor.7:10; Phil. 2:12; Col. 1:22-23; James 1:21-22; 2:14; 5:20; 1 Pet. 4:18).
3. Indeed the immediate privileges, to which believers are urged at once, are staggering. Paul travails that Christ be "formed" in them (Gal. 4:19); he expects that the crucifixion of the flesh to which they are committed be a subjective reality (Gal. 5:24); that they be identifiable as "spiritual" (Gal. 6:1); as "perfect" in the sense of total commitment (2 Cor. 13:9, 11, KJV); that the mind of Christ be established in them as their governing motivation (Phil. 2:5); that Christ dwell in their hearts by faith through the strengthening of the Spirit's dynamic power (Eph. 3:16); that they be thoroughly renewed in the spirit of their minds (Rom. 12:2; Eph. 4:23); that they exhibit the fervency in good works which marks the redeemed and purified (Titus 2:14); that they know the perfect love which flows from a pure heart and a good conscience and faith unfeigned (1 Tim. 1:5). Here is the norm, not the far-off goal. It is

from this base that growth proceeds.

4. *Beacon Bible Commentary.* 8:313.

5. Only the verb form is in the New Testament, Matt. 17:2; Mark 9:2; Rom. 12:2; this passage. The punctiliar sense of the aorist tense respecting the transfiguration of Jesus is obvious from the event; here the tense is present, hence "our being transformed." But in either case the emphasis is on the visible, recognizable likeness.

6. See Robertson, *Word Pictures.* "Stop being fashioned"; cf. NIV, "Do not conform any longer." No license is given to stop gradually over a long period of time.

7. *Hagioi,* "holy ones," a general designation for all believers, similar to "Christian."

8. A Christian who is out of joint, and hence fails to achieve that harmony which belongs to the "proper working of each individual part," needs yet a lot of "perfecting," if not *crisically* by purging, at least by much discipline and instruction.

9. For further discussion see Harvey J. S. Blaney, *Beacon Bible Commentary,* 10:367f.

10. When Christ is the Center, nothing else can be: neither money, health, nor happy circumstances (2 Tim. 1:7).

11. When Christians become infected by a lust for religious excitement, simple goodness gradually begins to seem tame. The passion for holiness is displaced by a passion for religious *fireworks.* This quickly degenerates into pseudo-spirituality.

12. The translation of *epkhoregesate* by "add" (KJV) misses the full strength of this aorist imperative. It rather signifies "to supply, furnish, present" (Thayer), and is so translated with slight variations by ASV, Moffatt, and NASB. But Goodspeed, Williams, and NEB, as well as RSV, use the word "supplement," which probably most accurately expresses the idea. The inference is that unless this process of supplementing goes on, the character will become lopsided and perhaps even distorted.

13. Knowing God is primary, but we must also know *about* Him, otherwise we will foolishly misrepresent Him. The same word is used in 2 Pet. 3:18, where we are told to grow in the "knowledge of our Lord and Savior Jesus Christ."

Chapter 20: The Ongoing Warfare—The Flesh Against the Spirit

1. N. T. Wright, *Following Jesus: Biblical Reflections on Discipleship* (London:

SPCK, 1994), 72.

2. These words come from Krister Stendahl, "The Apostle Paul and the Introspective Conscience of the West," in *Paul Among Jews and Gentiles and Other Essays* (Philadelphia: Fortress, 1976), 78-96.

3. See also Ps. 51, where David speaks of his "sin as ever before me" (v. 3) and of his having "done what is evil" (v. 4). But he also knows the source of such sin, the evil heart, which he refers to in vv. 5-6.

4. See the discussion in *God's Empowering Presence* of Gal. 5:13-15, 16-17, 19-23, 24-26; 6:7-10; Rom. 7:4-6; 8:4, 5-8; 13:11-14; Phil. 3:3.

5. For further reference to recent scholarship on this question, especially the position of J. D. G. Dunn, to which some of the following is a response, see Fee, *God's Empowering Presence*, 816-22.

6. But does so inconsistently. It uses "sinful nature" when "flesh" implies a negative moral judgment (e.g., see 1 Cor. 5:5; Gal. 5:13, 16, 17 [twice], 19, 24; 6:8; Rom. 7:5-8:13; Col. 2:11, 13; Eph. 2:3), but "worldly point of view" in 2 Cor. 5:16 (cf. 1:12, 17; 10:2) and "flesh" in Phil. 3:3-4!

7. This contrast does not occur nearly as often as we are sometimes led to believe, being found basically in Gal. 5:13-6:10 (cf. the analogy in 4:29); Rom. 8:3-17; and Phil. 3:3—although see also 1 Cor. 3:1.

Chapter 23: Thirsting for the Holy God

1. Unless otherwise indicated, all Scripture quotations in this chapter are from *The Holy Bible, English Standard Version®* (ESV®), copyright © 2001 by Crossway, a publishing ministry of Good News Publishers. Used by permission. All rights reserved.

2. Taken from the hymn "O Jesus, Jesus, Dearest Lord" by Fredrick Faber.

3. Taken from the hymn "Satisfied" by Clara Tear Williams.

4. A. W. Tozer, *The Pursuit of God* (Harrisburg, PA: Christian Publications, 1963), 15.

5. Taken from the hymn "Jesus, Thou Joy of Loving Hearts" by Bernard of Clairvaux.

6. Lindley Baldwin, *Samuel Morris: The March of Faith* (Minneapolis, MN: Bethany Fellowship, 1942), 48-49.

Books by Ralph I. Tilley

Thirsting for God (2011)

Letters from Noah (historical fiction, 2013)

The Mind of Christ by John R. MacDuff,
edited reprint (2013)

A Passion for Christ (2013)

*How Christ Came to Church: An Anthology of the Works of
A. J. Gordon*; edited reprint
with Introduction by Ralph I. Tilley (2013)

Breath of God (2013)

The Christian's Vital Breath: An Anthology on Prayer
Ralph I. Tilley, editor (2014)

Christ in You: Living the Christ-life (2014)

Not Peace But a Sword by Vance Havner,
reprint with Introduction by Ralph I. Tilley (2014)

The Bow in the Cloud by John R. MacDuff,
edited reprint (2014)

Called to Be Saints: An Anthology on Holiness
Ralph I. Tilley, editor (2014)

Coming . . .

The Christian's Native Air: An Anthology on Prayer
Daily Renewal: 365 Daily Meditations
Changed by the Spirit: An Anthology on Conversion

**Books available at Amazon.com; for *discounts*, contact
Ralph I. Tilley, editor@litsjournal.org**

For all available books, go to litsjournal.org.

www.ingramcontent.com/pod-product-compliance
Lightning Source LLC
Chambersburg PA
CBHW071951040426
42447CB00009B/1306